FRENCH CONNECTION

ALEXIS BERGANTZ is a historian of Australia's entanglements with France and the French Pacific. He is currently a lecturer at RMIT University in Melbourne, where he teaches in Global and Language Studies. He has a PhD in history from the Australian National University.

In the late 1800s, for Australians, France was the land of *haute cuisine*, *haute couture* and high culture, but also a country of dangerous revolutionaries and menacing colonialists. Alexis Bergantz's well-researched and very engagingly written history of the French in Australia offers revealing portraits of individual lives, deftly assesses the way the two societies saw each other, and explains how the French helped create modern Australia.

– Robert Aldrich, University of Sydney

In *French Connection*, Alexis Bergantz transcends 'contribution' or 'ethnic' history in explaining how Frenchness in Australia was among the ingredients of an antipodean culture that has been more cosmopolitan for much longer than most imagine. This superb cultural history is as stylish as the images of France and Frenchness that it so brilliantly interrogates.

– Frank Bongiorno, Australian National University

French Connections is a lively, spirited and historically informed account of the history and legacy of French–Australian relations. Bergantz deftly weaves together stories of individuals and groups who together paint an intricate portrait of the connections between the two nations. The engaging snapshots rest upon profound and rigorous historical research. *French Connections* is a significant contribution to this important historiography and will be essential reading for those interested in 'Frenchness' and 'Australianness'.

– Natalie Edwards, University of Adelaide

Though France failed to colonise Australia, French cultural connections and entanglements have continued longer and stronger in Australia than most of us know. Alexis Bergantz's wide-ranging, stylish, and thought-provoking book reveals how French immigrants and culture have infiltrated our dreams from the battlefields of Gallipoli to the palettes of our artists, and the couture and cuisine of our urban boulevards.

– Iain McCalman, author of *The Seven Ordeals of Count Cagliostro* and *Darwin's Armada*

With insight, wit and humour, Alexis Bergantz explores the multi-layered history of the Australian Francophilia and Francophobia detailing how, since the earliest days of English settlement, the French in Australia, and from afar, have played a vital role in shaping the Australian identity. An absorbing read!

– Margaret Sankey, University of Sydney

FRENCH CONNECTION

Australia's cosmopolitan ambitions

Alexis Bergantz

NEWSOUTH

A NewSouth book

Published by
NewSouth Publishing
University of New South Wales Press Ltd
University of New South Wales
Sydney NSW 2052
AUSTRALIA
newsouthpublishing.com

© Alexis Bergantz 2021
First published 2021

10 9 8 7 6 5 4 3 2 1

This book is copyright. Apart from any fair dealing for the purpose of private study, research, criticism or review, as permitted under the *Copyright Act*, no part of this book may be reproduced by any process without written permission. Inquiries should be addressed to the publisher.

ISBN: 9781742237091 (paperback)
        9781742245256 (ebook)
        9781742249803 (ePDF)

 A catalogue record for this book is available from the National Library of Australia

Design Josephine Pajor-Markus
Cover design Peter Long
Cover image The Swing, Jean-Honorè Fragonard (top) and *Down on His Luck*, Frederick McCubbin

All reasonable efforts were taken to obtain permission to use copyright material reproduced in this book, but in some cases copyright could not be traced. The author welcomes information in this regard.

Contents

Introduction: Frenchness in Australia   1

1. A glittering, raucous ritual: French cafés and culture   12
2. A battle for control: *Alliance* and misalliance   35
3. The scum of France: A reckoning with Australia's convict past   59
4. French migrants: The 'crème de la crème'   81
5. A matter of honour: Frenchness on trial   100
6. Fading family ties to France: Two diarists' views   119

Epilogue: France and ideas of the 'feminine' in 20th-century Australia   135

Appendix   145
Select bibliography   153
Abbreviations   164
Notes   165
Acknowledgments   187
Index   190

Note on translations

All translations are my own unless otherwise stated. An asterisk (*) following an author's name in the endnotes indicates a quotation that was originally in French. The original French can be found in the Appendix, pages 145–52.

Introduction: Frenchness in Australia

The French acting vice-consul in Australia could barely contain himself. 'Disillusioned', Eugène Lucciardi had just attended a public exhibition showcasing the work of Victorian State pupils in Melbourne. Many heresies were committed on that early spring day in 1906. For one, the children had drawn the Union Jack on a world map above Madagascar, which was under French colonial rule. On a more minor scale, but just as dumbfounding to the vice-consul, one student had written a fanciful report that mixed up Marat, the revolutionary martyr so famously assassinated in his bath in 1793, with Joachim Murat, the 'Dandy king' and brother-in-law to Napoleon I, who died a whole twenty-two years later. Lucciardi was adamant: the exhibition was 'an automobile accident translated into text'.[1] Had France not been, since the time of Louis XIV at least, the quintessence of civilisation? A mighty military power commanding all nations? Had not all artists and aristocrats, dandies and diplomats, connoisseurs and courtesans turned their eyes towards France, its art, its literature, its language and its fashions? What exactly *were* those children learning at school?[2]

People's ideas about France and French culture are diverse and sometimes contradictory. They can be influenced by a person's class, gender, nationality, education or social aspirations. In contrast to those ignorant school children, Australian author and socialist Christina Stead thought Paris in 1929 'not so much ... the French capital, as the capital of the modern world'.[3] The French themselves provoked a gamut of responses. The same year as the state exhibition, the Premier of Victoria, Sir Thomas Bent, absentmindedly castigated one of his political opponents for 'shooting in the back' like a Frenchman.[4] Not everybody thought highly of France, its culture or indeed the French.

A connection to France mattered quite a lot to some people – and this book endeavours to tell their story. To Lucciardi or Christina Stead, *Frenchness* (a sense of being French or displaying a connection to French culture) had a role to play in the way they lived their lives and how they thought of themselves. This book goes some way in unpacking the complicated relationship the Australian colonies, and later the Australian nation, had with a country that was on the other side of the world – a country that commanded a competing empire in the Pacific. But more importantly, *French Connection* aims to explore why a connection to France or French culture held meaning to some, and what they did with it, whether they were French migrants or Australian Britons (those of British descent whose culture was an extension of Britain's but often distinct in many ways).

The French have been a part of the Australian story since the beginning of white colonisation, from lowly cooks and diggers on the goldfields to the dynasties of wool buyers who arrived in Melbourne and Sydney in the late 19th century and whose families formed the social mortar of an elite francophone world. To many French migrants and their descendants, being French was a crucial part of their identity; it defined them as individuals and as a people. Take for instance the case of a group of French businessmen in Sydney and Melbourne at the time of the political scandal known as '*L'Affaire*' (the Dreyfus Affair, 1894–1904). During this time, the young Third Republic wrongfully condemned the Jewish army officer, Alfred Dreyfus, for treason and exiled him to Devil's Island off the coast of French Guiana. In New South Wales, the blunder-prone governor, William Lygon, the Earl of Beauchamp and Queen's representative, abandoned diplomatic restraint and proclaimed at an official function that the trials were 'a parody of justice', and made him feel proud to be English rather than French. Deeply offended, the businessmen closed ranks to defend the values of liberté, égalité, fraternité and their honour as Frenchmen. At the same time, many of these very same men were embroiled in internecine libel cases in which they questioned each other's nationality in order to sway the course of justice. Australian judges were mystified at the implication that someone was of immoral character *because* he was not really French. I will leave the particulars of these stories to chapter 5, but they do illustrate the broader point that Frenchness is not straightforward, even for the French.

These migrants never had a monopoly over French culture, which was by and large disembodied and global, existing outside of France. Often consumed and changed by Great Britain over centuries, Frenchness was part of the fabric of Britain's settler colonies. Since the time of William the Conqueror (or the Bastard), France served as a mirror through which to imagine Britishness. Mercantile and Protestant 'Britons' in the 18th century shored up their identity in opposition to the way they imagined the Catholic French to be: 'superstitious, militarist, decadent and unfree'.[5] British men were stoic and masculine in opposition to effeminate, passion-consumed French fops.[6] And yet at the same time ruling elites looked to French arts and culture to assert the boundaries of their own social class.[7] Many of these ideas travelled to Australia with convicts and military personnel from the late 18th century onwards. Throughout the 19th century, colonial newspapers repeatedly reproduced these stereotypes by simply copying content directly from British tabloids. And each successive wave of free migrants tried to recreate the social and cultural order they had left behind. But the place France and French culture held in the minds of these exiled Britons started changing as they became Australians. The faultines and cracks around the competing ideas of Frenchness are fascinating and revealing. They show us a world that did not quite exist but was a crucial part of the Australian imagination. Frenchness influenced the lives of people as diverse as wandering Australian bohemians, aspiring artists, women of the leisured class, or escaped French convicts in need of a new identity. Their stories say something about Australia's imagined place in the world during the 19th century and cast a new light on the largely forgotten groups of French and francophone people who called *l'Australie* home.[8]

When I moved to Australia from France some fifteen years ago, I was surprised to be met with so many unconditional 'ooh la las'. Despite France's complicated and problematic history in the Pacific, it did not seem to affect the way people saw me: croissants, baguettes, la dee da, Paris (*cringe, cringe!*). This was in sharp contrast to the mocking condescension I had experienced in England a year earlier as an undergraduate exchange student. Back then, I was expecting people to fawn over me because I was French (what *were* they teaching us at school?). But upon hearing that I was French, an English dinner-party host, with affected sadness, looked at me despondently and offered his condolences in a hushed voice. Perhaps it is due to distance, both temporal and geographic, but some of the almost familial bickering between France and Great Britain seems to have evaporated here in Australia.

Like most French overseas, I have played with my Frenchness – perhaps more consciously than some – to court favour. I grew up in Alsace, a region historically contested by France and Germany, and with a strong and vibrant identity and culture of its own. Snails are few but pretzels are plentiful, washed down with beer rather than wine. My parents' first language is Alsatian, then French. One generation further back, French was my grandfather's third language, after the Alsatian dialect and German. The Third Republic's dream of homogenising France by turning 'peasants into Frenchmen' by eradicating dialects and *patois* was never fully realised.[9] But I was an ideal candidate for such a transformation. I internalised the process and was part of the first generation in my family to actively reject my ancestors' language, doing my best to Frenchify myself. However, *les Français de l'intérieur* ('the French of the interior'), still often think of people from Alsace as French-speaking Germans. So I have always been aware of the performative aspect of culture and identity; *how* people have used Frenchness is as noteworthy as how it has been represented.

Introduction

Most histories on cultural encounters between France and Britain focus on moments of Francophobia or Francophilia – arrived at through reading the press, often during times of international conflict. Historians show that these moments of tension often underline a class divide between a cultivated francophone elite and a more popular dislike of the French. In the 19th century, low-water marks include the Dreyfus Affair, the Fashoda Incident (a flash point of imperial territorial rivalry between France and Great Britain in East Africa in 1898), and even French support for the Boers in the war in South Africa. These moments of British disdain for the French are offset by celebrations around the signing of the 'Entente Cordiale' in 1904 between the two enemy empires, which heralded a new era of improved diplomatic and cultural relations. In Australia, too, colonists could look to France with more love than hate, hate than love, or an 'inextricable' mixture of both.[10] Many events in Europe had antipodean echoes. Fort Denison in Sydney Harbour was ostensibly built in the 1850s to answer colonists' fears of a Russian invasion during the distant Crimean War. It was not finished until 1857, after the end of the war, but politicians built it as much to ensure a defence against the more realistic threat posed by the French or even the Americans.[11] The opening of a French penal settlement in New Caledonia around the same time also unfurled strong condemnations of France in the colonial press. Some warned of the dangers of the proximity of the 'licentious French nation' and that the penal colony was but a ploy by Napoleon III, whose 'moustachioed sons of Gaul' could invade in a matter of days.[12] On the other hand, the pendulum swung in the opposite direction when the world-famous actress Sarah Bernhardt toured Australia in the early 1890s and kindled a feverish new popular enthusiasm for '*l'art Français*'.[13] In all these stories, the French themselves are usually left out. In Australia, they have tended to be confined to the role of 'good migrants' who, through blood, toil and sacrifice, contributed to creating a successful modern nation. This was a particular interpretation of migrant history, particularly in the

1970s when Australia was reinventing itself as a multicultural nation. But the problem with the 'ethnic' approach is that migrant groups are still left gravitating around a core Anglo–Australian culture that remains homogenous and insulated, without being an integral part of the story or calling it into question.[14] The stories in this book challenge these clear separations by showing how French and Australian people alike have used a French connection in myriad ways to define who they wanted to be. They could do so in part because of the unique role France had played in the definition of Britishness. Not only did this influence reverberate as far as Britain's Australian colonies, but it echoed in the most incongruous of places, as Paul Maistre, another French consul in Australia, discovered during a trek through the ancient forests of East Gippsland in Victoria at the turn of the 19th century.

Maistre will feature prominently in chapter 2, as party to a decade-long war for control of Melbourne's *Alliance Française*. But in this instance he was simply taking some time off his consular duties (which he did as often as he could) to explore the area surrounding Melbourne, where he was posted. In a series of biographical sketches, Maistre gives a brief description of an exchange he had with his Australian guide. One detail the consul deemed worth recording, maybe with some self-satisfaction, was that even though his guide understood very little French, he 'always' carried with him a miniature book written by one great French author or another.[15] Reading this for the first time, I was deeply intrigued. Why would this Australian guide carry with him a miniature Balzac, Flaubert, Dumas or Hugo, a book probably printed in Paris, which he could not read, into the unbroken forest chain on the land of the Gunai/Kurnai peoples, amid rainforests, alpine woodlands and thickets of giant ferns? I imagined a rugged bushranger, hirsute and clad in waterproof sheepskin and leather boots, a swag strapped over his back, standing tall in front of a huge alpine ash. I saw him stretching out his arm to reveal a tiny French book nestled in the palm of his open hand while at his feet brush-tailed wallabies bounded away.

Introduction

And in the distance a native owl woke from its slumber to greet the outlandish apparition with a single deep slow 'woo-hoo'.

Two ideas at the centre of this book are captured in this scene. The first is a certain prominence of the idea of French culture in the British imagination, both in Great Britain and its colonies. What we call French culture the guide might have called French civilisation. In the 19th century, it was a widely held and powerful idea (and still sometimes is today) that various groups of peoples (be that by nationality, race or religion) had achieved different states of organised social life, and that some were further along the civilising process: the passage from barbarity to civility. So people would talk of British or French civilisation.[16] British civilisation was widely admired for its genius in commerce and industry, while the French were thought of as champions of the arts, music and literature; and both were seen as contributing to the forward march of a universal civilisation yet to come. Indigenous peoples were either relegated to the bottom rung of the ladder or denied a place on it altogether. Through their belief in ideas about different types of civilisations and their presence in Gippsland, Maistre and his guide were both directly implicated in the dispossession of Indigenous peoples that was the foundation of settler colonial societies. As European settlers took the land and cultivated it, they also continually internalised the 'civilising' process to show in their manners and the ways they behaved towards each other that they were civilised, as individuals, as colonies or as a new nation.[17] France occupied a dominant position in this game because the British aristocracy and ruling elites had long associated it with refinement and politeness. So Sarah Bernhardt's success in Australia was not just because colonists loved French art (their Francophilia), but because showing their appreciation of it said something positive about their level of cultural development, of civilisation. People attending her performances at the Princess Theatre in Melbourne in 1891 were even described as behaving in a more well-mannered and courteous fashion than would otherwise have been expected. Despite the 'overflowing house', they found their seats with decorum, without jealousies or resentment. There was 'no tumult – no crushing or struggling inside or outside the theatre'.[18]

Second, there is the idea of social distinction. Put simply, the guide probably thought that the little French book made him look good. Even if he could not read it, the object made him look civilised or like he knew what being civilised was about, even in the depths of an ancient forest. This is what the sociologist Pierre Bourdieu calls cultural or symbolic capital. Frenchness here is not something the French inherently possess (though they might think they do), but rather a social strategy or a tactic that allows people to draw upon various strands of a global culture to exhibit certain qualities through signs or behaviours. It can be something as incongruous as that miniature book, having the right accent, or belonging to a learned society like the *Alliance Française*.[19]

All these ideas and many more were contested in the practice of everyday life. French culture could be many things to different people. I recount the stories of men and women, new settlers and old, French and Australian, whose world a French connection helped define. We start by sitting down at a café in Paris with Norman Lindsay to watch the world go by. Australians in the 19th century were fascinated by France and French culture, its arts, literature, fashions and food. But to Lindsay and others, it also offered the possibility to embody another way of life, more attuned to the body and the senses, a way of life that offered Australians an alternative to the future laid out by their fealty to Britishness. At the same time, in Melbourne, the Australian women on the first Committee of the *Alliance Française de Victoria* looked to the past rather than the future. To them, a French connection harked back to British ideas of aristocratic refinement and prestige. The French society offered a cosmopolitan veneer of taste and decorum that sanctioned female sociability and served as a trophy of cultural status in a colonial society where class distinctions needed to be firmly asserted. So when Paul Maistre, the French consul in Melbourne, joined the Committee to open the *Alliance* to French migrants, men and women

Introduction

of all social ranks, two worlds collided, threatening fire and brimstone. But France was not just an abstract idea, it was also a competing empire in the Pacific, involving real people. When the French annexed New Caledonia to turn it into a penal colony, new demons awoke old fears. The arrival of hundreds of liberated and escaped French convicts to the eastern coast of Australia in the second half of the 19th century created an opportunity for the colonies' governing elites. They capitalised on the shame of the colonies' convict past and fears of security to further their own agendas and enforce a particular vision of a moral white Australia freed of its shameful beginnings. While some escaped convicts were extradited back to New Caledonia, many others, liberated convicts or otherwise, disappeared into the general population. Some cashed in on their Frenchness to buy respectability. Others left no trace and merged with the few thousands of largely forgotten French migrants who came to Australia from the second half of the 19th century to the First World War. Traditionally seen as good 'contributing' migrants, the Frenchmen and women who wanted to make *l'Australie* their home had reasons to migrate as diverse as their numbers. And not all succeeded. Among those who did put down roots here, a small self-selected elite group of French and francophone migrants and their families formed a subset of Sydney society from the late 19th century. In that world-within-a-world, centred around the wool trade, being French was also performative. Nationality could be wielded as a shield or a sword to define a collective bourgeois and respectable identity in the host nation, or to exclude those who had done wrong. As migrants and their descendants became more rooted in Australian soil, their connection to France changed. For example, Lydia Delarue, whose diaries we look at in chapter 6, was born in Australia but always thought of herself as French. Things changed when she arrived in Pau in the Pyrénées and was confronted with the repressive gender order of traditional and rural French society. In their diaries, Lydia and her father sketch out a different France from the clichés repeated in the colonial press or by travellers who seldom ventured out of Paris. The gaze they cast on the country of their forebears speaks to the significant role the French countryside played in defining British and Australian ideas about tradition and civilisation.

The timeframe of this book is roughly from the 1850s to the First World War, when diggers fought and died beside the French. Most stories take place during what would in retrospect be called France's *belle époque*, a time of perceived economic and cultural prosperity. In Australia it was a time of nationalist assertion, when separate colonies federated into a white imperial nation.[20] It was also a time when historians imagined the supposedly 'essential' Australian values of egalitarianism, mateship, irreverence towards authority and anti-imperial patriotism were fostered by contact with the Australian bush (how many bushmen carried miniature French books with them, I wonder?). Largely imagined by the urban intelligentsia of the 1890s – excluding women, Aboriginal people and migrants – these ideas continue to hold sway in the way we talk about ourselves as a people.[21] This book is another step in recognising the polyphony (and cacophony) that has always constituted our multilingual and multiracial settler colonial society. I have drawn on a wide array of sources, from colonial newspapers, private diaries and state archives. I have read Australian material in light of French documents, particularly the archives of the Melbourne and Sydney French consulates. These had seldom been studied before because they had been languishing in a Melbourne garage until 1988 before they were finally repatriated to France, looked after, cared for, sorted, and then forgotten.[22]

The stories recounted here are not the whole picture. But taken together they reveal something of the play of empires and the invention of a nation in a region thousands of miles distant from what people thought of as the centres of civilisation. The assemblage of cultural encounters, with their mix-ups and bruised egos, matter because they reveal one of the many ways in which Australia was always entangled with international cultural influences beyond the British realm. In between proud or perhaps arrogant Frenchmen and women, and some

Introduction

occasionally envious or peeved Australian colonists, we can glimpse a more connected and cosmopolitan Australia, one that was half imagined and half real.

CHAPTER 1
A glittering, raucous ritual: French cafés and culture

The man who gave us *The Magic Pudding* was on hallowed grounds. In fact, for Norman Lindsay, Parisian cafés were the very essence of Frenchness. On a short visit to the French capital from London in 1912, Lindsay wasted no time in finding one such holy site. Ruffled but unscathed from a frantic taxi ride, the Australian artist and writer sat down at the Café Tourtel, Place de la République, to practise the French art of people watching. On cue, a picturesque scene unfolded around him. The lazy blue smoke of cigars and pipes seemed to carry an ethereal parade of beards and moustaches whose shapes and sizes defied his Anglo-Saxon imagination. They ranged from the lofty haughtiness of a full-squared beard paying tribute to the King Leopold of Belgium down to the bushy military moustache sported by a canine patron. Appended to the unthinkable Gallic whiskers came men. Men of all types. Men in caps and work blouses and men in hats and frock coats. They read the day's papers and argued politics. They gesticulated with passion in arcane quarrels or buried their heads in their lovers' hair, succumbing to feminine charms. Newspaper boys were yelling 'like demons' while waiters conjured up cups of coffee and bocks of beer unperturbed by the dance of strange and feathered hats set in motion by the lively chatter rising from the tables.[1]

The mystical scene was reproduced all across Paris. The same electric ritual, gay, glittering and raucous was taking place in the gilded establishments of the grand boulevards and the modest small cafés, called estaminets, of Montmartre and Belleville. 'Here is what Australia needs, an institution made especially for us', wrote journalist Henry Mackenzie Green, one of Lindsay's contemporaries. The cafés brimmed with 'sunlight and easiness' and an 'easy unconventionality'.[2] More than just sanctums of contemplative hedonism, French cafés were a manifestation of a certain way of existing in the world. It was indeed with an eye to the future that people like Green and Lindsay observed foreigners and their ways. Many Australians in the early 20th century and colonial Australians before them had for a long time derived a sense of belonging by looking out to a wider British world. But as the colonies edged closer to Federation and nationhood and for some years after, people asked questions about what made them distinctly Australian. Ideas about what was then called 'national character' changed little throughout the 19th century. Australian Britons looked at the French in the same ways the British had for centuries. The French were at once shallow, vain, histrionic, volatile and cowards, but also philosophers, revolutionaries and epicures. France itself was seen as a paradox. It was at the same time the fountainhead of the arts and a bottomless pit of social and moral corruption. It was a harbinger of modernity, and a repository of tradition. But for all their strange ways, there was something about the French and France that captivated the imagination and provided a counterpoint to what Britain had to offer.

Civilisation and culture are embodied ideas; they are internalised, consumed, worn and put on show. For the few Australian Britons who went to France in the 19th century – artists, students or the rare wealthy tourist – as well as for those who stayed in the antipodes, embodying Frenchness – *trying it out* – could serve to mark social and class distinctions. But it also offered the possibility of a more fully realised relationship to the self, to food, the body and sex. So while Australians discussed French fashions, cuisine, literature and art at length, the larger conversation they were having was about themselves and who they wanted to be.

A taste for France

In the 19th century, Australian ideas about France came largely from Great Britain. They were repeated in half-understood, authoritative pronouncements about the nature of the French. In the colonial press, ideas about French luxury and refinement were used to sell products and services, while that same connection served to attract dining patrons in French restaurants in Sydney and Melbourne. In the early 1880s, the acclaimed Australian novelist and journalist Tasma (Jessie Couvreur) was living alone in a hotel in the Latin Quarter in Paris. From her room she wrote articles for the *Australasian* newspaper that gave her readers back home a rare glimpse of the artistic and political life of highbrow Parisian circles. Through Tasma, Australians could sit at the literary salons of the famed Juliette Adam, the founder and editor of the *Revue*. They could read about performances at the Comédie Française, or about various art exhibitions at the Salon. They read about controversial political debates around divorce laws, or the strange punctilio of the Académie Française.[3] But Tasma's Australian voice and point of view were exceptions. Travel to France from the antipodes at the turn of the 19th century remained rare and largely an elite privilege. Colonial Australians had few opportunities to visit, hear or read about France directly. Knowledge fell prey to the tyranny of distance and the gridlocks of empires, so most interactions between France and Australia were mediated by Great Britain.[4] It was not until 1882 that the French steamship company the Messageries Maritimes opened a regular service linking Marseille to Noumea in New Caledonia via the Australian colonies. And commercial exchanges remained limited, Australia imported very few items from France except for luxury goods, wines and spirits, and exported only a few primary products, especially wool.[5] So leading Australian newspapers mostly reproduced British content. The *Sydney Morning Herald* in 1894, for instance, simply reprinted a piece from the *London Speaker* about Arthur Conan Doyle's 'impressions' of France and the French. But the mind that gave us the beloved detective Sherlock Holmes was somewhat unimaginative on that day. Doyle himself only really paid lip service to British ideas of France that had been commonplace since the early 19th century. To him the French came across as histrionic, keen on duelling, too proud and honour-loving. Their saving grace was their devotion to pleasure, the arts and culture.[6]

In 1836, the English novelist and historian George PR James had made very similar comments in a satirical chapter comparing the English and the French under the Restoration and the July Monarchy. He began by writing that 'An Englishman is proud, a Frenchman is vain.' Further, according to James, the Englishman fights coolly, while the Frenchman is hot-tempered. When talking, the former are efficient and to the point; the latter are volatile and frivolous yet make an enjoyable art of it. Indeed, the French were seen as having a profound love of pleasure. When eating, the Frenchman will describe 'every sensation it produces in his mouth and throat, from the tip of the tongue down to the stomach, and winds it up with a smile'. In the end, James concluded that 'the Frenchman is constitutionally a happier animal', he is born a philosopher, 'he enjoys today, he forgets the past and lets to-morrow take care of itself'.[7] A French connection, then, could stand for epicureanism and pleasure, but it also denoted exclusiveness and sophistication, especially in fashion and food, even in far-flung British colonies.

In 1883, the British (and French-educated) journalist Richard Twopeny visited the Australian colonies and noted with satisfaction, and a little tongue in cheek, that new wealth had allowed colonists to buy themselves some class. 'If one considers the distance from Paris, and the total want of a competent leader of fashion', the women of Melbourne 'do not dress badly'.[8] Enriched by capital drudged up from the auriferous arteries of Victoria, diggers and their wives could now adorn their bodies with items of clothing signifying their new status and affluence.[9] In the definition of social and class boundaries in a colonial society, as in the Old World, French was code for *bon goût* (good taste) and refinement. The use of French words in 'the feminine art of clothing' such as 'crêpe de Chine', 'fil d'Ecosse', 'chiffon' and 'voile' conferred a certain cachet upon ordinary items.[10] Australian weeklies and dailies reflected this practice, publishing much advertising material that used 'French' as a synonym for upmarket and elegant. The *Sydney Morning Herald* in 1906 advertised as a 'French frock' a respectable heavy dark cloth tunic of the turn of the century with puffed-out shoulders, a bolero collar and 'smart diminutive tie'. On the eve of the First World War, it promoted a 'frock for the races' (an airy, floral chiffon evening gown) as one good enough to be worn on the French Riviera. The advertisement suggested that for the right price a woman could don the glamour of European elites to make a splash at this quintessential Australian social and sporting event, where not only the horses were on show.[11] A fondness for French high fashion trickled down to department stores. In 1890, David Jones claimed that its 'elegant millinery' was coming from 'the best English and French sources'. And if the national connection of La Maison Parisienne in the new Sydney Strand Arcade, purportedly 'the only French glove house in Sydney', was not self-evident, it was highlighted nine times in a single advertisement, with each pair of gloves on sale prefaced with the adjective 'French'.[12]

The French aura of cultural pre-eminence had deep and old roots, but France appeared to reach a zenith in the arts, culture, taste and fashion particularly during the reign of Napoleon III, symbolised by the ubiquitous crinoline dress of the empire.[13] The Second Empire and the ensuing Third Republic capitalised on long-held ideas about French luxury and taste by putting in place economic policies that embraced more artisanal modes of production, focusing on style and quality, rather than seeking to emulate Britain in the mass production of cheaper goods. This seemed to confirm the idea that the French simply had better taste. So-called *articles de Paris* were in high demand: products like fans, buttons, musical instruments and artificial flowers.[14] *Appellation* and *terroirs* and the legal restriction on the use of regional names for products like champagne and cognac further entrenched ideas of exclusivity and lavishness.[15] Some items were of more dubiously 'French' provenance than others (hair removal cream, 'freshly gathered' French flowers and ceramic toilet ware).[16] But whether real or not, the made-in-France label served as a signifier of taste and quality. By the early 20th century the list of French items on Australian import lists had grown but still largely reflected the specialisation of French industry and the desires of Australian consumers. Millinery, musical instruments, silk goods, clocks and watches, clothing, dress feathers, shoes, ceramics, confectionery, alcohol, glassware, jewellery, toys and pipes were joined by items more symbolic of modernity such as the phonograph and the motor car.[17]

The attraction of French culture extended from the adornment of bodies to the means of nourishing them. Restaurants became popular in England in the 1830s and the new gastronomy was heavily influenced by French cuisine. In Britain it was fashionable for the elite to boast of a French cook, an acquisition made easier by the arrival of French exiles following the 1789 Revolution.[18] Such prized staff were in more meagre supply in the colonies. But several establishments offered French food for a range of budgets. In 1900 on Melbourne's Hunter Street, Adolphe's Diner Parisien promised 'a combination of French Cooking and Bohemian freedom' – the latter facilitated, perhaps, by the inclusion of free wine with a meal. Luca's Town Hall Café on Swanston Street announced that its recently renovated interior came with a new genuine French chef, while many smaller tea salons advertised French pastries for ladies out shopping.[19] The most notorious of all French dining establishments in Australia between 1890 and 1920 was the inimitable Paris House on Phillip Street in Sydney (see images 1 and 2 in the photo section). The founder, Monsieur Desneaux, also owned a popular charcuterie around the corner on King Street which sold andouillettes (a kind of sausage) and pâtés. Paris House was later taken over by another Frenchman from Lille, Gaston Liévain, and his Belgian wife. Described as an 'ultra-moderne' restaurant, with private rooms and a dining balcony, it boasted an à la carte menu serving international and French delicacies such as venison, truffle omelette, bouillabaisse, foie gras and caviar.[20] The ground floor was a popular bistro, the second was more expensive and more private, while the third was a champagne lounge sponsored by Moët & Chandon.[21] On Fridays in the 1920s, in the downstairs section, the poet and scholar Christopher Brennan entertained Sydney's literati in one of his conversation groups called Les Compliqués. Attendees were expected to converse in French, but it made for some disparity in loquacity. Brennan himself was known to launch into eyebrow-raising soliloquies that belonged more to the 17th century literature he was reading than to everyday spoken French.[22]

In the 1880s, self-styled colonial bohemians also frequented French establishments. For the group closely associated with the early days of the nationalist, racist and misogynist *Bulletin* newspaper, it was Paris House and Le Café Français (see image 3) in Sydney, and La Maison Dorée in Melbourne.[23] These bush balladists, short-story writers and black-and-white sketchers – the generation of Henry Lawson, AB Paterson, and AG Stephens – are often singled out as being part of an artistic and journalistic 'golden age' in Australia during which this new, predominantly Australian-born generation defined a particular vision of Australian nationalism that centred their artistic and intellectual fervour on Australia itself and on the Australian bush, departing from the tradition of an older generation of British-born migrants and moving away from Great Britain.[24] Yet their efforts were, ironically, still conceived through a European frame. They prided themselves on their radicalism and France embodied many of their ideals: it was republican, secessionist, socialist and revolutionary. Their idea of French bohemia was one largely popularised by British writers. In particular, George Moore and his *Confessions of a Young Man*, published in 1888, which portrayed to English-speaking audiences for the first time the life of Bohemian Paris in the 1870s and 1880s and the early Impressionist art scene. It did more to influence British perceptions of France than 'all the works of Flaubert and Zola'.[25] The idea of *la vie de bohème* had first been made popular in 1851 in the stories of French novelist and poet Henri Murger and further popularised in Puccini's opera *La Bohème* (1893–1896) and George du Maurier's 1894 novel *Trilby*, set in the bohemian Paris of the 1850s. These works held out the promise of an alternative world of café-concerts, absinthe, poetry and licentious encounters with *grisettes* ('shop-girls' of 'easy virtue').[26] This was the attraction for many, including the group associated with *The Bulletin*. France and bohemia allowed them to imagine and *live*, for a time, an alternative life, freed from the conservative moral and artistic restraints of the Victorian era. Their wives and companions were left to bear the brunt of their liberation.

No one took this affected Francophilia as far as the founding editor of *The Bulletin*, JF Archibald. Born John Feltham, Archibald reinvented himself later in life as Jules François, pretending to have a French-Jewish mother.[27] He was anti-clerical, republican and an avid aficionado of French art and literature. The transformation allowed 'Jules Frankwa', as it was sometimes butchered, a Warrnambool policeman's son, to manifest his unique blend of radical and xenophobic politics with the commanding appearance of old-world prestige and authority.[28] Few Sydneysiders today pause to read the plaque of the Archibald Fountain in Hyde Park dedicating it to Franco-Australian friendship during the First World War, but if they did, they would learn that Jules François bequeathed the money in his will. He also gave specific instruction that the commission go to a French artist.[29] However, the pub-going, all-male environment of Australian *bohème* still leaned more towards British social practices and harked back to British literary traditions.[30] None of the main characters in *Trilby* were in fact French; Bohemia was made in France but for a foreign audience. As Peter Kirkpatrick puts it, the Francophilia of Australian bohemians was a 'revolution in style, not substance'.[31] And yet, it is clear that they were looking for something else, perhaps something more, and some went directly to the source to find it.

Paris: Capital of the modern world

After arriving in Paris, Henry Mackenzie Green sat down at a small marble table in a café off the Boulevard St. Germain. He might have gestured to the *garçon* and ordered a coffee, a 'bock' of beer, or even a glass of absinthe. There, he took stock of his surroundings and contemplated the 'very real charm' of Paris.[32] Green was a man of many qualities, bright, erudite and athletic. Born in 1881 in Sydney's Double Bay, he would go on to make significant contributions to Australian intellectual life until his death in 1962, as a journalist, a librarian, a literary historian and sometime poet. He belonged to Sydney's prominent literary circles and brushed shoulders with the likes of Christopher Brennan, Miles Franklin, Mary Gilmore and John Le Gay Brereton. He was typical of men of his generation who saw no contradiction in sharing an allegiance to both Great Britain and Australia, but the question of what it meant to be Australian was in many ways also at the core of much of his work. Only twenty-six years old in 1907, Green embarked on a trip to Europe after his studies at the University of Sydney in logic and mental philosophy to see, travel, write, learn and study the arts.[33] And to him, the French capital was quite unlike anywhere else.

Perhaps aided by alcohol or feeling lightheaded from the novel experience as well as the heavy tobacco smoke of the café, Green gazed around to try to put his finger on the unique pulse of the city. The 'quickening touch is in the atmosphere', he decided. And maybe the 'sort of atmosphere about the place' came from 'the small twinkling eyes of the dirty, old, bottle-nosed cab-drivers', or the way men shrug their shoulders and nonchalantly swing their canes, or 'the way the women carry themselves'. But above all else, he thought, it came from the cafés.[34]

Thousands of cafés populated Paris at the turn of the 19th century. They ranged from gilded and luxurious establishments off the Boulevard des Italiens, the Avenue de l'Opéra and the Champs-Élysées, with some café-concerts offering high-value entertainment, to much more modest estaminets that provided simple comforts like heat, cheap food and company to the 'little people' of *Paname*, the working-class Paris of Belleville or the Faubourg Saint-Antoine.[35] Cafés had fascinated British visitors for a century. They appeared less threatening to morality and health than London's gin palaces and offered a more open environment for sociability than the taciturn British pub. They provided a space for men and, gradually, women of all classes to while time away day and night.[36] British visitors often noted the surprising sobriety of patrons: cafés were spaces for a different type of sociability. Green himself observed the apparent civility with which the men and women conducted themselves. French civilisation seemed indeed to improve social behaviour.[37]

Certainly, equating Paris to its cafés and France to Paris is reductionist. Claire de Pratz, an English-raised Frenchwoman, dedicated an entire book in 1912 to debunking the enduring synecdoche. 'The average Englishman's impression of France is based upon Paris', she protested, in a *cri de coeur* echoing down the centuries, 'or rather, upon that portion of Paris known as Montmartre and re-joining in the Moulin Rouge and entertainments of a similar character'.[38] She was waging a losing battle. Green was adamant, 'it is in the *cafés* Paris lives, in the cafés where her fascination lies' and this, he thought, was especially true 'for an Australian'. After 'London's huge invulnerable gloom' Paris presented a mirror through which Green and others could reflect upon their 'own people', Britons of a different ilk coming into their own under a new sun.[39] Paris, the city many thought of as the capital of the civilised world, and which philosopher Walter Benjamin called 'the capital of the nineteenth century', and Christina Stead 'the capital of the modern world', presented enviable images of modernity and artistic fervour, as well as sometimes enticing warnings of decadence and vice.[40]

The Paris through which Green and Lindsay wandered in contemplation – dodging cars and trams, and putting their lives in the hands of 'lunatic' taxi drivers – was a physical embodiment of the modernity and progress that defined the end of the century.[41] Large parts of the old and insalubrious Paris had been gutted by Napoleon III and his prefect Georges-Eugène Haussmann in the 1850s and 1860s to make way for the now characteristic radial boulevards and symmetrical avenues. The 'chalk-coloured facades' bored the American writer Henry James 'with their pompous sameness', but Christina Stead in 1929 found them 'so light, so bright, so chic and so charming'. She was perhaps unaware that Napoleon III partly designed them with his new aristocracy and bourgeoisie in mind, and that they displaced the lower classes to the edges of the city.[42] The wide and brightly lit avenues contributed to the spread of the sobriquet of Paris, Ville Lumière – Paris, City of Light – which by the turn of the century had gained wide currency, a manifestation of the symbolic light shining from the city since the 18th-century Enlightenment.[43]

Hailed by modernisers as a new step in the universal civilising process, Haussmann's improvements cleared slums, increased public health by bringing in fresh air and light, and brought in a new moral order to previously crime-infested back streets by facilitating mobility and commerce.[44] Alongside similar changes to the German cities of Cologne and Berlin, Paris inspired colonial plans for the improvement of Australian cities. In the decades before the First World War, plans were afoot to transform Sydney's William Street into a Parisian-style boulevard. The depression that hit New South Wales in the 1890s left it in an architectural and social limbo from which it arguably never recovered. But only a few hundred metres from where the Archibald Fountain still stands, it is not hard to see how the thoroughfare, which connected the already exclusive suburbs of Potts Point, Darlinghurst and Elizabeth Bay to the city, was being imagined as a large and exclusive avenue adorned with local sandstone mouldings and with shops, terraces and cafés dedicated to bourgeois taste.[45] On 'Marvellous Melbourne's' own Collins Street, affluent people could be seen 'doing the Block' in a ritual social emulation of Parisian *flâneurs*.[46] And when Australia was deciding on the shape of its new capital city of Canberra through an international competition, the sketches of the Parisian planner Hubert Agache came in third place. His Haussmann-inspired design divided the city into specialised quarters split by the distinctive straight lines, converging to a 'Concordia Place' where the Court of Justice faced 'a Triumphal Arch inscribed in an Exhedra' (see images 4, 5, 6, 7). Enticing as the Parisian plans were, they did not penetrate the core Anglo-Saxon inclinations of the judges (could the plans have been *too* French?). Instead, they selected the proposal of an American, Walter Burley Griffin, a tribute to the English Garden City movement.[47]

Napoleon III had wanted his empire to be built under the dual ideals of etiquette and taste.[48] The Third Republic in turn sought to legitimise its regime by telling a story of progress and reason. It painted itself as the inheritor of the French Revolution and the science of the Enlightenment. It promoted such ideals through recurring 'universal expositions' and the Eiffel Tower became the most potent symbol of French modernity, built for the centenary of the French Revolution in 1889, and never taken down. So in addition to luxury, France became a leading industry in new technologies.[49] 'Paris is undoubtedly the home of the motor cycle' cheered the *Sydney Morning Herald* in 1898. This was during the Australian tour of the female motorcyclist Madame Serlopette, who donned racing skirts and pushed her engines to 26 miles per hour at the Sydney Cricket Ground. The bicycle, automobiles, the cinema and aeroplanes put France decisively in the international electric spotlight. When the world-renowned French pilot Maurice Guillaux completed the first Melbourne-to-Sydney mail flight in 1914, he inspired a number of Australians to become pilots themselves, including a then seventeen-year-old Charles Kingsford Smith.[50]

Art in the air

France, and Paris in particular, had an aura that seemed to elude explanation, especially when it came to the arts. Its 'art atmosphere' seemed to have no equivalent anywhere else. Alice Foy, an amateur

Sydney artist and teacher with the means to travel spent three years in the French capital from 1905. She went there because of the 'atmosphere of strenuous work and of association with the master minds of the old art world'. This is what 'the Australian artist misses, unconsciously', she explained, 'until one has lived in the art colony of Paris amongst teachers, students, and artists, who think and live art to the exclusion of all else'. Mrs E Paul, another Australian student, piled on: 'In London the true artistic element is sadly lacking.' In the heart of the British empire, teaching still followed a tedious 'rote and rule' tradition, whereas the studios of Paris encouraged individuality, 'there you live in an atmosphere of art: it permeates everything'. To the artist Leslie Beer, on the eve of the First World War, it was not the aloof, 'fat and prosperous' French professors who made 'life in the Latin Quarter worthwhile', but again the elusive 'atmosphere', the sense of aliveness and importance, the 'bustling activity and progress in everything connected with art'.[51] There was something in the air.

The French capital was often seen as 'the magnetic centre of the world of Art'.[52] Other European cities, Berlin and Vienna in particular, were gaining in repute. New York would eventually take over the title in the 1940s. But Paris had a longer pedigree as an artistic and intellectual hub that went back to the Middle Ages. And the French penchant for centralisation had heavily concentrated libraries, museums, salons and galleries in the capital; what historian Christophe Charle calls the 'symbolic resources' of the nation.[53] The city was full of 'artistic treasures' with 'its fine buildings' that made you *feel* art' as 'a living, growing reality of importance'.[54] When Alice Foy and other students were not formally studying, they went to the galleries to study 'the masterpieces of the marvellous ancients and moderns' and learn the radical innovations of the time such as impressionism and symbolism.[55] Men and women the world over were drawn to this hub of creativity.

Many leading Australian artists, including some associated with the Heidelberg School, travelled to Europe, and often especially

France and Paris, as part of their training. John Longstaff studied at the atelier of Fernand Cormon, a leading historical painter, and more Australian artists followed suit, practising in the studios of the École des Beaux Arts, the Académie Colarossi or the Académie Delécluze.[56] Rupert Bunny was the first Australian to receive a *mention honorable* at the Salon de la Société des Artistes Français (Old Salon) in 1888. Emmanuel Phillips Fox was the first Australian to become a *Sociétaire* of the Société Nationale des Beaux-Arts in 1910,[57] and in 1922 Bessie Davidson became the first Australian woman elected as a member.[58] This increased mobility in the 19th century and its appendant technological improvements had become synonymous with the fast pace of an unfurling modernity. Foreigners were themselves a constitutive part of the feeling that Paris was *modern* because they contributed to its 'cosmopolitan' feel.[59] Before 1914, they made up 7 per cent of the population of the French capital, three times more than in London, Berlin or Vienna. Between 1872 and 1899 nearly one thousand Americans exhibited at the Salon.[60] But not everyone saw this 'foreign invasion' with a kind eye.[61]

French students at the Académie Julian eventually rebelled against the growing number of foreign students by circulating a protest pamphlet and making a show of setting up a phonograph blaring the Marseillaise, 'the glorious song of democracy', non-stop for days, until an enraged student smashed the record to the floor.[62] Foreigners themselves, in search of an authentic experience, sometimes resented each other. Americans in particular had, by the early 20th century, swarmed the old Latin Quarter and Montparnasse in great numbers, displacing Alice Foy and many others to the cheaper Student's Quarter. These 'sham bohemians', as she called them, came with fat purses to buy into and feed an already clichéd image of bohemia carefully curated and commercialised for a growing tourist industry.[63] And clichés about life in Paris were hard to shake off.

When Alice Foy returned to Australia after three years in the French capital, she was exasperated that people back home expected her to be transformed. They thought she should have come back 'Parisianised in some mysterious way', complete with an accent and pretty hats and gowns. But her studious years were far from 'a du Maurier-like notion of artistic diversion'. She parried clichés with descriptions of the 'poisonous' air of the city, of the crowded, stuffy and 'unhealthy' studios. Above all, she had gone to France to learn, not to go gallivanting on the boulevards. Life as a 'serious student' was hard. Dressed in plain garb, they sometimes worked fourteen hours a day, six days a week, with few opportunities for distractions bar a few social evenings of music 'washed down with hot chocolate and coffee'.[64] What frustrated her most about these reductionist ideas of Paris was the cultural cringe they revealed about her fellow Australians, many of whom assumed that a foreign culture must be superior. Not without pride — or perhaps arrogance — she concluded that for all the abundance of art in Europe, some was 'worse than anything ever known in Sydney'.[65]

More radical nationalists went further and outright criticised the influence French art was having on Australian artists. At the turn of the 19th century, when newspapers were abuzz with talks of a federation of the Australian colonies and the birth of a new nation, art took on a new importance. It was seen as a gauge of the talent and the level of cultural maturity of a distinctly Australian nation. The painters of the Heidelberg School adapted techniques of the French 'plein air' movement to express the feelings of Australian urban and rural life. They did so with the intent to contribute to the development of a discrete national art form.[66] But to some, painting Australian scenes 'in the light of French teaching' was a betrayal of the imperial idea of Britishness, and a bastardisation of the coming Australian nation. One commentator noted in the *Argus* in 1891 that there was 'a note of discord in all this French enthusiasm'. The exodus of young artists to France and their passion for 'l'art Français' was a distraction from their British roots and stunted the growth of an Australian school of art as their style merged with that of 'dear France'.[67] Besides, France was not only seen as a paragon of civilisation to emulate. To many, it represented a cautionary tale of the *mal du siècle*: the decadence, the melancholy, and the seeming moral dissolution spreading across Europe.

Decadence and sex

Modernity had a flipside. Paris symbolised high art, culture and progress, but it was also a site of revolutions, radicalism and corruption. The civil war that followed the Franco-Prussian conflict and the radical social and anti-religious Commune government that ruled the French capital for a few months in 1871 had left many scars, including a legacy of burnt architectural ruins in many parts of the city. Until 1900 the last remaining walls of the Palais d'Orsay stood as skeletal mementoes of the fratricidal conflict.[68] The physical decay of the city represented an outward manifestation of inner dissolution. For many, the Prussian defeat of France marked the beginning of a descent into the abyss. Novelist Victor Hugo called it 'l'année terrible' and, for his younger contemporary Émile Zola, it was 'la débâcle'. The economic depression that followed lasted until 1896.[69] The national birth rate was stagnant, the army defeated. France was seen as emasculated.

On the international scene, the French bowed to the British at Fashoda in 1898. In Britain, they received vastly negative press coverage over their opposition to the British in the Boer War, and around the Dreyfus Affair, the ongoing antisemitic political and judicial scandal that engulfed the Third Republic for more than a decade. The expression 'fin de siècle' came to signify not only the end of the century, but a perceived decay in moral values accompanying the profound economic, political and social mutations which followed the fall of the Empire.[70] The French, along with the rest of the world, wondered if it was the end of their civilisation.[71]

In British thought, literature was an expression of French artistic genius. AG Stephens, the literary critic and editor, talked of 'the literary grace that seems a Frenchman's birthright' when discussing the French-Australian writer Paul Wenz.[72] As such, modern literature came under forensic analysis for proof of French moral and psychological failings. The *Argus* in 1892 denounced the writing of 'the tribe of Zolas, Renans, Bourgets, Daudets, and Maupassants'.[73] Puritans and conservatives condemned realism as a pathological obsession with the gloom and gore of human life. Real literature and real art were supposed to edify the soul through the contemplation of higher ideals, not the crassness of human existence. In the *Sydney Morning Herald*, Guy de Maupassant's life was brandished as a telling moral tale of the sinfulness of earthly pleasures (Maupassant had tried to kill himself, was committed to an asylum and died from complications of syphilis). Paris itself was the culprit, 'the sensual unbelief of the Parisian world must answer for the mental disease to which Maupassant succumbed'.[74] As Australians reached unprecedented levels of mass literacy, the authorities decided that what foreign material people could get their hands and eyes on should be tightly controlled. In 1888 Alfred Deakin, then Victorian Chief Secretary (and an avowed Francophile), went on a three-year crusade against local booksellers and publishers. In vain he tried to find copies of an infamous translation of Zola's *La Terre*, for which the British publisher Henry Vizetelly had been prosecuted for obscene libel. Deakin himself did not find any but in 1889 the *Victorian Customs Act* did stop a shipment of Vizetelly books. By 1901 the Victorian control system was extended to the whole of the Commonwealth. As historian Frank Bongiorno explains in his book *The Sex Lives of Australians: A History*, more prosecutions of booksellers followed, sometimes around the sale of books that had already been available for years, though cases could be dropped on account of the supposed literary merit of the works in question.[75]

These censorship laws had a lasting impact on public culture. One day in 1921, Alan Rowland Chisholm, aged thirty-three, 'very short, tanned and dapper', was on his way to the University of Melbourne Library. This Mallarmé specialist might have had a new spring in his step, as he had just been appointed lecturer in charge of French at the same university (where he would stay for the rest of his eminent career).

When he arrived at the library, he looked around but could not find his order of the works of Zola. After Chisholm made inquiries, a librarian directed him to a remote cabinet, cautioning that 'we simply couldn't put Zola on the open shelves!'[76] This quarantining of Australian cultural life no doubt encouraged many intellectually curious (and frustrated) Australians to leave, even temporarily. And the censoring of French books surely only reinforced the association of the French with licentiousness and with sex in particular.

Indeed, after fashion, the most widely advertised 'French' items promoted in the Australian press were 'manhood' tonics, contraceptives for both sexes and abortifacient drugs. In 1895 'Professor Robert Herman' of Collins Place in Melbourne, a 'French specialist' paid for two advertisements side by side, apparently without irony, the first a cure for 'lost manhood' and the second an item labelled 'woman's salvation' to put the 'wife's welfare under her own control' (both to be mailed in a sealed envelope). Madame Joubert offered a French remedy to restore female 'regularity', and another advertisement sold 'Parisian female powders' to the same effect. Monsieur Leon sold 'Superior Elastic French Goods' for 5s per dozen. If the 'French' provenance of the items remains dubious at best, so too is the authenticity of the many purportedly French names selling them, but both provided authority. 'French Goods' generally fetched twice as much as British products.[77] The assumed candour of the French in matters of sex was on both Green's and Lindsay's minds during their visits to Paris. The French seemed to be doing it better, or at least to not be so bashful about it. This invited reflections about Australians' relationship to sex and to the body as well as on the nature of the self and the possibility of a more liberated Australia.

Sitting at his café, Green observed that the shameless lust of the French was on full display around him. To an Edwardian intellectual rebelling against the leftover prudishness of the Victorian period, such embodied and raw sensuality was a taste of freedom he seldom experienced in Australia.[78] 'The men look always as if they were thinking of the women, the women as if they carried the men in the corners of their eyes and all their thoughts.' He paid lip service to the established creed that 'Parisian morals' were inferior to British and Australian morals, but his observations took him to a different conclusion. Much as George James did in 1836, Green carefully compared and noted what he saw as a fundamental difference between the French and the British. The 'central god' of the British is money, while that of the French is sex. In turn, sex 'tinges all the rest, the whole tone and atmosphere of the national mind'. Green, too, concluded that people seemed happier and more alive in France.[79] To Lindsay, the sensuous pleasures of the French capital echoed a 'Golden Age of innocence' that unravelled the Puritan order of his youth, 'half the importance that the British give to what they call vice is due to the secrecy with which they practise it. And a lack of respect for that vice is what constitutes the essential innocence of the Parisian mind.'[80] Sitting at the Olympia Café, he sketched a 'youth and a girl reclining with lips languorously clamped together' but with one eye on Lindsay, 'adding the charm of exhibitionism to their ardour' – or perhaps the charm of voyeurism.[81]

The relationship between the sexes Green and Lindsay observed suggests a larger concern about femininity, of the self and of the nation. Paris itself was often personified as a woman. 'Cosmopolitan as she is, [she] stands out clearly as a woman, a Parisienne.' The city, like a woman, would change a man, wrote Green, make him shrug his shoulders, drink absinthe, stroll with a jaunty cane, forget 'his bath and his insularity', 'smile out of his amazement' and breathe 'a lighter-hearted, wittier and more irresponsible air'.[82]

Along with the city, the Parisienne became an emblematic figure and a recurring trope in the often-voyeuristic commentaries of male visitors such as Lindsay.[83] She could be portrayed as a working-class *midinette* (a young, pretty, sentimental and sometimes frivolous girl), a *demimondaine* (a courtesan, a prostitute, or a convention-breaking woman), or a married upper-class *dame* in haute couture. But the femininity of Paris and the Parisienne extended to the whole nation and its inhabitants.

France and the French were largely seen as a feminine country and a feminine people, the counterpoint to a masculine England. 'If England is the masculine country of the world, France is essentially the feminine country,' explained Clair de Pratz in 1912. The main qualities of the French are those ascribed to women: they are charming and graceful; they possess manners; they are more passive, less entrepreneurial, less frugal, more delicate and artistic; they lack emotional discipline and tend towards exuberance.[84] Since the 18th century, England's 'rampant Francophilia', particularly among the elite, the vogue for French culture, its language (the borrowing of 'frenchisms', as historian Linda Colley puts it) and the import of luxury items and fashions had produced anxieties about their impact on British masculinity.[85] But to middle-class intellectuals like Green at the turn of the 19th century, the apparent femininity of the French showed the fallacy of the strict gendered and sexual roles they had been raised with. Instead, the French confirmed Green's belief that men and women each possessed both 'male' and 'female' qualities.

British men considered women as 'an inevitable expense', Green explained. They were 'necessary' to complete oneself, although they could sometimes be 'a nuisance'. The Frenchman, on the other hand, already possessed the feminine qualities that made him 'more complete in himself'. And herein lay the explanation to the artistic inclination and genius of the 'Latin races' to whom the French were thought to belong. The abundance of feminine qualities also put French women in a category of their own, 'enormously more feminine (and female, too)' than their British counterparts.[86] Moving on from the young couple he had been sketching, Lindsay observed 'two women passionately kissing' while ignoring a third, male, party (see image 8). The sketcher tried to explain the Sapphic embrace away as innocent affection or an attempt to charm the men in the café.[87] If Frenchmen were more complete individuals for their feminine qualities, this particular episode shows that contemplating the complete obsolescence of the 'male observer' still remained, for Lindsay, beyond the pale.[88]

Australian feet

French, their mores, their fashion and art were not just discursive curios comforting exiled Britons in their sense of self. At the turn of the century, colonial Australians were preoccupied with the grand task of federating six British colonies to create a new nation within the British empire. With the development of scientific racism, social Darwinism and racial anthropology gradually worked their way into considerations of foreign cultures. People used words like 'Gallic', 'Anglo-Saxon', 'Teutonic' or 'Celt' to discuss their origins and measure their attributes and achievements. Differences of history and culture were increasingly understood as a reflection of something innate and immutable. An article published in 1902 in the Melbourne *Argus* could therefore state with authority that 'the French foot is narrow and long', 'the foot of the Scottish is high and thick; that of the Irish flat and square; the English short and fleshy'.[89] But with a nation then not quite two years old, questions about the shape and size of Australian feet still dangled. So when Australians talked about France and the French, they were talking about a national type they believed could bring something to what was often thought of as 'the Coming Man' (it was usually a man) in Australia.

The belief in the usefulness of comparative studies of national character for the betterment of one's own culture, and a belief in the complementarity of mixing different groups, was not new. Many thinkers in the Anglosphere, such as the English poet and cultural critic Matthew Arnold in particular, admired the Germans for their morality and vitality, and so did Green. Others in the United States also saw themselves as the inheritors of the Germanic Teutonic tribes and their qualities of individualism and competitiveness.[90] But France provided a different choice, one many saw as more *civilised* because of its focus on culture and the arts. It was also a widely held belief that countries such as the United States, England and Australia were too materialistic. The idea that England – the nation of shopkeepers – was too money-oriented and acquisitive was cemented, unsurprisingly perhaps, by a French intellectual, Guillaume Guizot. But his ideas were particularly influential in the thinking of his British contemporaries John Stuart Mill and Matthew Arnold. Civilisation, according to them, did not mean, or should not mean, solely material progress (steamships, railroads, canals, and so on) but also enlightenment and culture: the cultivation of the self and the nation for the betterment of 'mankind'.[91] Australia was already too focused, some thought, on 'business and money making'; more of these material resources should be spent in emulating France in its love of art and science, which would lift the spirit, and the soul, of the nation.[92] And so the French were praised for the qualities they could bring to the British stock in the antipodes, the 'strength and determination of the English character should have blended with it the grace, the brightness and the gallantry, and chivalry of the French'. There was an 'element in the mental condition' of the French that was lacking in Australia and which should be blended to the coming type, 'their poetry, their art, and their élan – qualities which had made the French a great and progressive nation.'[93]

While Australians looked to France with awe or revulsion, it got them thinking. Each first-hand account published in the colonial press, every restaurant or department store advertisement alluding to Parisian sophistication or promising a bohemian experience were small components of a larger picture. The seemingly innate abilities of the French with the arts and literature and their different relationship to gender and sex were as many small tiles building a much larger mosaic which overall showed Australians a different way of life, half imagined and half real. For a new nation avowedly 99 per cent British, the Australian fascination with France suggests a space of possibility where Australia and Australians were imagining themselves as a cosmopolitan nation-in-the-making.

FRENCH CONNECTION

And yet this fascination with France and all things French helped to anchor Australians to the past as much as propelling them towards an undecided future. To some, the British aristocratic ideals of exclusiveness and refinement that Frenchness evoked could serve to assert bourgeois hierarchies in a colonial society where social boundaries needed to be constantly defined and jealously guarded.

CHAPTER 2

A battle for control: *Alliance* and misalliance

On 23 April 1908, white flags adorned with the cross of St George were flying across the British empire to celebrate the saint's Feast Day and the victory of good over evil. But if a dragon had been slain somewhere in Europe, heralding a season of plenty and rebirth, Melburnians were daily being reminded of their antipodean condition. It was the middle of autumn and it had been one of the driest in living memory. Threatening clouds had been gathering over the city for days, but to mock rather than relieve. They delivered scarcely noticeable light rain flippantly alternating with bright sunlight.[1] Cattle all over country Victoria were nothing but 'staggering bags of bones', and a mysterious disease had been killing them by the dozens.[2] In Melbourne, the capital city, fire and brimstone threatened. At the start of the week, huge swathes of smoke engulfed a block of buildings between Flinders Street and Flinders Lane. The fire, which started in a storeroom, was contained moments before devouring supplies of kerosene, benzene and other flammables.[3] On that most joyful and holy of occasions that was the Feast of St George, after a portentous week brimming with bad omens, two unmarked boxes with no return address were left at the French consulate, one made of tinplate, one of cardboard. Who had sent them? Saint or dragon?[4]

Here be dragons

The anonymous boxes signalled the closing of one act, and the opening of a new one. The drama had been keeping Melburnians enthralled for years. Two factions, dubbed by the society paper *Table Talk* as 'the studious and the frivolous', had been at war for the better part of two decades. The former was headed by the French consul in Melbourne, Paul Maistre, who wanted the *Alliance Française* of Victoria to fulfil its role of disseminating the culture and language of his *patrie* to the far reaches of the British empire. The young French Third Republic, buoyed by a belief in the universalism of its values wanted the light of French culture and civilisation to shine on all, regardless of class or sex. But the latter group, the 'fashionable', all-female Australian faction, was reluctant to abandon its control of one of its social and elitist sanctuaries.[5] And after all, they had been in charge almost since the society's creation. The *Alliance* connected them to an older France of aristocratic ideals and refinement. It provided respectable women of the bourgeoisie – the middling echelon of society with no aristocratic lineage – with an opportunity to maintain or enhance their social status by promoting exclusive membership and by hosting stylish balls and 'At Home' receptions. In the hodgepodge of colonial and post-Federation Australia, women were often the guardians of a genteel social order that needed to be shielded from outside forces. These parties were not just fun and games, and they were *not* an exercise in democracy.[6]

Both the French consul and the aspiring *mondaines* of the original committee played their parts well. Act one ended in a cliff-hanger finale where the feminine counsels orchestrated a walk-out on the consul and his allies, leaving them alone in the room. Act two would be the consul's revenge, and act three his downfall. Beyond the seemingly petty squabbling for control of the direction of the *Alliance Française* lies the unbridgeable gulf that separated the sealed-off bourgeois world of colonial Australian women and France's male representative in Victoria. At the same time, shifts of seismic cultural significance were taking place in the world. France was losing its global pre-eminence and its culture was being consigned to the realm of feminine accomplishments. It only made the fighting more bitter. The epic battle between saints and dragons had only just begun.

Shaky foundations

It all started innocently enough. On 6 June 1890, in the plush suburb of St Kilda, Madame Berthe Mouchette read a letter from Paris out loud to a small group of interested people. The letter invested her as the local delegated authority of the *Alliance Française* of Paris and officially launched the *Alliance Française de Victoria*. This first meeting took place at 'Oberwyl', now a luxury, heritage-listed property. From the Basses-Alpes department, Mouchette had been living in Paris before moving to Australia in 1881 with her husband and sister, Marie Lion. After the death of her husband she and her sister purchased 'Oberwyl', as an already well-established and reputable girls' boarding school in 1885.[7] The *Alliance Française* was only two years old then.

Created in Paris in 1883, the core mission of the *Alliance* was to disseminate the French language and French literature, both within France's formal empire and to the world at large. As such it was quickly embraced by the government of the fledgling Third Republic, who saw it as serving the public interest of France through proselytising its civilisation abroad – what the French still talk of as the idea of cultural 'rayonnement' ('influence' but with a particular divine quality). At the time, Jean Jaurès, the future socialist leader – then only a young professor at the university of Toulouse (and still a moderate republican) – believed that the *Alliance* would ensure that Frenchmen and women living overseas remained faithful to their nation. It would also help to make France loved in foreign countries and compensate for low French migration by making foreigners more 'French' in their 'minds and in their hearts'.[8] The messianic rhetoric of political leaders like Jaurès and the administrative, financial and political links between the *Alliance* and the French government position the French cultural institution firmly as a secular inheritor of the French Catholic civilising mission. It also places it clearly within a form of righteous expansionism and cultural imperialism espoused by France since the Revolution of 1789. It makes evident the tensions and paradoxes at the heart of France's unique form of 'Universalist nationalism', still so much in evidence today: a cultural model all should embrace but that remains firmly in the service of a particular vision of France.

Oberwyl, a Greco-Regency mansion with a columned front porch and French shuttered windows, one of St Kilda's oldest, is only a five-minute walk from the current seat of the *Alliance* at Eildon Mansion on Grey Street, an even grander building. Although the location has changed, Madame Berthe Mouchette remains celebrated as the founder of what is now known as the *Alliance Française de Melbourne*. This is true, in part, but the circumstances that saw her propose the formation of this first committee are as fraught as the early history of the society itself.

At the beginning of 1888, Maurice Astruc, a Mauritian working for the Francophile Australian solicitor Joseph Woolf in Melbourne, took it upon himself to write to the *Alliance* in Paris, suggesting opening a Victorian branch. But the then consul for France, Léon Dejardin, reportedly feared the opprobrium that could befall the new society if it was headed by a man 'of colour'. Instead he asked Woolf himself to set up an 'action committee', recommending him 'because of the high esteem our compatriots have for him, and his demonstrated taste for the French language and French literature'.[9]

Berthe Mouchette herself was connected to the French consulate world and the contiguous French-speaking Melbourne community through her late husband's position as deputy chancellor and in her own right through her reputation as a teacher and painter.[10] She put her hand up to create a *comité de dames* ('ladies committee') for the new venture. Woolf, however, withdrew his services due to ill health and, with the approval of headquarters in Paris, deferred to Mouchette, whose own committee was ratified in 1890 at that first *Alliance* meeting at her grand home.[11] That the idea for a Melbourne *Alliance* had initially come from a Mauritian man, a French-speaking product of French colonial history, but was, in the end, enacted by a Frenchwoman, herself chosen as the second best choice after an Australian man, speaks volumes about the paradoxes of both the little French society of Melbourne and the wider society in which it operated. In both cases, despite their universal aspirations, their inner workings and social prestige in Melbourne hinged on defined racial and gender hierarchies that were largely shared between the French metropolis and the British colonies. Because of the peculiar circumstances of its foundation, the tone within the Melbourne *Alliance* was established from the outset. For want of a *comité d'hommes* ('gentlemen's committee'), the *Alliance* was, almost by default, one of women.

The Melbourne branch was already six years old when Paul Maistre arrived with his wife and children to work at the consulate after a posting in London. In his mid-thirties, he dabbled in creative pursuits such as poetry and other writing, and cherished his time away from work. He spent two substantial periods of time in Melbourne (interrupted only by a shorter stint back in England) as vice-consul and eventually consul for France, between 1886–1898 and 1901–1908.[12] He was very much a career diplomat, and it is easy to see him as an apostle of the Republic, intent on reforming the *Alliance* to the core so it would serve his France well, but his interest in the institution was fleeting at best, at least until his second posting. He and his wife Charlotte, née Allen, were honorary members to start with, as befitted his position, but he showed no particular desire to actively participate. He was eventually pressured by Paris and the Sydney consulate-general to become more involved, which might go some way in explaining his ham-fisted methods, and why he rarely attended meetings and then seemingly only to express his disapproval – but misogyny was a potent ingredient in the mix.[13] If the creation of the *Alliance* can be seen as a portent of the crisis of French hegemony, if things were not going so well in the global conquest of minds and hearts, Maistre did not do much at first to nudge the *Alliance* in the right direction. Instead, he left the French society in the hands of Australian women, who quite reasonably used it as a stage for bourgeois sociability.

A woman's world

Through her connections in Melbourne society, Berthe Mouchette was able to secure the support of leading society women whose social clout was derived in part by an attachment to the ideals of a landed British gentry, complete with honorific titles.[14] Aside from Mouchette's social skills, the fact that the newly created *Alliance* attracted some illustrious women also connects back to British and aristocratic attraction to things French and the feminisation of that culture over time. By the late 18th century, what historian Linda Colley calls an 'invasion of Frenchisms' gradually came to be perceived as a threat to British ideas about masculinity, even as it helped to define it.[15] Over time the very linguistic qualities of French, its 'softness and musicality', its 'melting tone', came to be opposed to the virility of the English language. Mastery of foreign languages became the domain of women. A century later it was common for the English gentleman to frown at the very idea of speaking French.[16] In 1903, Isidore Maurice-Carton, Lecturer in French at the University of Melbourne, remarked that if boys did study French (or even German) it was to boost their commercial careers, but they 'have never been taught to like or take an interest in the subject'.[17] In 1905 in Sydney, all of the twenty-one laureates at the annual *Alliance* exams were girls from local ladies' colleges: Kambala, the Presbyterian Ladies College of Croydon and St Catherine's Clergy Daughters (now St Catherine's School) in Waverley.[18] So much for the language of diplomacy.

The first *Présidente d'honneur* of the *Alliance* was Lady Janet Clarke, wife of the exceedingly wealthy Sir William Clarke, the largest landowner in the colony, who had been made baronet for his role as president in the 1880–81 Melbourne Exhibition. Born in Victoria, she first worked as governess to William Clarke's children. After their marriage, the Clarkes were renowned for their parties and charities. They entertained on a lavish scale, with guests arriving on foot or by carriage and in the hundreds at 'Cliveden', their sumptuous East Melbourne mansion of grand proportions, or arriving by train at their private railway platform at their property in Sunbury, some 40 kilometres north-west of Melbourne. Through her wealth and her social work Lady Clarke became a leading figure in Melbourne society for over thirty years, in turn becoming the vice-president of the Austral Salon and president of the Dante Society.[19] The first *Présidente* of the *Alliance* was Mrs Holroyd (later Lady Holroyd), whose husband was also the president for many years of the Imperial Federation League, and the Athenaeum and Savage Clubs.[20]

Lady Clarke, as honorary president, would remain untouched and detached from the unfolding drama. But her role as figurehead of the *Alliance* and other societies shows the significance of such organisations as spaces of appropriate sociability for an imperial and aspiring aristocratic world where the games of social inclusion and exclusion could safely take place. It also points to the divisions that existed among the sexes in these privileged social institutions where men and women occupied separate spheres.[21] The Austral Salon, founded in 1890 and located on Collins Street in the Austral building, was exclusively reserved for women professionally engaged in the literary and artistic world to discuss literature, drama and the arts for the advancement and the edification of their sex (though men could attend lectures and social events).[22] The gendered schism was reproduced at the Melbourne *Alliance*: some of its events even took place at the Austral Salon or during 'At Home' receptions where the 'sterner sex was somewhat scarce'.[23] In late April 1900, members of the *Alliance* were entertained at Lady Clarke's East Melbourne mansion overlooking the Fitzroy Gardens, where the 'fairer butterflies of Society', as *Table Talk* called the women in attendance, engaged in small talk over cups of coffee or glasses of champagne. In the background some of the most *en vogue* musicians could be heard performing, including the much-sought-after pianist and composer Madame Charbonnet, a cornerstone of the French artistic network of Australia, one-time teacher of opera singer Nellie Melba and the mother of swimmer Annette Kellerman.[24] Given the feminine and aristocratic ideas attached to French culture in the 19th century, the *Alliance Française* provided an umbrella of decorum and taste that sanctioned female sociability. The only man on the first committee of the *Alliance* was the secretary.[25]

Early troubles

The first classes given by the *Alliance* took place at Madame Mouchette's home, where she and her sister Mademoiselle Lion dispensed French lessons every Wednesday night at eight o'clock. The lessons consisted of spoken readings of modern French theatre and accommodated ten to twenty students. Some, however, found the location too far from the city and too difficult to access, and the number of classes insufficient. An anonymous French correspondent to *Table Talk* (likely Paul Maistre himself) mused that the *Alliance* had made its timetable unworkable for most people so it would not steal Sarah Bernhardt's spotlight during her Australian tour. He wondered why there were not more classes since there was an over-abundance of teachers in the colony (as we will see in chapter four). He signed his little epistle Paul 'Le Franc', in the double sense of frank or forthright, but also indicating that he was a native Frenchman.[26]

But the *Alliance* was impervious to criticism, and interference from the consulate was seen as an imposition. When prompted, the *Alliance* sent reports of its activities to Paris only reluctantly.[27] Matters became worse after Mouchette and her sister moved to Adelaide in 1894. The now predominantly Anglo-Australian committee steered the French society decidedly in the direction of the other social clubs they belonged to so that the *Alliance* became another site for the production and reproduction of their social world, to the exclusion of French nationals and Australians of a lower social class.[28] Maistre became incensed and dismissed the Victorian branch as a frivolous social club, nothing more than one of those 'mondaine Australian societies where, under the pretence of arts and classical literature, they organise "teas", "soirées" and "bals" … a pale copy of the Austral Salon', where French was little spoken.[29] But to the largely English-speaking membership, language was not the point. 'If one has a good command of English, it is silly to try and master French or German', suggested one guest at an *Alliance* 'At Home' reception at Cliveden in 1901.[30] Maistre was further revolted by the all-female composition of the committee, describing it with the loaded expression '*tomber en quenouille*', which has the double meaning of something falling under the authority of a woman, and of becoming obsolete.[31] And so with a vindictive eye Maistre paid close attention to the society's activities, waiting for mistakes to be made, so he could take control. The first blunder was the *Alliance* exams.

Teachers under examination

By most accounts, the first exams held by the *Alliance* in Melbourne in 1890 were a disaster. They were 'supposed to be an educational test', went one critique, but 'were little short of farcical in almost every detail'. Examinations that should have been public were conducted one-on-one in low tones between one competitor and a single examiner 'who passed or rejected the candidate according to individual fancy'. The examiners themselves seemed so at a loss that they were seen asking for help from some of the French teachers who had come to support their students. Pronunciation counted for more than grammatical accuracy, and one student was disqualified for having spent a few days in France, 'although it had not previously been announced that the breathing of French air … would be regarded as harmful to French students'. The list of grievances went on and extended to the written examination as well.[32]

Four years later, the *Alliance* tried to justify its declining number of students, paradoxically suggesting it was due to the respect the society was earning as a language institution. The low numbers showed that 'our exams are serious and that it is perfectly pointless to send us those of their students who are still learning to conjugate'. But some efforts were made the following year to give the examinations more credibility by employing more native speakers as examiners. These were from the establishment: the consulate in Sydney and the *Comptoir National d'Escompte de Paris* (the French bank) in Melbourne. Since at least two of the new examiners were Sydney-based and linked to the Consulate in Sydney, suggests the possibility of a more co-ordinated effort to redress the direction of the Melbourne *Alliance* rather than a decision by the committee.[33] When an *Alliance* proper was created in Sydney in 1899 (for a while it was just a lending library) it immediately played an important role in the public teaching of French in the colony. Due in large part to the efforts and stranglehold of the consul general, George Biard d'Aunet, the action of the Sydney *Alliance* focused primarily on language teaching rather than social events and linked the *Alliance* to public teaching in New South Wales, working towards the state-wide adoption of new methods of language teaching.[34] By 1908 the Public School Board of New South Wales required its candidate teachers to hold a diploma from the Sydney *Alliance* as proof of their competency in French.[35] This lent the institution a stamp of legitimacy and ensured its success. Melbourne went in the opposite direction.

Adieu Racine, Voltaire ...

Seeking relief from the scorching November heat in 1895, 'Nestor' stepped into the cool of the Athenaeum Club, the gentlemen's club on Melbourne's affluent Collins Street. In the upscale sandstone building he spent an hour in the company of the 'masters of French literature'. While his body cooled down, his intellectual thirst was quenched by the '*tour de force*' of the *conférencière* (speaker) regaling the pundits.

Slender and dark-haired, Mademoiselle Irma Dreyfus had a softly angular, defined jawline that gave her a determined and commanding air. She knew what she was doing. Over the years she had become adept at condensing centuries of work into short lectures for the general public. On this occasion in the span of an hour she left the audience's heads dizzy with a constellation of the leading lights of French literary and artistic history: Bossuet, Fenelon, Bourdaloue, Poussin, Le Brun, Le Notre, Racine, Voltaire, Lully, Boileau, Madame de Sévigné, La Fontaine, La Bruyère, La Rochefoucauld, Madame de Lafayette and Mademoiselle de Scudèri, to name only a few.[36]

Dreyfus, a Frenchwoman from Alsace, had migrated to Australia via New Zealand in 1890 with her sister Mrs Aarons. Both were French teachers and active in promoting French culture.[37] Dreyfus gave numerous public lectures in Melbourne with the patronage of the consulate and local men of letters.[38] Devoted to her country of birth and the arts, she donated half the profit of a talk she gave at Government House in mid-1897 to the *Alliance Française* Library.[39] Some of her earlier talks were eventually translated into English and published in book form. In 1898 the French government made her an *Officier d'Académie* in the chivalric *Ordre des Palmes Académiques* for her services to French culture overseas.[40]

Public lectures and literary soirées were another means by which the *Alliance* was supposed to help propagate French civilisation. Dreyfus already had a significant track record and several devoted students when she approached the committee in 1893 with a series of seventeen lectures. Her offer was readily accepted.[41] Yet after the first lecture was given, the minutes of the *Alliance* Committee meetings fall silent and never mention Dreyfus again. We know she *did* give the lectures, but with the support of Paul Maistre and without *Alliance* patronage.[42] Exactly what went on between the committee and Dreyfus is not entirely clear. It is a very distinct possibility that she was at least in part ostracised because of her Jewish name. Its association in many people's minds with Captain Dreyfus led her, in the middle of the

Dreyfus Affair in 1898, to defend herself against circulating rumours, stating that 'my family is neither closely nor remotely related to that of that man'.[43] In 1900 she left for Europe, where she founded a new *Alliance*-affiliated society in Paris, the *Alliance Littéraire, Scientifique et Artistique Franco-Britannique*, whose aim was to establish personal and professional bonds between writers, savants and artists of the two countries through international exchange and conferences.[44]

The rift between Dreyfus and the committee was also due in large part to a difference of opinion about the way the *Alliance* was run, and it became public. Dreyfus shared Maistre's view. Before leaving she wrote an open letter to the president, Mrs Holroyd, published in French in the society paper *Table Talk*, with a full-length portrait of herself. It pointed a polite, but firm, finger at the leadership of the *Alliance* for its lack of initiative in language teaching and, importantly, its elitism:

> When I am asked if we organised language lessons, the monthly reunions of our Melbourne branch, which due to circumstances only concern one class of society and the smaller class, might seem to not have been enough. I will defend these reunions which have some good in them, a lot of good, but which, we all agree I believe, cannot and do not really do much for the propagation of the language.[45]

Along with her name she included the new title the French government had bestowed upon her: she was an 'Officer' of the French Republic, an honorific title earned through merit, drawing a political and social line between herself and the Australian 'aristocracy' and bourgeoisie heading the *Alliance*.

Dreyfus was not the only person the *Alliance* rejected. The year she left, Isidore Maurice-Carton, who lectured in French literature at the University of Melbourne, also offered to give a series of public talks. Unlike Dreyfus, they did not let him give even one.[46] This rejection is even more peculiar. Maurice-Carton was touchy and punctilious, but his devotion to French culture and his academic credentials were well established. His love of the French language verged on what some thought of as gross 'linguistic megalomania' (which they also saw as a common attitude among French people).[47] For Maurice-Carton, French possesses a precision that 'does not afford any loopholes for misapprehension as to meanings', for 'a French sentence is easily comprehended, and cannot be misunderstood, like an English one may be by the misplacing of a full stop or a semi-colon'.[48] But there was a bit more to the psychological make-up of Maurice-Carton to position him as a defender of French culture overseas – if a quirky one. He had migrated to Australia in 1879 with the intention of taking up farming, but instead completed a Master of Arts at the University of Melbourne, where he stayed on to teach. Permanently haunted by the ghosts of the Franco-Prussian conflict, in which he had fought, he transferred those anxieties to the cultural domain and always remained wary of – verging on paranoid about – the German threat to France's cultural dominance and its interests in Australia. The *Alliance*'s German counterpart, the *Deutsche Schulverein von Victoria*, was at the forefront of his mind, and it was in a combative spirit against Germany that he redoubted his efforts to promote the spread of French in the colony.[49] French-language teaching at the university gained momentum under his stewardship, first as part-time lecturer in 1902 and then full-time from 1905 until his retirement in 1920. Besides the classes he offered in language and literature, he was able to build on the predominance of French in secondary schools in Victoria, enticing students to take up French literature and language at the university by creating numerous prizes (sometimes at personal expense). He supported the creation of a French Club by students at the university which awarded a £4 prize (the Pierre Corneille Prize) to the first runner-up of the Senior Public School (Honours) exam each year.[50] Two years after its foundation, in 1903 the club reportedly had a library of 300 volumes of French literature and eighty members, and organised monthly meetings to discuss history and literature – in French. It did what the *Alliance* should have been doing. Their motto appeared on their stationery: *'c'est en forgeant que l'on devient forgeron'* ('it is by forging that one becomes a blacksmith' – practice makes perfect).[51]

So how are we to understand the *Alliance*'s rejection of two qualified and established lecturers? And if the *Alliance* did not give public lectures on French literature and culture, what, then, was it for?

A Frenchless society

In lieu of educational soirées and public lectures the *Alliance* became increasingly concerned with social events, in particular the Annual *Alliance* Ball. The 1907 ball was 'the most successful this society has yet held, both numerically and socially', according to the society paper *Punch*.[52] But the 'French' component seemed almost an imposition, at least aesthetically. 'The decorations, entirely the work of the committee, were very artistic, and this is saying much, for the tricolour (blue, white and red) does not admit of any possibility in the way of soft contrast.' Only 'pale and dark green foliage' could be used, but it was 'very tastefully done'.[53]

The ball, and the problems surrounding the exams and lectures, show more than the inadequacy of a group of colonial Australians who were not qualified to run what was supposed to be a language institution designed to promote another country's cultural interests abroad. It shows that the committee only saw the *Alliance* as a place of social significance, sanctioned by its purported links to French culture, but where French itself in fact held little importance. This goes some way in explaining the committee's attitude towards both Maurice-Carton and Irma Dreyfus. But class was another important factor.

Maurice-Carton and Irma Dreyfus, individually and through their careers, represented a threat to the control of the *Alliance*, for they embodied precisely what the committee was not: they were both French nationals and knowledgeable in the language and its culture, and both played an important role in the emerging discipline of modern language teaching in Melbourne. Both would quickly have shown the committee members to be grossly inadequate in their roles and that French to them was just an element of genteel performance. Excluding them was necessary to retain the power to define what the *Alliance* was, and whose interests it served. It also shows the significance of the *Alliance* to the tight-knit group of socialites as a site through which to maintain their status and rank in the small world of late colonial Melbourne. But fostering belonging along gender and class lines meant that many others were excluded, including Australian colonists and French migrants of a lower social class. And it became increasingly difficult for the committee to justify its isolationism.

The treasurer of the *Alliance* until 1907, Mrs Sybil Maud Cave, was far from being against education. She would become the Honorary General Secretary of the Victoria League of Help after the First World War, helping to create libraries for returned servicemen and for Australian children in the bush. The League of Help – an imperial charitable organisation run by women – even named a high school prize after her.[54] But when in 1901, in response to the early fiasco of the *Alliance* exams, it was suggested that teachers of French could become more involved, she dismissed it as 'inadvisable'.[55] In 1906, when Maistre was on leave, his temporary replacement, the vice-consul in Sydney, Eugène Lucciardi, mentioned that French residents felt they were under-represented at the *Alliance*. When he suggested several French names for the committee, some of whom were also teachers, the committee replied that they were decidedly against the membership of teachers, giving the outlandish explanation that they wished to 'avoid any suspicion of unfairness in the examinations'.[56]

When Lucciardi did manage to bring more French people on to the committee it backfired. One of them was Madame Charlotte Crivelli, the wife of Dr Crivelli, the French physician to the Melbourne French community, and the daughter of his predecessor Dr Duret. Including the Crivellis was designed to tip the balance in Maistre's favour – the 'French' side – but had the opposite effect. Though she was of French extraction and her family was a cornerstone of *le tout Melbourne*, Madame Crivelli, through her upbringing in Victoria, sided with the Australian members of the committee. The Crivellis' connections in France in fact expanded the reach of the committee and allowed them to make noise in high spheres in Paris, and plant the seeds of Maistre's eventual downfall. They complained that under the French consul's influence, 'wigmakers' and 'corset-makers' joined the committee and that 'seeing this, the wife of the Governor, who was expected at the meeting, sent her chambermaid instead'.[57] If the complaint was hyperbolic, their point was that Maistre's efforts at democratising the *Alliance* were doing more harm than good. To them, it was leading to a carnivalesque upending of the social structure of a colonial world in which class boundaries could be at times uncertain and needed to be jealously guarded.

Gloves off

Paul Maistre became more actively involved with the *Alliance* around 1901, after his English posting.[58] By now well into his forties, he had the self-deprecating tendency that often comes with self-assurance. Paunchy and red-nosed from drinking (he himself uses the adjective '*bourguignon*', after the wine, to describe his nose), he tried to extend France's largesse to the committee to coax it into submission. Gifts of books (including his own), free use of consular mail services to avoid stamp duty, and the occasional medal were wielded as many carrots to cajole the *Alliance* into following the example of the Sydney branch and give the society a larger reach. But if gifts were accepted, it did not give him free rein, particularly because the treasurer, Mrs Cave, fought him tooth and nail.

The first priority for Maistre, in order to gain the authority he needed to effect change, was to encourage more regular contact with Paris. That this relationship was written in the statutes of the society left the committee members little choice, but they dragged their feet.[59]

During the few years of his membership it became apparent to Maistre that none of the women involved seemed aware of the *Alliance*'s statutes, which certainly partly explained how matters could have gone as they did in the preceding decade. It also provided him with the opportunity for staging an effective coup.

In 1907, Maistre wrote a scathing pamphlet explaining what the *Alliance* was and what it should do. He sent a copy of his *Notes sur l'Alliance Française de Victoria: Sa fondation, ses statuts, son but et ses moyens d'action* ('Notes on the *Alliance Française* of Victoria: Its foundation, its statutes, its goal and its means of action') to Paris but also handed a copy to the committee. Vindictive, if not vengeful and outright brutal, the document attacked the committee members themselves and their way of life by pointing out the similarities between the *Alliance* and other society clubs such as the Austral Salon. When his notes were read to the committee meeting in August of that year, their understandably vexed response was that 'the Committee can only say that if in its meetings there have been omissions or if it has not strictly observed regulations, all have always sought what is best for the Society'. But herein lay the crux of the matter. The society, as it existed, hinged on the strictly defined class and gender boundaries of Melbourne's elite social circles, which excluded those which the *Alliance*'s messianic mission sought to include.

The first point of Maistre's *Notes* was about the structure and membership of the committee. Though a trivial technicality in appearance, it was of paramount importance in the struggle for effective control, for it signified a progressive erosion of the monopoly of its leadership. Second, the *Alliance* was supposed to be as much a refuge for French citizens to maintain contact with their national culture 'whatever their social situation and their fortune' as a place to promote French interests in foreign lands. So far French nationals had largely neglected (and been neglected by) the *Alliance*. One way to remedy this, Maistre hoped, would be to introduce more French members to the committee, who would, in turn, attract more memberships. But

Maistre also wanted these new members to be men, who could bring to the Committee 'that habit of affairs, that calm judgment and the logic that are not, usually, the preserve of the fair sex'.[60] Maistre's desire to change the gender composition of the *Alliance*, to make it 'truly' French, ironically lays bare some of the paradoxes at the heart of French society. It highlights the dialectic between a strong form of nationalism defined through a universalist rhetoric but which dovetails with deeply entrenched stereotypes about the place of women in society, which the young Australian Lydia Delarue would find so contemptible on her visit to France, as we will discuss in the final chapter. Maistre used transparent tactics to convince Maurice-Carton to join the committee by appealing to his ego and questioning his patriotism.[61] He dithered for a while but eventually gave in to stay in the consul's good books, though not without expressing his distaste 'since to this day everything they have done seems directed against the University, the University can naturally only be hostile to them'.[62] In fact, all Maurice-Carton's suggestions to reform the *Alliance* would have seen it become subordinate to his own program and the French Club at the university. In the end Maistre stuck to the statutes of the *Alliance*. The ideas he presented to the committee were nothing more than what the *Alliance* headquarters advised and what the society did elsewhere, in Paris and the provinces: exams, monthly literary soirées, liaising with primary and secondary school teachers, and ensuring the complete ascendancy of the French language and French music in all aspects of the society.[63]

Molière's return

Some changes started taking place slowly but these were seen by the committee as a further attack. In the last months of 1907 Rosa Aarons, sister to Irma Dreyfus, one of the most active new – French – members of the committee, proposed that the *Alliance* give a series of 'Soirées-Lectures' not only for members, but also non-members and school pupils. These should be of interest to 'all who study our language and our literature, without any distinction of age or social condition, and will educate through entertainment'.[64] The first was given on 23 September to a packed room at the 'Independent Hall' in Fitzroy where many committee meetings also took place (it is now another heritage-listed luxury house, known to millions of Australians as the home of the fictional detective Jack Irish, played on television by Guy Pearce).[65] In more ways than one it was a landmark event. First, it offered special entry prices to public school students and their teachers, thus extending the reach of the *Alliance* to the general population and cementing its links with the education sector. It saw an immediate spike in *Alliance* memberships.[66] Second, the play that was selected, Molière's *Les Femmes Savantes* (*The Learned Women*) was an audacious choice. One local newspaper noted the universality and timeless nature of the characters of the play. The author's satire was aimed 'not at ridiculing ephemeral follies, affectations, absurdities of language, and manners, but at making comedy from characters which exist, with modifications, in all ages'.[67] *The Learned Women*, for Molière, represented a new archetype of women he was wont to satirise: women whose affectation of clothes, dress and manners he had decried in his earlier *Les Précieuses Ridicules* (*The Pretentious Young Ladies*), but who had now grown older, along with their century, and in order to keep shining in society affected scholarship in all the branches of the tree of knowledge. He derided the main protagonists, three women belonging to the high bourgeoisie, for their superficial and affected erudition, grotesque to the point of ridicule, in the sciences, high arts and philosophy. He mocked their attempts to use arcane jargon without understanding the deeper meaning, their preoccupation with form without substance. Could the message have been clearer or more vindictive? In any case, it seems to have been received. Neither Lady Holroyd, Lady Clarke nor Mrs Cave attended, nor any of the following soirées.[68]

The coup

Part of Maistre's plan to make the society more French was to integrate it more effectively with the interests of the French and French-speaking community in Melbourne. As such, he wanted the funds of the *Alliance* to be entrusted to the *Comptoir National d'Escompte de Paris* in Melbourne, the French bank, as was customary elsewhere in the world. Mrs Cave insisted that the funds remain with the Union Bank, especially because the former director of the French bank, M Phalempin, had in the past rejected their account because it was too small. The matter was put to a vote and Maistre won by a large majority, with only Mrs Cave and one other voting against the proposal.[69] The new director of the *Comptoir National*, Monsieur d'Orgeval, probably on the advice of Maistre, opened an account with his company and paid into it his and his wife's first membership fees, sending a receipt to Mrs Cave. Though the transfer had been voted in, Cave was still the treasurer and not a simple secretary, and the d'Orgevals' membership had not yet been approved by the committee – even if it was a formality. The constant encroachment on her and her friends' authority, and by men, must have been a hard pill to swallow. A heated exchange of letters between Cave, d'Orgeval and Maistre followed, where she was accused of anti-French sentiments and where she denounced d'Orgeval's actions as illegal. Cave also took offence at the suggestion that the accounts in her care should be examined by an independent auditor (to save the *Alliance* money, she had had the accounts done for free, by her husband).[70]

At the following monthly meeting, in Maistre's absence, Cave tried to overturn the vote on the transfer of funds and block the membership of the d'Orgevals through absurdly punctilious readings of the statutes of the *Alliance*, which did not hold against the common sense of the other committee members.[71] But after reading her correspondence with d'Orgeval to the committee, they agreed on an amendment that the transfer would only occur once a more courteous director was appointed to the French bank. How much Cave's own vendetta was directed against the transfer, against d'Orgeval or simply against Maistre is unclear. Certainly d'Orgeval's accusation that she was anti-French was unfair (she had supported the election of French committee members). But while she was not being explicitly accused of malpractice, her stubborn insistence on keeping the funds at the Union Bank, and her refusal to have the books audited, for whatever reason, was not a good look. The story started filtering into society papers such as *Table Talk*, a form of social opprobrium Cave and the other committee members would have been very concerned about, considering the *Alliance* was meant to be a social haven, with a jealously guarded entry, precisely to avoid such damning public exposure, which could damage one's reputation.[72] It is also interesting to consider the influence Maistre had on the committee, certainly through his position in Melbourne but also as the only man present. His sheer (if sporadic) presence was always enough to tip the balance of votes to his point of view. But Cave stood her ground. On 12 December 1907, a fateful last meeting of the committee took place at the Independent Hall. Within the small enclosed space of the rented rooms of the brick building in Melbourne's north, tensions were rising high. The summer heat probably did nothing to ease tempers, but pressure had been building for years.

Maistre and the treasurer started politely enough but were quickly at each other's throats, firing regulations and statutes across the room to try to control the proceedings of the day. By that point *Table Talk* was deriding the situation by calling it a 'confusion akin to Babel'. But if anything, tongues were loosening: Cave all but told the consul to shut up, telling him that the committee was composed of only fifteen members and that he was not one of them, that he could therefore 'neither talk, nor vote'. Maistre parried, explaining that his position of honorary president gave him the right to take part in deliberations and that he had the vote by proxy of another absent member. He went further and, aided by other statutes, cancelled the amendment Cave had introduced in his absence that would delay transfer to the French bank because of the character of M. d'Orgeval. Checkmate? Not quite. Cave simply did not budge from her position. Both were out of ammunition; it was a stalemate. This did not sit well with the consul, who towered over the committee members, 'hotly' arguing that as consul for France and honorary president, he regarded the rejection of the d'Orgevals, two respected members of Melbourne's French community, as 'an absolute scandal'. On that last remark, Cave twice gave the *présidente*, Lady Holroyd, the nudge until she stood up and called the meeting to an end. This was the culminating point in the tangled conflict of the past decade. It involved too many egos and too many incompatible vested interests. Following Lady Holroyd's lead, the Australian women got to their feet and left the room in concert, leaving behind Maistre with four of his acolytes.[73]

From here Maistre staged a legal coup. When his first attempt to call a meeting without the assent of either of the two *présidentes* failed, he sought advice from J Woolf and, with some legal gymnastics, called a general meeting in late January 1908, two months before the next scheduled official meeting. The presidents did not attend. During that rogue meeting, Maistre took charge and made business the *ordre du jour*. It included a petition addressed to Holroyd and signed by thirty-five members to have accounts of the previous years audited. It also made provisions for the election of new members as well as a program of soirées-lectures for the coming year.[74] By March, at the first official meeting, the power balance had shifted too much for the old committee to regain its ascendancy. To legitimise his actions, Maistre produced two letters from the Paris *Alliance* lending him their full support for his reform agenda (though the letters preceded his coup).[75] In April, Lady Holroyd, Mrs Cave, Mrs Crivelli and four others presented their resignations to Paris and to the members of the Melbourne branch.[76] A week later on 23 April, on the Feast of Saint George and the anniversary of Shakespeare's death, the two unmarked boxes with no return address were left at the French consulate: one made of tinplate, one of cardboard, containing the account books of the *Alliance Française de Victoria*.

Winners and losers, saints and dragons

Victory, in the end, came at a price. For if the Australian committee resigned after vicious infighting with Maistre and his allies, its members did not leave quietly. Maistre probably felt entirely justified in his actions; he was supported by the statutes of the *Alliance* and had the support of Paris to effect change. He also had the upper hand as a man and as the official representative of his country in Australia. And he was, after all, only serving the greater cause of France, of his France. Yet he underestimated his adversaries and the hurt he caused them. Secure in their own right as the first committee of a society that had, in the end, been theirs from its inception, the Australian women retaliated. On a visit to Paris Mrs Crivelli used her personal contacts to discuss Maistre's manoeuvres and get word to the Ministry of Foreign Affairs.[77] In April 1908 the consul general in Sydney also received a formal complaint from the former committee members, which he had to relay to Paris.[78] Four months later a despatch arrived in Melbourne from the French capital, instructing Maistre that by his actions he had compromised his position, and inviting him 'to make arrangements to come back to France'.[79] He left for good in February 1909.[80]

To this day, Maistre's legacy endures, and the *Alliance* remains a strong presence in Victoria, working towards its mission of promoting French culture and language through public events and by maintaining strong links with high schools. Every year, thousands of Victorian students of French take part in the Berthe Mouchette competition in poetry recitation.[81] Yet setting the Melbourne branch on a path consistent with the ideas of the original institution had been a challenging task.

For the French nationals involved, it had been a matter of personal as well as national honour: it was about the seemingly fading prestige of their language and culture in the world, defending the egalitarian patriotic ethos of the young republic and reclaiming the social place it could confer upon them in Australia. For the Australian women of the committee, French culture was largely detached from the realities of the contemporary French nation. It held meaning as an expression of a cosmopolitanism with its roots further back in time, in the 18th century and an era of generalised Francophilia in Europe. For them, French culture represented another asset in the game of refinement and prestige that helped define the boundaries of their social world. The French connection gained through the *Alliance* thus became a significant prize. It allowed both groups to catalyse opposing beliefs into concrete manifestations of social power. The *Alliance* was the site for a struggle between two competing and, in the end, irreconcilable visions of what French culture represented, where saints and dragons fought for old-world prestige under a new Australian sun.

But to colonial Australians, however, from the 1850s onwards, the French also came to represent a much more tangible and real problem as they made ventures into the Pacific and laid to rest Australian dreams of complete British supremacy in the region. More problematic even for the image the colonists wanted to project of themselves to the rest of the world was the establishment of a French penitentiary in New Caledonia.

CHAPTER 3

The scum of France: A reckoning with Australia's convict past

On the eve of Federation, the French consul general in Sydney complained to Paris that 'a feeling of reciprocal friendship' towards France had 'not yet arisen' in the Australian colonies. Georges Biard d'Aunet was an egotistical character. Many of his colleagues found him arrogant and overtly punctilious. The Ministry of Foreign Affairs kept telling him to drop the noble surname that had been his mother's but to which he had no legal right (his mother was the writer Léonie d'Aunet, better remembered for her affair with Victor Hugo). And as a career diplomat he also seems to have struggled to reconcile the discrepancy between a generalised Francophilia in English-speaking countries, like Australia, and an evident distrust towards France as a competing empire in the Pacific, and as a geopolitical rival to Great Britain. He had 'observed all too often' that 'the Australian colonies are not very cordial ... towards our country'. He thought this attitude was 'unfair' – not least of all because it reflected poorly on him. But international suspicion was the spirit of the time and France had done little to earn the colonies' trust.[1]

Australian colonial governments had become increasingly wary of European moves in the South Pacific from the 1870s. They fretted and beseeched Great Britain to take over New Guinea before the Germans did. They feared the New Hebrides (present-day Vanuatu) would fall into French hands. Russia always seemed to loom. By the time of Federation, the perceived threat became a military Japan and an overcrowded China. These fears underpinned the national plan of Federation, which was, from the beginning, a white and British imperial project.[2] When France annexed New Caledonia in 1853 to turn it into a penal colony modelled on Botany Bay, new demons awoke old fears.

From the small group of islands about 1500 kilometres off the coast of Queensland, hundreds of French convicts came to Australia in the second half of the 19th century. The Australian colonies had no authority to stop the comings and goings of liberated French convicts, and the power to extradite escapees rested with the French government. And yet the stakes were high. In the 1840s and 1850s the Australian colonies had won the intertwined and hard-earned right to partial self-government and the abolition of British transportation.[3] These victories had placed them, many believed, on the path to nationhood and on a higher rung of the civilising process.[4] The 'scum of France' were an unwelcome reminder of the shame of criminality and Australia's penal foundation.[5]

But what role did France play in the story of Australian nationalism and the development of Australia's border protection paradigm? The arrival of the convicts from New Caledonia both disrupted and intensified Australia's attempts to disavow its convict past. Politicians and vested interests in turn saw the episode as an opportunity to advance their own agendas. To many of the French colonists already in Australia, the convicts cast a shadow over their respectability. Some resented being 'looked at from head to toe' and being asked with suspicion if they came from New Caledonia.[6] But if they were rattled by the association they could simply wait for the political storm to pass, and so could many ingenious convicts.

An invasion of the 'moustachioed sons of Gaul'

It is hard to imagine what the men of the First Fleet must have felt when they saw the two ships of the La Pérouse expedition arrive at Botany Bay. This was one of the most remote outposts of the British empire. Yet here were the French, again. In fact, this was not the first time the French had ventured into the Pacific region in recent decades. But France's colonial ambitions had remained ill-defined and timid in the face of British might.[7]

In the early 19th century, the French presence largely meant French Catholic missionaries. Even in Australia and New Zealand, the first priests were French. They spread the word of God and promoted the interests of their country. As historian Robert Aldrich put it 'Catholic and French were almost synonymous, just as were Protestant and Anglo-Saxon'. From the 1830s, Marist Orders tried to gain a foothold in the Protestant-dominated New Hebrides. This would keep anti-Catholics in Australia on their toes for decades and encourage the Presbyterian lobby to advocate for Australia to annex the group of islands later in the century.[8] Gradually, French adventurers, entrepreneurs and administrators also made their way to the Pacific, with a permanent consul in Sydney from 1842 (1839, officially, but it took three years for the first consul to arrive).[9]

Since the beginning of white settlement in Australia, the French had also considered penal colonisation as a way to further their imperial designs in the region and of dealing with France's social and penal problems. They briefly considered south-west Australia. They also tried to claim the south island of New Zealand through a private deal with local Māori at Akaroa.[10] When this failed they took over the Marquesas islands in the southern Pacific Ocean in 1842 and briefly sent convicts there between 1851 and 1853.[11] When France annexed New Caledonia in 1853, several Australian newspapers warned it was only a cover and a prelude to an invasion by Napoleon. The *Moreton Bay Courier* alarmingly informed its readers that 'a good steamer, or a north-easterly breeze' could bring over 'swarms of the moustachioed sons of Gaul' in a matter of days.[12]

France's incursions into the region were faltering at best. But they made the Australian colonies uncomfortable.[13] Historian Stuart Ward has noted that if Fort Denison in Sydney Harbour was ostensibly erected to answer colonists' fears of a Russian invasion during the Crimean War in 1854, it was more realistically built against a French attack.[14] Henry Parkes remarked later in life that at the time war with Russia had seemed 'remote' but a rupture between France and England 'imminent'.[15] To the colonies the best defence was a good offence. Repeatedly they tried to force Britain's hand in turning the Pacific into a 'British Lake'. They convinced the imperial power to annex the Fiji islands in 1874 and in 1883 the Queensland government unilaterally took possession of the eastern half of New Guinea in the name of the British empire, fearing the Germans would beat them to it. When London disavowed the move, the colonies set up an Intercolonial Convention in Sydney to put plans in motion for a Federal Council of Australasia. One of the goals was to speak with a united voice to London about the need to curtail further European interference in the region.[16] The Victorian premier, James Service, spoke of 'the bitterness of feeling' that the New Guinea disavowal had created between the 'mother country' and the colonies.[17] It was already becoming apparent that the expansionist desires of the Australian colonies were exceeded only by Britain's lack of interest.

Until the establishment of a condominium in the New Hebrides in 1906 (a legal arrangement whereby the French and British shared judicial control), the Australian press relentlessly called for a British or British-backed annexation. But while the French did station troops on the islands briefly in 1886, the idea of a military invasion belonged, as the *Queenslander* newspaper put it, 'to the depth of an alarmist imagination'.[18] The French were no longer seen as a military threat, particularly since their defeat in the Franco-Prussian war in 1871. So the main argument in favour of annexation was to stop the French from sending their convicts there. Similar arguments were marshalled about the penal colony in New Caledonia. Charles Pearson, an intellectual and politician, wrote an influential book called *National Life and Character: A Forecast* in 1893 which depicted the forthcoming plight of white nations soon to be under siege from their non-white subjects in their colonies. Pearson did raise the possibility of a French invasion from New Caledonia, but by convicts with military training, rather than all-out war.[19] 'The Vagabond' – the journalist Julian Thomas – echoed these sentiments, perhaps less convincingly: 'It may be said that France would hardly arm her convicts against Australia; but all is fair in love and war.'[20]

Certainly not everyone in Australia framed France's penal colonial project in New Caledonia in such doom-laden terms. 'To grumble alone is a real solace to an English mind', one phlegmatic commentator wrote in the *Sydney Morning Herald* in 1873.[21] He saw the 'uncomfortable company' of the French in the Pacific as a natural development of the same great enterprising liberal spirit that had made the mighty British empire. He hoped the French colonisation of New Caledonia might help develop commerce in the region. The French might in time replicate their luxury industries in New Caledonia and the island might provide 'a new market for the coarser workmanship of English hands'. The adventure might even correct the French cardinal sins of centralisation and over-administration, which many thought undermined free individual enterprise and made the French worse colonists than the British. In the Pacific, the French would be forced to embrace a more liberal political order and 'recognise the great truth that every man possesses equal rights under the law to do and enjoy according to his pleasure.'[22] But it was precisely this cornerstone of Britishness, the belief in individual right and freedom and the rule of law, that French convicts coming from New Caledonia put to the test.

Forgetting interrupted

For thirty-odd years, from the first shipment of convicts in 1864 to 1897, the French government sent more than 30 000 people into exile to its island-prison. Of these, about 22 500 were hard-labour convicts, 4000 were 'Communards', political prisoners exiled after the civil war that followed the Franco-Prussian conflict in 1871 and the Paris Commune, and 3800 were *récidivistes*, or second-time offenders, exiled after a relegation law was passed in 1885.[23] Of the total number of convicts transported during that period, hundreds gradually found their way to the eastern coast of Australia, once liberated, or as escaped convicts, hidden on commercial liners or having survived the perilous five- to ten-day sea journey on stolen boats or makeshift rafts.

Although the British government ended transportation to the eastern coast of Australia in the 1840s and 1850s (1867 for Western Australia) after fierce local and global campaigns by anti-transportationists, the French saw the Australian experience as a benchmark to create the nucleus of a similar settler society in New Caledonia that would advance the cause of French civilisation.[24] Some experts in the study of the punishment of crime argued that Australian colonists should have taken this with pride as it proved the success of the redemptive and regenerative properties of transportation, including Australians' rejection of the system itself. Had transportation not produced in Australia thriving, civilised and politically mature bourgeoning nations? Instead, many colonists argued that transportation as a means of colonisation did *not* work, and that the success of the Australian colonies came precisely from their political unity against the system.[25] But as French convicts started arriving on Australian shores, they disrupted the tales of moral respectability the colonies were telling themselves and the rest of the world. They also kindled discussions about the colonies' limited sovereignty.

When news that France had colonised New Caledonia first reached Australia, the *Sydney Morning Herald* was up in arms about the 'unlimited collection of Parisian brigands' that could so easily travel to the east coast. 'No sooner ... have we got rid of British convictism, than we are threatened with French convictism'.[26] Victoria had just passed two acts (never sanctioned by the Colonial Office), in 1852 and 1854, to prevent Van Diemonian convicts from crossing Bass Strait.[27] The anti-transportation campaign had hinged on the fear of moral pollution (the extent to which Australian settler colonies could self-govern was often linked to the degree of perceived moral contamination by the convict element). So the rhetoric and imagery of contagion was ready to be applied to the French. Thus the *Argus* posited French convicts as a disease that seeped into the soul, while 'cholera was merely a physical evil ... the evil of convictism affected both body and soul'.[28] But the French were slow to develop their scheme and it took them another eleven years to send the first group of convicts to New Caledonia. In the interval, if we look beyond the initial outrage, the issue faded from public debate, and when it resurfaced it had lost some of the momentum of the earlier anti-transportation campaigns. Instead questions were raised in government circles and in the press about the legal powers of local parliaments in such matters of international law, until theory met with reality.

In 1866, as British transportation was being wound back in Western Australia, three French prisoners escaped as their ship lay in harbour in Sydney on its way to the island-prison. To the Australian authorities' relief they were quickly captured again by the French on Parramatta Road and unceremoniously shuffled back onto the boat taking them to the penal colony. The incident raised important questions about the legal ambiguity surrounding the convicts and about the powers of the colonies: the treaty for the mutual extradition of criminals between Britain and France had recently expired, the prisoners had committed no crime under British law, and it therefore seemed that they could be considered free men once 'beyond the shadow of the ship in which they were imprisoned'. Had they sought asylum, what should the colonies' response have been? And was their arrest on shore by the French not a violation – if a fortunate one – of British sovereignty?[29]

When Henri Rochefort, one of the most notorious Communards, escaped New Caledonia in 1874 with the help of a British ship that took him to Newcastle, his fame preceded him. According to his own rendering of the events, when he reached New South Wales, *le tout* Sydney welcomed him and his companions with open arms. Australian colonists cheered and celebrated the freedom of political prisoners who had escaped the stranglehold of an enemy power.[30] The *Sydney Morning Herald* on the other hand pointed out Rochefort's ill-gained fame as a political revolutionary and the danger his radical ideas represented to the order and 'the steady commercial development' of the British colony. They were glad to see the back of him.[31] More worrying than his ideas, Rochefort's escape seemed too brilliantly orchestrated to have been realised without the knowledge of the local authorities in Noumea and this raised the probability that more would come.

When rumours started circulating a couple of years after Rochefort's escape that the French government was going to allow 600 Communards in New Caledonia to petition for a remission of their sentence, the colonial authorities in Australia once again were on the qui vive. The Colonial Secretary of New South Wales urgently telegraphed his counterparts in New Zealand, Queensland and Tasmania, and the Chief Secretaries of Victoria and South Australia, to ask if any of the colonies had legislation in place to prevent the Communards from reaching Australia. He further suggested an objection could be addressed to the Imperial Government. New Zealand, Queensland and Tasmania were intent on joining the protest and authorised New South Wales to speak on their behalf.[32] Victoria, at this early stage, 'could not see grounds on which we could reasonably base such remonstrance.'[33] The South Australian government raised the point that the Communards were political offenders rather than common criminals and should be offered protection under British law. Still, if the French intended 'to release criminals', South Australia too would 'heartily join in the protest'.³⁴

The problem was referred both to London and to the French. The Governor of New South Wales, Sir Hercules Robinson, wrote to the French consul in Sydney, Eugène Simon, and the government of Queensland wrote directly to London, objecting at having 'pardoned convicts' coming to their territory.³⁵ The French ambassador in London, the Duc Decaze, and Simon in Sydney professed the good faith of their government and passed on the complaints, while carefully reminding the British and Australian authorities that if granted, pardon would restore the full rights of the Communards as French citizens and that no coercive measures could be used to curb their movements.³⁶ On 29 August 1876 a small notice appeared in a bottom corner of the *Journal Officiel*, the official journal of the French Republic, warning of Australian animosity towards the *déportés*, and advising their families to kindly redirect them somewhere else, if they could.³⁷ In any case, most opted to go back to France when the amnesty was granted in 1879.³⁸

Neither the French nor the British understood what the fuss in Australia was about. To the *Sydney Morning Herald* the idea that the Australian colonies could become an offshoot of 'the penal settlement of some other country' was abhorrent. Australian colonists had already 'vigorously protested against … being any longer regarded as a penal settlement themselves'.³⁹ But there was a gulf between the aspirations of the colonies to be seen as civilised polities (which to them meant free of the convict element) and what France and Great Britain actually thought of them.⁴⁰ The Governor of New Caledonia could not wrap his head around why the Australian colonies fretted so much about the idea that the Communards could be allowed to leave the island en masse. Since New Caledonia was welcoming of Australians, he thought it would be a simple 'mark of kind and neighbourly feeling, for reciprocity to be shown' – the implication being that in his eyes, Australians were also, and still, liberated convicts. He piled on, suggesting the Communards would surely be 'much less objectionable' to Australians than Australians were in New Caledonia, many of whom were 'addicted to drink' and had 'more than once caused difficulties with the native tribes'. Scorned, the New South Wales Colonial Secretary conceded that Australians 'may possibly be drunkards,' but insisted 'they are not criminals ... they are free citizens'.[41] Unfortunately, these distinctions were often lost on the British as well. A *Pall Mall Gazette* article scolded Australian colonists, telling them they 'should look at home and see whether Sydney and Brisbane are not now nourishing a whole class of ruffians of the very worst order' before they protest 'against the possible infection which French criminals may communicate to their society'.[42] The shadow of convictism loomed large over the colonies' bid for self-definition. But regardless of these disagreements, colonial governments had taken the swift action and replies of the French ambassador in London and the consul in Sydney as a binding guarantee that no convicts from New Caledonia, of any ilk, would set foot in Australia. Yet from the early 1870s, more and more began to arrive. These were, to the colonists, a confusing mix of amnestied Communards, liberated hard-labour convicts, convicts on tickets of leave and escaped convicts under sentence.

A taste of 'la vie Austral'

In 1919, the Baron Emile de Chastel died in Rockhampton at the respectable old age of seventy-four and was survived by four sons. He had held many occupations during his lifetime. He had been a labourer, a gardener, a licence-holder in a hotel and a teacher. In 1882 he advertised French lessons with the credential of being a 'Professor from the Besançon Academy of the French University'. He also gave freely to the community, helping raise funds for the local Alton Downs Town Hall, the school and the cemetery. His death certificate listed his profession as 'gentleman'. In 1874, the French government had sentenced him, under his real name Claude-Emile Charmier, to fifteen years' transportation and life in exile in New Caledonia for indecent assault.

Five years later he escaped with nine others, heading for Queensland on a stolen rowboat with makeshift sails made from repurposed hammocks.[43] If the name change was necessary to avoid notice, the addition of a nobiliary title was a nice touch. Who would suspect a French baron of being an escaped convict? His own descendants only discovered the subterfuge almost a hundred years after his death when digging into the family's history.[44] Claud-Emile Charmier's success points to the ease with which many could reinvent themselves in far-off colonies (and with the added bonus of a French aristocratic connection in British colonies). Well-to-do French migrants might have been worried about what people were saying behind their backs because of the association with criminality, but what triggered Australians was the New Caledonian connection; being French and a baron was enough to remove suspicion. Another French convict illegally staying in Australia, Paul Trottet, wrote to a friend still in New Caledonia to encourage him to come, 'there's no documentation, behaviour is the only proof of what you are'. But he warned 'they hate Caledonians'. 'If you wanted to get caught you'd only have to tell them that's where you've come from.'[45] Paul Trottet had been condemned to five years of hard labour in 1882 for attempted murder, but because he could not find work in New Caledonia he was given a ticket-of-leave to go to Buenos Aires for a few years – along with a formal injunction forbidding him from staying in Australia.[46] The penal system in New Caledonia applied different sentences to different convicts. Common criminals sentenced to five years or fewer of hard labour were meant to stay on the island once 'liberated' for a length of time equal to the duration of their sentence. Those condemned to eight years or more (the greater majority: 80 per cent) could never leave the colony, except if a leave of absence of up to three years were granted to them if they could not find work on the island.[47] How many liberated convicts and ticket-of-leavers found their way to Australia? Some could have gone to another French colony such as Algeria, the biggest settler colony of the growing French empire, or to the United States or South America, where burgeoning French communities thrived in the second half of the 19th century.[48] Trottet's story was probably more the norm than the exception. His experience highlights the impracticality of a regulatory system devised by a distant government in the French *metropole* which provided few if any measures of enforcement. After a four-day crossing that had been hard on his stomach and a couple of weeks roughing it out, he had found work as a kitchen porter at the Grand Hotel in Melbourne, where he toiled in exchange for board and lodging. He was learning English and flirted with '*les Anglaises*': 'Ah! There are some pretty English ladies here, there are … a few where I work and who have very pretty eyes.' He wrote to his friend in New Caledonia that he still had 'a mind to go to my country of choice, America, but I will wait I want to have a little taste of *la vie Austral*'.[49]

The exact number of convicts like the Baron and Trottet who chose to stay in Australia, for a while or for life, is impossible to know. Many needed to not leave a trace and their legal status created a lot of confusion and made contemporary estimates tricky. In 1889 the New South Wales government put the number of French convicts in the colony at 800, reportedly an increase of 300 in just two years.[50] In Victoria the police thought there were only 62.[51] How many were unaccounted for? How many were liberated convicts or ticket-of-leavers? When it comes to escapees, French records show that the number of convicts who managed to escape the *bagne* (penal colony) between 1864 and 1913 was somewhere between 675 and 720.[52] But of those probably far fewer tried to cross the Coral Sea to Australia, or succeeded. Many likely sought refuge in New Caledonia itself, with friends or hidden away in indigenous villages. Some, however, were repeat offenders. In 1898, three men, Ernest Laurent, François Roca and Antoine Vernay, were apprehended in the Papua New Guinea island of Samarai. The authorities were convinced they were on their way to Queensland. Roca had already been extradited once, Laurent twice, and then again a third time under the name Louis Chrétien. It was Vernay's first attempt. It is unknown if he managed to stay at large, but one of his tattoos augured nothing good; it said 'pas de chance' – no luck.[53]

What matters more than numbers is the public perception of the convicts and the issues they raised about sovereignty and morality. As reports in the press multiplied and numbers seemed to swell, so too did the perception that the French government was unconcerned and that the authorities in New Caledonia would turn a blind eye to escapes, 'too glad to be well rid of such customers, so long as they are able to save appearances.'[54]

Colonial legislation and the first Federal Council

To compensate for the failures of the French, the British colonies tried to deal with the problem with the legal means at their disposal but found them wanting. France and Great Britain had signed a new Extradition Treaty in 1876 for the mutual extradition of criminals (excluding political prisoners), but it did not give colonial authorities much to work with. Article 16 of the treaty outlined measures for extradition proceedings from colonies or possessions of the two imperial powers, but they needed to be initiated by representatives of the government from the colony or possession from which the criminal had escaped.[55] With some linguistic gymnastics, the Attorney General in Sydney tried to reinterpret the treaty to give the onus of extradition to the colony or possession where the criminals resided and justified going against the spirit of the treaty 'in light of the great dangers to which this Colony is exposed from its proximity to the French penal settlement in New Caledonia.'[56] But this was not enough. Even if the meaning was turned on its head, the Extradition Treaty still only applied to escaped convicts. Liberated convicts retained their freedom of movement – bar returning to France – and this was the problem.

The crux of the matter was that colonial governments wanted the power to keep all convicts from New Caledonia, regardless of their legal status, from entering their territory. A speaker at a Melbourne Bastille

Day celebration in 1890 explained that this caveat was due to the British belief in the rule of law and individual freedom unequivocally. Australians 'do not *deny* the legal right [of those convicts]', the *Argus* reported him saying, 'but ... few individuals in this world desire to, or can, *act up* to their *full legal rights*. If we all attempted to enact our utmost dues from every person we came into contact with, the world would not be worth living in.'[57] For the colonies to realise the society they wanted, free of the moral stain of convictism, the legal rights of French former convicts under international law had to be denied. Individual colonies tried to put measures in place to do just that.

In New South Wales in 1879, Henry Parkes attempted to introduce a bill in Parliament 'to make provisions against the Influx of certain Foreign Criminals into New South Wales'. Significantly, 'Foreign Criminals' referred to both escaped and liberated convicts who were all 'coming into New South Wales in numbers sufficient to cause alarm to Her Majesty's subjects in the said Colony'.[58] Queensland, which would sometimes frame separation from New South Wales as a separation from the stain of convictism, also tried to pass a *Criminals Expulsion Act* in 1881, which was disallowed by the Colonial Office.[59] The new resolutions, which set up the groundwork to create the Australian Federal Council, protested against France's plan to soon transport relapsed criminals to the Pacific and expressed the hope that the entire region would never again be host to any penal settlements in the future. A few years later in 1887 the Federal Council itself (which did not include New South Wales) made a more strongly worded address to the Imperial Government about what it now called 'this grave and national evil and wrong' and warned it could be forced to take 'measures of self-defence'.[60]

The Australian colonies, through their repeated complaints to the French and the Imperial Government, did achieve a small level of success, though this did little to change the perception their concerns were not a priority for the European powers. The measures did too little and too late: in 1880 a ministerial despatch reduced the number of tickets-of-leave issued and four years later holders of tickets-of-leave were forbidden to set foot on Australian soil. The length of leave was reduced from three years to one in 1887 and the scheme abandoned in 1889.[61] But as Australia was an obligatory port of call for many ships leaving New Caledonia, disembarking and starting afresh would have been tempting – 'here, it's freedom' wrote Trottet.[62]

Within a context of heightened imperialism and developing nationalism, when the possibility of the colonies federating in the near future was under discussion, the arrival of the French convicts underlined the porosity of the colonies' borders and the limited powers of colonial governments that depended on the decisions of a distant imperial authority. The unanimous opposition of the colonies to French transportation also suggests that for them the issue was not simply about stopping human bodies at the border but was also about asserting to themselves, to the Imperial Government, and to the world, that they rightfully belonged to a community of civilised self-governing polities. And this assertion of moral respectability was precisely evidenced by their rejection of convictism, wherever it came from. By the mid-1880s, with the constant arrival of convicts and by then seemingly worse convicts from New Caledonia, the problem snowballed from a point of international relations between the colonies, London and Paris, to a full-blown domestic political scare campaign about the threat of convictism. The idea of convictism itself tapped into a fear of moral contamination where (white) criminality and race still intersected at a time when immigration restrictions were becoming a growing preoccupation.

Scapegoats and straw men

In 1889, the *Illustrated Sydney News* printed a feature article on a 'Sydney Celebrity', the Communard artist Lucien Henry. Henry spent twelve years in Australia from 1879 to 1891, before returning to France, where he died in relative obscurity. In Sydney, on the other hand, he and his wife, Juliette Henry, had become well known and respected artists and intellectuals. Juliette gave French lessons from their flat on Victoria Street in Potts Point and hosted a regular literary salon, the *Cercle Littéraire Français* (1893–1898) either at her home or rented rooms at the YMCA near Central Station.[63] Lucien was one of the first art teachers appointed at the Technical College in Sydney and an early champion of a distinct Australian art school based on indigenous flora and fauna. His only works still on permanent public display are the two main stained-glass windows in the Main Hall of the Sydney Town Hall. One is an allegorical figure of New South Wales depicted as a young woman, with strong echoes of Marianne, the personification of the French Republic since the Revolution and the Goddess of Liberty. The second represents Captain James Cook as an explorer. Henry was praised for his republican, socialist and cosmopolitan views of art, which dovetailed with a romantic understanding of the emerging national sentiment in Australia and the need for it to be represented in art.[64] The *Illustrated Sydney News* rejoiced in 'the glorious privileges of a young and free country' to receive 'the impress of advanced thinkers whose far-seeing originality has secured their banishment from the older lands of beaten tracks and conventional hedgerows'.[65] Henry, as a talented artist and a political exile, enriched the tapestry of national maturity, cultural growth and respectability the Australian colonies were trying to weave. But other convicts were pulling at the seams.

Political and public conversations about the convicts throughout the second half of the century hardened over time, particularly after the relegation law was passed in 1885. Distinctions were increasingly being drawn between different types of convict: between the Communards as political prisoners, and the *récidivistes*. The distinction was part of an active disavowal process through which the colonies tried to distance themselves from their own convict past – tried and often failed. The renewed convict problem united the colonies in a search for security in the Pacific that was not solely about defence but also about a common search for a moral respectability that was projected on a global stage.

The more the colonies protested their morality and outrage at the French convicts, the more they were being reminded of their own past, the less they, and the world, were able to forget. Politicians and other interest groups, in turn, saw in the popular outcry a chance to advance their own agendas, further feeding a generalised discourse of moral panic and territorial anxiety which often was a far cry from the lived experience of humanitarianism and empathy between convicts and colonists.[66]

Although about 80 per cent of the *récidivistes* were transported for minor larceny and the other 20 per cent for vagrancy, they were described in the Australian press as pure 'moral rubbish', 'men and women who are villainous by training, habit, and by nature' and 'skilful in murder, burglary and fraud'.[67] With the issue of the *récidivistes* public discussion once again took on the colours of the discourse about moral hygiene it had during the earlier anti-transportation and anti-convict demonstrations of the 1840s and 1850s. In 1886 the *Queensland Figaro and Punch* once again admonished that the 'pestilence of criminals is worse than cholera'.[68]

The *récidiviste* was the true criminal, the epitome of the worst woes of convictism. And it lent itself well to grotesque caricature in fictionalised accounts. A story published in 1907 in the *Australian Town and Country Journal*, full of deceit, treachery and murder and written with all the verve characteristic of the period exemplifies this well.[69] In it, the swindling ways of the false Count de Nerac were eventually exposed, not by the police, but by the greed of a liberated convict, a former prison fellow (Bismark), whose attempts at blackmailing the Count had repeatedly failed. Still uncertain of the count's true identity, Bismark needed to confirm his suspicions before he could denounce him and exact his revenge. The author tells us that 'it is well to state that Bismark was tattooed all over his body'. And here lies the *dénouement*. A waiter in the hotel in which the Count resided remarked on Bismark's tattoos and told him that, impressive as they may be, they were nothing compared to the ones Nerac hid under his clothes, which he had glimpsed when the Count was asleep. This was all the proof Bismark needed; swiftly, he went to the police, told what he knew, and together they confronted the false Count, who ended up in solitary confinement. Bismark's tattoos, the tattoos of a liberated convict, were exceeded in artfulness and sinfulness only by those of the escaped convict Criquet.

Public ideas about the *récidivistes* were politically infectious. They had the potential to build on the anti-transportation campaigns of the preceding decades against British convicts. In 1887 Parkes attempted to pass another bill to deal with 'foreign criminals' (it did not pass its second reading either).[70] It resembled the first bill but was more extreme in its drafting. Under the new proposal, captains of vessels on which convicts were found would be considered accomplices and sentenced to five years' imprisonment. Vessel and cargo would be confiscated. If any passengers were unaccounted for before docking, all communication with the shore would be prohibited and the master of the ship liable to pay a £100 fine for each missing passenger.[71] To the director of the French steamer company the Messageries Maritimes, the bill was so extreme that it seemed a thinly veiled attempt at disrupting French commerce in the region and an added incentive to force the French to relinquish their rights over the New Hebrides.[72]

Yet such stringent measures were not uncommon. They were part of a larger emerging legal apparatus aiming at socially and, increasingly, racially quarantining undesirables through the regulation of colonial borders. As historians Alison Bashford and Catie Gilchrist have shown, financial deterrents against shipping companies bringing in prohibited migrants were a well-established practice in Australia, Canada and the United States – though they were more draconian in Australia. Eventually, the *Immigration Restriction Act 1901* would make the owners of vessels transporting unwanted immigrants liable for a £100 fine.[73] The director of the Messageries Maritimes might have been right, but Parkes' proposal also shows the enduring potency of the issue of convictism in the Australian colonies well into the second half of the 19th century and of the continuing efforts to enforce a particular vision of racial as well as moral purity through exclusionary measures.

In Victoria, threats to the perceived moral respectability of the community were employed to rally opinion for support of Federation. In the 1880s, the anti-Catholic and nationalistic liberal Victorian premier, James Service, was quick to capitalise on the anti-convict and anti-*récidivistes* mood.[74] Addressing the Intercolonial Trade Union Conference in Melbourne in 1884, Service pleaded for federal unity on the back of the vilified French convicts, who were once again compared to a viral disease – smallpox this time. Federation and anti-convictism were framed as natural and mutually defining steps towards national maturity so that Australia would 'command the respect of the whole civilised world'.[75] By 1889 the issue in Victoria was also framed as a labour problem. The French consul at the time reported that at the general elections that year the Melbourne Trades Hall Council demanded its candidates swear to work towards passing a bill prohibiting the import of 'criminal, native and asiatic' labour into the colony. 'Concerning the criminals, they all agree', he went on, 'they are only hesitant as to the natives and asiatics'.[76] That the rhetoric coming out of Victoria was so inflated is remarkable for two reasons. First, the consul's report suggests that by the late 1880s the increasingly racialised discourse of exclusion did not completely trump moral prejudice against convicts, again highlighting the importance of the issue in Australian minds. Historian Karin Speedy has shown that local authorities in Australia could read the 'Arabness' of some escaped convicts as a sign of criminality, and indeed their status as escapees as a sign of moral corruption, but here, it is also remarkable that convicts, broadly defined, were seen as *more* problematic than non-white labour.[77] Second, this anti-convict prejudice was not grounded in lived experience. In 1892 the French consul denounced to his superiors the ongoing rhetoric of the 'danger of moral contamination … to the virtuous population of Victoria' which he thought was nothing but 'exaggerated lies'. In the past seven years, he had himself overseen the extradition of only one convict.[78] Even if we make allowance for the fact that the French had limited resources or the will to extradite convicts and allow for the unreliability of contemporary figures, as we have seen, at the time of the general elections the Victorian police itself had tallied up the number of 'ex-convicts' to only sixty-two.[79]

Community

In 1873, the author Marcus Clarke was taken to see a runaway Communard hiding in Melbourne, just a year after the publication of the final instalment of the serialised form of his classic *For the Term of His Natural Life* in *The Australian Journal*. The police had been looking for Michel Seringue for the past three days after he had escaped the transport vessel *L'Orne* and swam to shore. When Marcus Clarke met him, Seringue had no stockings on and was wearing a canvas suit. His frame was lit by the insufficient light of a single candle and a wooden fire. In 'volubly-spoken' French that made the Australian writer's head ring, Seringue recounted his life tribulations from humble beginnings in the wine trade in the southern region of Occitanie, his years in the navy to his reluctant role in the Commune, his condemnation and his recent escape.[80] Clarke then wrote a plea in the *Argus* newspaper on behalf of the 'poor devil'. He called on his readers' empathy to see Seringue as a victim of fate rather than 'the ferocious being painted by the police *affiche*'.[81] In contrast to the often intransigent and bellicose rhetoric of colonial authorities, the historical record is replete with similar encounters framed by compassion and humanity towards the convicts themselves, be they Communards or common criminals. In 1883 the Collins family, who owned a cattle station about 15 kilometres north of Rockhampton, rescued five escaped convicts who had washed up on shore. The men were sunburnt, dehydrated and in such a sorry state that one of them could no longer walk. The Collinses nursed them back to life. The authorities eventually caught up with them and extradited them back to New Caledonia. Mrs Collins was distraught and pleaded with the French consul for their release but never saw them again.[82] And in 1879, fifty amnestied Communards had taken residence in a restaurant on George Street North in Sydney. A couple of them were 'men of good education' and many appeared 'to be of high intelligence'. Most were 'carpenters, masons, hatters, butchers, and ordinary labourers'. Some had already found work. The only problem the others faced was that they did not speak 'a word of English'. The journalist who made inquiries about the men reasoned that their number was a far cry from the 600 the authorities feared, and appealed to the Australian public to 'give them a fair chance' as they 'may prove themselves excellent colonists'.[83] Not unlike the range of responses to refugee arrivals by boat nowadays, arguments about human decency and for the social and economic potential of the convicts run parallel to politicians' rhetoric about 'border control' and threats to public culture.

The arrival of the French convicts tugged at the heartstrings of colonial polities in search for global recognition and self-respect. Anti-convictism and the push to further self-government were wielded in a way that reveals the social and political weight of the convict legacy in the psyche of colonial Australians well into the second half of the 19th century. They rejected that which they no longer wanted to be by focusing their anger, rhetorically and legally, on a partly imagined foe, ironically bringing to light the very past they wanted to forget.

Carried away by the momentum of his push for federal unity, Victorian premier James Service once argued for a total ban on French migration to put an end to the convict problem. One lone newspaper article supported the idea on moral grounds as 'we know the licentious character of the French nation'. But while stereotypes about the French abounded, few took the xenophobic bait.[84] French convicts were largely left alone and rapidly disappeared into the general population.

In 1923, Charlotte Crivelli's son, Georges Crivelli, echoed the sentiments expressed by the French consul general Georges Biard d'Aunet almost 25 years earlier and deplored 'the malevolent prejudices' in Australia 'against our country'. But to him these negative feelings were not caused by French imperialism in the region nor just the 'escapees from New Caledonia'.⁸⁵ No, Georges Crivelli lay the blame at the feet of other French migrants. These did not meet his bourgeois sensibilities, and were not the champions of French civilisation and culture he probably had in mind.

1 and **2**: Paris House opened in 1890 and was frequented by the Sydney intelligentsia, high society and the French community for several decades.

1 *Paris House, SLNSW, 'Paris House, 173 Phillip Street, 1917', H Searle in PXA 1408.*

2 *Paris House Menu, 1904, private collection.*

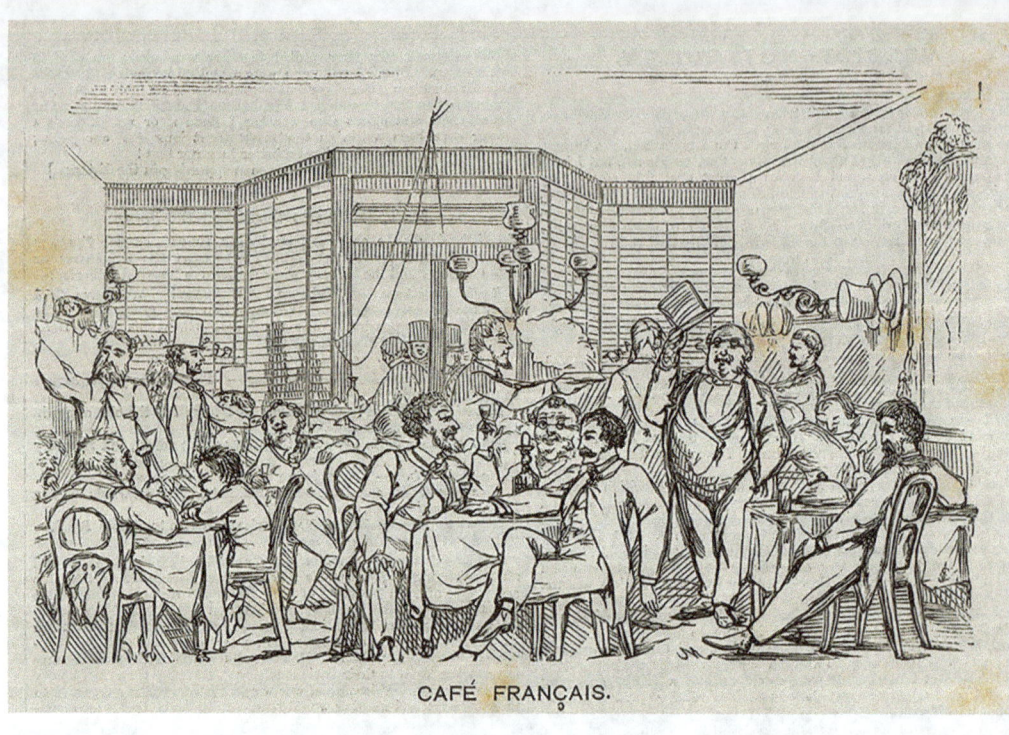

3 Colonial Australians were fascinated by French cafés, with their easy and carefree sociability. This cartoon in the satirical paper *Punch* seems rather to mock the style and drunken stupor of the male patrons of the *Café Français* on George Street in Sydney.

'*Le Café Français*', Sydney Punch, 3 September 1864, 4.

4, 5, 6 and **7**: Hubert Agache's plans for the design of Canberra proposed key features of the Parisian architectural landscape such as radial boulevards (**4** and **6**), a *Place de la Concorde* (**5**) and an *Arc de Triomphe* (**7**).

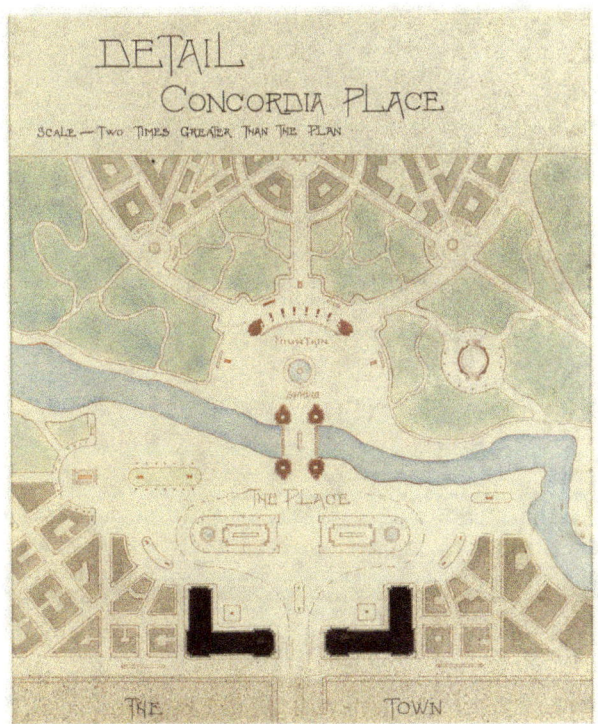

4 'The Federal Capital of Australia: quarters', NAA: A710, 3.

5 'Detail Concordia Place', NAA: A710, 7.

6 *'Prospect view number II'*, NAA: A710, 9.

7 *'Triumphal Arch'*, NAA: A710, 17.

The Olympia Café.

Drawn by Norman Lindsay.

8 In this drawing Norman Lindsay assumes the role of voyeur, observing two women embracing and ignoring the male party at the Olympia Café in Paris.

Norman Lindsay, 'The Olympia Café', The Lone Hand, *1 July 1912.*

9 *J Baptiste, 'Hair cutting, shaving and shampooing salon, Hill End, NSW', 1870–1875, SLNSW, ON 4 Box 9 No. 70020.*

9 and **10**: These two photographs of a hairdresser and barber shop suggest a story of financial triumph. Did the use of the name 'Paris' contribute to the success of J Baptiste's 'Saloon'?

10 J Baptiste, 'Paris hair cutting, shaving and shampooing salon, Hill End, NSW', 1870–1875 (detail), SLNSW, ON 4 Box 8 No. 18819.

11 At street level we can see the clock adorning the shop of the Delarue family below the much more imposing GPO clock.

Alfred Tischbauer, 'George Street, Sydney', 1883, oil on canvas, Dixson Galleries, SLNSW (DG 210).

CHAPTER 4

French migrants: The 'crème de la crème'

In 1856, as the port of Dieppe in Normandy in northern France came into sight, Antoine Fauchery metaphorically threw an old travelling companion overboard. Drawing closer to the fishing port, Fauchery felt he could finally let go of the tenacious nostalgia that had clung to him for four years – he had come home.[1] Fauchery, born in Paris, was a minor bohemian writer, journalist and photographer who brushed shoulders with Henri Murger, Charles Baudelaire and Gérard de Nerval. The poet Théodore de Banville described him as having 'sparkling eyes' and 'Olympian hair in frizzy disorder'.[2] Fauchery boarded the *Emily* in 1852 bound for Port Phillip, via London, to try to make his fortune on the Victorian goldfields. His *Letters of a Miner in Australia*, first serialised in *Le Moniteur Universel*, the official journal of the Second Empire, offer one of the most vivid accounts of life in goldrush Victoria. Written with a sympathetic eye for the underdog – the diggers, the Chinese, the Jews and the emancipists – and a beef against capitalists and squatters, the letters convey in vibrant prose a rare French point of view on a typically anglophone adventure.

Fauchery was not alone in wanting to try his luck in Australia – and not the only one in the end to throw in the towel and go home. From a surprising number of places across the globe, hundreds of prospective French migrants and their families wrote to the consulates in Sydney and Melbourne. They asked for information, for help, for hope, and taken together their letters reveal a polyphony of French perspectives: from men and women whose stories were bound to Australia, sometimes for an instant, sometimes forever. Building on the letters that have survived to this day, I revisit the traditional understanding of French migration to Australia that sees the French cast as 'good contributing migrants' and I explore the varied reasons they sought to come to this land at the end of the earth.[3] For the most part, they were also not born ambassadors of culture or defenders of the halcyon days of French grandeur. Here we encounter people who at times thrived, at times floundered, and simply tried to get on with their lives as best they could. Their unique experiences of migration point to the complexity and difficulties of their lives and of the equally complicated waves of comings and goings that made Australia.

They are loath to leave their native land

In his satirical notes lampooning French society, jotted down in the 1870s under the Second Empire, Flaubert wrote that people should 'register sadness' when talking of the French colonies.[4] By the late 19th century it had become a bit of a cliché for writers and thinkers to lament the sad state of affairs in France's empire, underpopulated by settlers, underdeveloped and with untold riches lying in wait. Many complained that the French empire was crumbling under the weight of its own administration, while the British expanded theirs ever more, carried both by instinctive flair and genius as well as by more liberal policies that encouraged private ventures and the flow of capital.[5] For the travel writer Gerrit Verschuur, the French lack of enterprising spirit was conspicuous even in French colonies, where 'serious traders are foreigners' and the French migrant population limited to 'the ubiquitous hairdresser, women selling gloves, some bankrupt fellow turned photographer or café-owner … and swarms of civil servants'.[6] Verschuur laid this sad state of affairs squarely at the feet of the French themselves, blaming their inflexible, unflinching, home-loving quality. 'The Frenchman only reluctantly emigrates so that a young man capable of creating a lucrative and independent position for himself on the other side of the ocean prefers to lead a life of privations where he was born, struggling to make ends meet.'[7] The reluctant French migrant cliché does have a basis in reality. Between 1880 and 1890, only about 10 000 French people left France annually compared to somewhere between 200 000 and 230 000 of their neighbours across the Channel.[8] A traditional understanding of this comparatively low mobility is that there were few reasons for a predominantly rural population, culturally attached to the soil and economically entrenched in its modes of production, to leave their country.[9] In one of the first studies of non-British migration to Australia, first published in 1927, the demographer Jens Lyng put it simply: the French are 'loath to leave their native land'.[10] The majority of those who did leave went to neighbouring countries. Those who ventured further afield than within Europe tended to favour migration outside the French empire. In preference to Algeria and Tunisia, they went to the United States, Argentina, Brazil or Chile.[11] Not until the 1890s did colonial lobbies and the French government start promoting French migration to its own colonies in a more concerted way.[12] But the French empire had little bearing on the national imagination until at least the First World War, unlike the British empire did in England and on the rest of the world.[13] And so, many prospective French migrants turned to the Anglosphere. Some were already in British colonies when they considered moving to Australia. In 1913, a group of four French friends and their families, for example, could no longer stand the 'harshness of winter' in English-speaking Canada and dreamed of the warmer southern continent.[14] And Marie le Callee had been teaching French in Cork, Ireland and was, in 1905, similarly seeking a warmer, dryer and – she specified – 'Anglo-Saxon' climate for her health.[15]

Those who took the plunge

As Fauchery boarded the *Emily* in 1852, the change of scene was immediate. Thirty years before the Messageries Maritimes connected France directly to Australia, most travellers bought passage on British ships. Fauchery right away found himself in that 'Anglo-Saxon' climate, in very close proximity to men and women of the English middle class, whose quirks he found amusing – at first. 'They are regular Chinese! – *Tea! Tea!* And the workman leaves his bench, the shopkeeper his counter, the beggar his begging.'[16] But the tediousness and boredom of life onboard crept in quickly, and the *Emily* was not a large ship. As time passed, measured by the fading shade of the silk ribbons adorning women's hair as they passed through the tropics, the British got on Fauchery's nerves. Feeling trapped by the mass of pell-mell bodies and odours in the confined space of the lower-deck common area, sweltering and gasping for air, the Romantic traveller sought refuge above deck to relieve the ennui of the long voyage. But his fellow passengers followed him wherever he went: 'I pushed them, bumped them, sat down on them, walked on their feet without ever being able to drag out of them a start of surprise or a spurt of ill temper.' In despair, he went for a walk, and they were 'treading on my heels and bumping me'. 'Is this, on the part of the English, a systemic tormenting, a determination to be disagreeable to the *Frenchman*?'[17] In the end Fauchery philosophised that it might not have anything to do with him at all but rather with the nature of the English. The French have 'this exquisite sensibility of mind' to 'treat and interpret questions of art and taste', whereas the English have a 'rough-and-ready' way, are cold and egotistic, qualities which 'will serve them powerfully' in their new world.[18] And so, not without a certain haughtiness and conceded respect for his travel companions, Fauchery disembarked at the head of Port Phillip Bay, amid the forests of ships' masts congregated in this new Eldorado. He was one of a slow trickle of a few thousands or so of French migrants and adventurers who came to Australia between the 1850s and the beginning of the First World War.

Napoleon III's coup d'état in 1851 marked the end of the Second Republic, the restoration of the empire and the beginning of a decade-long spike in French emigration. Many who had supported the Revolution of 1848 left (Fauchery was himself an ardent Republican). They were joined by those whose living conditions were affected by a worsening economy, a series of agricultural crises, a slowdown in the export of luxury goods and the increasing pace of industrialisation. Some of these trickled down to the Australian colonies, but never in great numbers – more usually as individuals or small families. Many were tradespeople, farmers, winegrowers and the ever-present French teachers, and most had a stint on the goldfields to start with.[19] In those early days, the majority seemed to come from Aquitaine and Normandy, regions linked to major sea routes, but generally they arrived from all over France.[20] By 1871 there were just over one thousand Frenchmen and women in Victoria, under a thousand in New South Wales, and approximately a couple of hundred in both Queensland and South Australia. The vast majority were men, especially outside the urban centres.[21]

Australia was certainly not an obvious choice. Information was scant. Gold was an attraction but some could not even locate the continent on a map, and thought it was a mere province of the Californian goldfields.[22] A handful of memoirs and personal accounts by French travellers published around the time of Fauchery's own work provided the only source of reliable and practical information on migration written in French. They were also the only source of information about the history of a country at the far ends of the earth.[23] In Fauchery's account this is achieved by way of a portly, sweltering French Catholic priest (whose existence remains dubious) he encountered in Heidelberg in a broiling and precarious church made of wood planks. In one long and sanctimonious breath the man of God covered the history of the colonies, from Cook, Botany

Bay, early settlement, transportation and the brutality of early days, to the redemption of the criminals, the discovery of the auriferous deposits beckoning the poor of Europe and the opening of endless and bountiful land beyond the Blue Mountains.[24] Being of a more artistic and philosophical inclination, without much ability for manual labour, Fauchery eventually left the goldfields to open his *Café Estaminet Français* on Little Bourke Street East. Still with no fortune in sight, he eventually made his way back to France.

Not all accounts of the goldfields were as generous as his. One gold-seeker of note was the Count Lionel de Chabrillan. From an affluent aristocratic family, Lionel liked to live a little too fully for his family's means and to gamble away their fortune. Destitute, he first came to Victoria of his own accord to recover his fortune in 1852 on the goldfields, but did not last long there either.[25] He came back to Australia not long after, this time helped (or pushed?) by his family, who obtained a position for him as the first French consular agent in Melbourne. On this second journey he came with his new wife, Céleste – the 'harlot spouse', a former high-end courtesan who brought his family shame on top of his financial ruin. When Lionel de Chabrillan and Céleste left Paris for Melbourne, Céleste hoped for a new beginning. Unfortunately her much-anticipated, scandalous memoirs reached Australian shores before she did. Ostracised and snubbed by Melbourne society, she wrote a vengeful novel denouncing the depravity of the Victorian goldfields, *Les Voleurs d'Or* (*The Gold Robbers*), published in 1857 and later adapted to the stage by Alexandre Dumas. The novel compounded ideas about Australia as a land of wickedness and exile that had been commonplace since the beginning of white colonisation.

Imagining Australia

The idea of the antipodes, a land of inversion on the other side of the world, had existed in the European imagination for 2000 years before the beginning of white settlement in 1788. All but a fantasy at first, it was an idea and a scientific theory (a large land mass to counterbalance the weight of Europe) that mattered greatly, for it set the mental framework through which Australia later came to be perceived. It set the trope of inversion through which early European explorers saw the worlds and peoples they encountered.[26] And it was those same explorers of the late 17th and 18th centuries who matched the geographical land mass of Australia and the islands of the Pacific to this existing European mental map.[27]

The voyage accounts of Louis-Antoine de Bougainville and James Cook went through many successive editions in the late 18th century in France and promoted interest in the mysterious and exotic Pacific region. The establishment of the British settlement in New South Wales in 1788 fascinated the French and a number of books on the topic, both scientific and fictional, were published as early as 1789, at the time of the French Revolution.[28] So from the beginning of European settlement Australia came to be associated with the idea of political exile in French minds. The first play to have Australia as a setting was written neither in Australia nor in London but in Paris: *Les Émigrés aux Terres Australes* was a one-act drama depicting the ordeals of exiled enemies of the Revolution as they strived to rebuild their lives in the antipodes.[29] By the time Jules Verne published *Les Frères Kip* in 1902, tropes of Australia as a place of banishment had become fixed: in the novel, the protagonists are sent to life imprisonment in Port Arthur in 1885, despite the penitentiary having closed eight years earlier. Verne also relied on descriptions of Hobart written by the explorer Dumont d'Urville in the 1820s and 1830s.[30]

Fictionalised publications that took Australia as a setting were few and far between but defined a certain view of the 'ends of the world'.[31] Jules Verne's *In Search of the Castaways* or Alexandre Dumas' *Journal of Madame Giovanni* crystallised visions of Australia as a land of exile and exoticism to a French audience in the late 19th century.[32] But Verne and Dumas never set foot in Australia. In fact, only four

French fiction writers in the 19th century are known to have travelled there.[33] The others were armchair travellers (Fauchery called it 'playing at travel') who relied on second-hand information, borrowing liberally from the growing volume of publications from various geographical societies, feeding from and responding to an expanding market for the exotic and the unknown.[34] Similarly, in the iconography of mass publications such as *Le Tour du Monde* and *L'Illustration*, depictions of the Australian environment remained largely unchanged through the 19th century. It was depicted as luxuriant and abundant, while the Indigenous population fell prey to the marriage of social Darwinism and the advent of modern anthropology, being gradually demoted from the status of 'good savage' to that of an anthropophagic 'dying race'. Australia was a masculine space of adventure evolving 'from penal settlement to frontier society'.[35] The recently settled colonies also gradually came under scrutiny as a fast-developing part of the British empire, where the progress of its rapidly urbanising towns served as a commentary on the superiority of the British and a critique of the failings of the French.[36] Writing to the French consul from Ismaïla in Egypt in 1910, a forty-year-old ship broker confessed of his 'love for the more extensive life of the English colonies'. He had his 'heart set on Australia, whose immense progress I admire'.[37] Other prospective migrants admitted knowing nothing about the place but were intrigued by the possibilities. In this spirit many wrote to the consuls – the only available avenue to express their desire to migrate. Henriette Repiquete from the Saône et Loire, with her 'primary school teacher diploma' wrote to the consul, explaining she could play the piano, give singing lessons, and sing in soirées. She wanted to know if she could honourably earn a living in Melbourne. 'If you cannot give me this information', she wrote, 'to whom should I turn?'[38] A recent graduate from the French medical faculty in Beyrouth who wanted to leave Syria was contemplating Australia but acknowledged he knew nothing about the place.[39]

A land for 'the underpaid and underfed'

In the European summer of 1880, the Australian writer and *conférencière* Tasma gave a talk to the *Société de Géographie Commerciale de Paris* at the fashionable Hôtel de Savoie in the sixth arrondissement in Paris. She spoke on the advantages Australia offered to French migrants. The confirmed Francophile started by teasing her audience, for whom 'to leave Paris, is to leave the world'. Why would anyone move to 'a place where cannibals and convicts are running in the streets'? But taunts made way for an attractive picture as she described a land of abundance and space with a population a fraction that of France. The 'underpaid and underfed' French could find that 'in Australia food costs half what it is here, wages are double what you are receiving, working hours are shorter'. Above all, Australia needed, wanted – she insisted – the French for 'this overflow of the artistic sciences that is brimming over here'.[40] The penny must have dropped at that point for Monsieur and Madame Mouchette (the celebrated founder of the *Alliance* in Melbourne), sitting in the audience in the 17th-century building. Walking out of the cobbled courtyard of the Société, through the wrought-iron gate and on to the Rue des Grands Augustins, Monsieur Mouchette turned to his wife and asked, half in jest, 'Shall we go to Australia?' She acquiesced with a 'Pourquoi pas?' – why not? One year later they were on their way to Melbourne, with Madame Mouchette's sister, Marie Lion.[41]

Tasma went on with her lecture. If the French learned that 'there are wealthy people willing to encourage the migration of producers, wine-growers, artists and foreign teachers', they will 'leave to the side savages and convicts and think about the profit to be made by expatriation'.[42] And perhaps she was right. From the early 1870s to 1891 the French population in Australia almost doubled. Trade increased, especially in wool, and the opening of the steam line passage of Messageries Maritimes made it faster and direct. Generally young and still predominantly male, French migrants now tended to slightly favour New South Wales. Some might have left France after the

Franco-Prussian war and the Commune, or come indirectly via New Caledonia, some as migrants, others as liberated or escaped convicts. Others simply wanted to better their lot in life. A Parisian dressmaker wondered if her *mode de Paris* would sell in Australia. In Monte Carlo, a croupier wanted to land a full-time job. A French cook in Chicago was about to move to Boston but was considering Australia as his next move if he was not more successful soon. A third-year student at the *École Nationale d'Agriculture* of Montpellier was wondering if his knowledge of English would give him an advantage. Another student at the *École Nationale* studying agriculture and viticulture wanted to know if he could rise through the ranks faster in the antipodes. For Marie Reynand, a piano and mandolin teacher in Marseille, her interest was sparked when several ship captains docking at the city port told her she could have a career as a pianist in Australia.[43]

As the fever for gold died down, migrants indeed came to work in agriculture, trade and services. Farmers outnumbered winegrowers (the French Bank of Melbourne reportedly financed the introduction of asparagus into Geelong) but French vignerons were particularly in demand for their 'hereditary' savoir-faire 'pursued throughout centuries'. In 1893 the *Sydney Morning Herald* explained that the French vigneron is 'one of the most useful immigrants we can have' because of 'this long and intimate knowledge of every detail of his business'.[44] Many others made a living as teachers, cooks or hairdressers, or worked in restaurants, no doubt capitalising on the prestige accorded by a link to France in British settlers colonies'.[45] In a photograph dated 1870–1875 we can see one J Baptiste's 'Paris hair cutting saloon' go from a modest and dirty wooden structure to a solid brick building with a shiny shopfront window. Baptiste, still short and still wearing a hat, traded his day-to-day grey clothes for a sharp white professional suit (see images 9 and 10). With the increase of trade in wool between France and Australia, by the end of the 19th century the skilled or semi-skilled migrants that constituted the bulk of French migration were joined by a small group of wool buyers and their families who formed part of the nucleus of a more elite group, to whom we will turn to in the next chapter. They came from the highly industrialised northern cities of Lille, Roubaix and Tourcoing and were followed by bank clerks and men whose professions linked them to the wool trade. Together this group formed a relatively well off and cloistered network of commerce, kith and kin, first in Melbourne, and then, following capital and wool in the 1890s, in Sydney.[46] By 1914 the Sands Directory listed thirty-four French or Belgian wool-buying firms in the New South Wales capital.[47] Trade activities meant that by the turn of the 19th century, half of Australia's French migrants lived in New South Wales and a quarter in Victoria, and by 1911 more than half lived in urban areas. But the economic depression of the 1890s in Australia slowed down migration and was coupled with a declining birth rate in France. At their 'peak' in 1891, French migrants, including those born in French colonies, only came to just over 4500 (a figure not reached again until the end of the Second World War). The same year there were almost 21 000 French migrants in Britain, including more than 12 800 in London alone.[48] In all, few French came to Australia. It was largely a case of individual rather than chain migration and they never formed a clearly distinguishable national or 'ethnic' community like the Germans, the Greeks or the Irish. Many also fell through the cracks of the migration system altogether and are unaccounted for.

Silent voices

The 19th century was a liberal era in international migration, with fewer, less systematic and less co-ordinated national border controls.[49] Still, the period between 1860 and 1920 saw an unprecedented spread in identity documents as nation-states solidified their monopoly over what sociologist and historian John Torpey calls the 'means of movement'.[50] But such documentation presents particular problems for historians. Because national identification was first concerned with the exclusion of specific groups, not everyone was counted and accounted for in the same way. Colonial and Commonwealth censuses, for instance, were initially more concerned with accounting for the non-white composition of the population, and thus the first Commonwealth census in Australia simply grouped all Europeans together.[51] In the era of the White Australia Policy, after Federation in 1901, there was still confusion about the differences and overlaps between race and nation-ality. Non-white migrants from the French empire, giving their nationality as French, might have in fact passed through the racist immigration net. Historian David Dutton has noted that as late as 1933 immigration officers had to be 'instructed to bear in mind that a person's name might not reveal their race, particularly people of French, American or Portuguese nationality'.[52] Another problem in this era is the representation of women. The *Naturalization Act 1903* meant that women automatically acquired their husbands' citizenship and lost their own upon marriage.[53] Yet women did not just follow their husbands, and more migrated alone in the 19th century than was once assumed.[54] And not everyone wanted to be counted, either. 'Not all the persons of actual French nationality are shown in the official records or known in ordinary ways', noted the *Sydney Morning Herald*. 'For reasons which are obvious, many from New Caledonia sink their identity upon settling down in Australia.' Whether they had escaped or were freed convicts, they kept their heads down, often living frugal lives on the margins, working in physically demanding occupations as wharf labourers or ironworkers.[55]

Many other migrants simply did not write and left us no trace. These could include 'those who died soon after arrival, the illiterates, entire families that left no close relatives behind, individuals who deliberately broke off contact with home, and a considerable portion of those who failed in one way or another'.[56] Of the consular letters that did survive, some highlight in harrowing ways the silence into which many migrants fell once they had left home, family and friends. Painful letters sent by family members who had sometimes been decades without news paint an upsetting picture of loss and powerlessness.

In 1886, Sylvain d'Héron was living in Brooklyn in the United States and had not heard from his estranged brother for twenty-nine years. Someone from Melbourne had tried to call on him when he was out. Could it have been his brother, or someone come to announce his passing? He was the only family he had left.[57] In Algiers, Emile Dennemont's brother had not heard from him in two years. In distress he asked the consul in Melbourne if his brother 'still exists'.[58] In Calvados in France, Victor Paysan's brother had also not received any news for three years. Roving, questioning, probing, he received a glimmer of hope from sailors at Le Havre who thought they had caught a glimpse of his brother navigating along the Melbourne coastline.[59] In a similar situation, Pierre Marie Guillerie, a fifty-four-year-old man working for the Messageries Maritimes, tried to extend his stay in Sydney to look for his own missing brother.[60]

General migration pictures are therefore not without limits. They often tend to homogenise migrant groups and reproduce the limitations of archival documents by playing down or ignoring differences of race and sex. They also fail to illuminate the personal stories and unique individual choices people made. 'Migration is a universal human experience so vast and complex it defies satisfactory representation', writes historian David Fitzpatrick.[61] This is all the more true for the French in Australia, who were few to come. Traditional migration history uses statistical data (naturalisation records, colonial and Commonwealth censuses) to identify a typical migrant, and that migrant is usually a man. It also pays much attention to so-called 'push and pull factors'. Certainly, events in France – successive revolutions, phylloxera outbreaks – or the promise of a better life elsewhere could motivate many to take the plunge but individual motivations could be far more diverse.[62] And often only those who stayed are deemed important because they or their children gave their life force to the new nation. Yet the lives of those who did not stay, or did not leave an official record, or who, one way or another, 'failed' the integration challenge, are also an integral part of the story of migration. They illuminate broader processes of decision-making and international movement. The letters gathered from the French consular archives offer a unique, albeit small, palliative to these problems, for they allow us precisely to glimpse the lives and minds of several migrants or prospective migrants whose decisions to migrate reflect their unique personal circumstances.

Unfulfilled dreams

In the end, whatever their reasons for choosing to migrate, many gave up: 'I am ready to leave, Australia is a beautiful country, but poverty is hard.' Marie Coing came to Melbourne in 1910 to work as a furrier. Her trip had been paid for by her new employers but 'the conditions were the complete opposite of what I was promised' so she moved to Sydney for a couple of years. Hard times sent her back to Melbourne, where she was still lining fur from a rented bedroom on the eve of the First World War. Winter was coming to an end, demand for her handiwork would soon subside and her savings were too meagre to take her back to France. She pleaded to the consul, 'If I am to be destitute, I might as well be destitute in my own country' and they paid for her return voyage.[63] Australia was not the economic Eldorado many had been promised or had imagined. Even when they did find work, the lack of familial or professional networks could make for loneliness. In 1886, George Henri d'Alphonse was doing odd jobs at the American Bar on Bourke Street but 'here in this country, in Melbourne, I scarcely make a living in a hotel with 12 shillings per week which is not enough … and I have neither friends nor acquaintances'.[64]

The closing decade of the 19th century drastically changed migration to Australia. It all but came to a halt in 1891. The Australian economy was shrinking, unemployment rising, exports and national production were stunted. The boom years were replaced by strikes, lockouts and an intensification of class conflict.[65] In 1891 the physician to the French colony in Sydney, Dr Laure, and other members of the community started the French Benevolent Society to provide relief to

French-speaking migrants in difficulty. But the French authorities in Australia would have preferred that prospective migrants think twice about coming at all.[66] In Melbourne in 1905, the consul Paul Maistre wrote back to Marie le Callee, the teacher of French in Cork, 'hasten … to dissuade you, if possible, from coming to Australia to seek, not even fortune, but a modest affluence'. Contrary to Tasma's enthusiastic promotion of Australia as a bountiful land of opportunity some twenty-five years earlier, the consul's advice was crushing, 'unfortunately for you there are already too many teachers of French in this country, where, in order to eke out a living, they are reduced to giving lessons at ridiculously low prices'.[67]

The 'immense progress' and 'more extensive life of the English colonies' came at a price.[68] The Australian environment was noticeably changing through habitat destruction and the introduction of non-endemic species. Rabbits, from the 1880s, started ruining pastures on the east coast. With ground cover disappearing, the soil was changing. During the eight-year-long drought that began in 1895, it turned to dust.[69] A handful of French vignerons' families who had settled at Minto, forty kilometres south-west of Sydney, were among those hard hit by the compounded misfortunes of the 1890s. Paul Maistre, in Melbourne, tried to dissuade others from following them to Australia where 'a rather acute crisis' awaited them, 'which will not facilitate your placement in a country where foreigners are looked upon suspiciously by a working class very hostile to immigration'.[70]

French vignerons were notoriously difficult to entice.[71] In 1905 the Victorian state government paid for recruiting advertisements in France and Algeria. The same year, at the British consulate in Algiers, Lord Jersey, former governor of New South Wales and now the NSW agent-general in London, waxed lyrical about the opportunities awaiting French winegrowers in Australia.[72] Three brothers, described by the consul in Melbourne as 'good wine-growers' bit the bullet and left their positions in Algeria for Victoria following Jersey's speech but encountered only hardship. Paul Maistre used their experience to issue a stern warning to the French Ministry of Foreign Affairs, the Ministry of Agriculture and the Government Office in Algeria, asking them to dissuade his compatriots from giving any credence to advertised offers:

> Completely ignorant of the language, the habits and customs of the country and consequently obliged to accept any offer, [French vignerons] are in general intentionally exploited until the day when their Australian employer, having amply profited from their specialised knowledge and experienced labour, dismisses them and they then realise they have lost their quarry in the shadows, and toiled for others.[73]

For some, however, Australia was more than an economic opportunity.

Escape and exile

On Bastille Day in July 1914, the French celebrated their last national holiday before the world changed. Politicians were monitoring the situation in the Balkans but there was no sense of urgency yet. On this day of carefree celebration, Fernand Gracin sat down to write to the consul in Melbourne about his missing son. There was urgency and his world had already changed. 'He might have fled to Australia', Gracin explained. At just sixteen years old his son had stolen large sums of money from the local bank and vanished. He had always had 'a love of travel and mainly for distant lands'.[74]

Distance could be appealing, and so was the possibility to start afresh in a new world, especially if the old got in the way of your plans. Dannie Favre in Latin America was 'separated from bread, board and assets' from her husband but wanted a proper divorce. In France it would take three years for the separation to be official. She was eager to move to Australia if it meant she could remarry immediately.[75] Madame Lusanne Chalauser in Burma in 1891 had a case of the missing newlywed. Her husband was nowhere to be found and rumours were circulating that he had married a German girl in Australia.[76] From Scotland Suzanna Thibault sent a photograph of her own missing husband, who had disappeared seven years prior.[77] Finally, in 1886 it was Monsieur Borelle who was writing, from Saigon, about his wife who had left him nearly a decade earlier. He knew she was in Melbourne working for an architect. He threatened her with a divorce if she did not come back, to which she promptly replied, 'I am very happy where I am' and enjoined him (through her lawyer) 'to always respect my peace of mind'. A dramatic 'you are the author of my ruin' concluded his side of the divorce proceedings.[78]

Lionel de Chabrillan was not the only one to be sent into a form of exile to Australia by his family. The family of one Henri Bocquet was intent on seeing the last of him as well. Their reasons are unknown but the intention was crystal clear. First they contracted him for seven years to the French army; perhaps they hoped the military stint would help him mature, or possibly make him into a more responsible man, a more trustworthy person, the son they wanted rather than the one they had. What we do know is that, as soon as he returned from the army, they immediately sent him away again, this time to Cairns in far north Queensland to work in the sugar industry. Flouting his family's instructions, he made his way down to Melbourne, using his charms to sponge off people along the way, which eventually attracted the attention of the consul, who wrote to his parents. Their verdict was final: neither his mother nor father 'wished to hear about their son', and did 'not want to do anything more for him' nor did they 'wish for his return to France'. Yet they were unwilling to set him free completely. After working for a time as an English and arithmetic tutor in Melbourne, Henri fell in love. But this time his charms failed him and Dolly Hickson, his love interest, refused to marry him. Visibly unwell and distraught, Henri walked into a pawnshop on Elizabeth Street, asked to see a revolver and some cartridges, and put the gun to his forehead. In broken English he threatened to kill himself – 'I am shoot; I will shoot!' – but the shop owner stopped him. The Melbourne *Age* wrote the scene off as 'a very ridiculous pretence at suicide on the part of a Frenchman'.[79] The bench remanded him for medical treatment. Henri must have gotten ahead of himself before his marriage proposal as he had made queries to have his legal documentation sent over from France. But his family's reach and hold over his life never wavered, even in his forced exile. Australia was far away, as far as his parents could send him, but not far enough away to lessen the fear of the disrepute an ill-advised match might throw on them. Knowing nothing of the girl he wanted to marry, they refused to send him his papers. He later moved even further away from France, to New Zealand, where his family's wishes were finally realised: he disappeared.[80]

The consular letters underline the diversity of points of origin of prospective French migrants, writing from inside as well as outside the French mainland, from within and without the French empire. The fragments of documents that have survived place them in Egypt, Brooklyn, Algiers, the Saône et Loire, Syria, Paris, Monte Carlo, Chicago, Montpellier, Marseille, Canada, Cork, Madrid, Latin America, Burma, Scotland and Saigon (Ho Chi Minh City). Not all came to Australia. Those who did hoped for better lives or adventure, or had little say in their fate. Not all thrived and not all stayed but as an innocuous set of migrants, travelling alone and hailing from a nation considered civilised and white, they quickly disappeared into the general population.

Georges Crivelli looked to his compatriots in Australia with little more than contempt: escaped convicts, ship 'deserters, a few hairdressers and cooks, and that's it!'[81] But Australian prejudices against France, which existed concomitantly with a love of French culture, probably had little to do with a few thousand French migrants of low socio-economic background and more to do with French meddling in the Pacific, France's penal colony and the complex millennium-long relationship between France and Great Britain. But to people like Crivelli, members of *le tout* French Melbourne and Sydney, especially the cloistered elite male microcosm of the French business community, being French was not just a nationality. It was an intrinsic component of their status and honour as gentlemen, and it defined their relationship to one another and to the Australian nation.

CHAPTER 5
A matter of honour: Frenchness on trial

'Exclusive, expensive and exquisite: welcome to Hunters Hill': this is how the leafy and secluded north shore suburb of Sydney is now promoted to the wealthy. 'Quiet yet connected', it is home to the 'Sydney establishment' and 'a few Hollywood A-listers'.[1] Encased between the Parramatta River to the south and the Lane Cove River to the north, the affluent peninsula owes part of its charm to its early French inhabitants.[2] The sloping land of Hunters Hill was originally developed by two entrepreneurial French brothers, Didier Numa and Jules Joubert, between 1847 and the 1880s. They subdivided the land, built an initial thirteen villas, all but one made of the local sandstone, and turned an insalubrious area into an exclusive and sought-after location. They connected the isolated district to the rest of Sydney through a competitive steam ferry line, breaking into the monopoly of Edye Manning's company and the services offered by 'French Louis', an ageing, frequently drunk runaway whaler who made a living by selling oysters and carrying passengers to and fro in an outrigger.[3]

In the 1850s, more French and French-speaking settlers joined the Joubert brothers. First were the Baron de Milhau, exiled after the 1848 Revolution; the French-speaking Swiss Leonard Bordier and the Australian-born Edward Jeanneret, who had French Huguenot ancestors. This group further developed the area.[4] More French-sounding names soon followed: Du Boisé, Vernay, Doublet, Boileau, and the Delarue family, whose fading ties to France will be the focus of the next chapter.⁵ The French consul lodged at Passy House, a mansion on Passy Avenue, built by the Joubert brothers in 1855, named after the sixteenth arrondissement in Paris, and on whose roof the tricolour flag could be seen waving high perched on a staff.⁶ On the southern shore, the French Marist Fathers took their seat at the aptly named Villa Maria, the Marist Brothers built St Joseph's College, and the Marist Sisters a high school for girls.⁷

For a few generations, then, there 'subsisted a sort of connection between the French in Sydney and Hunter's Hill'.⁸ Well into the 20th century, the suburb retained 'something of the atmosphere of a French provincial town: settled, reclusive, standing apart', with 'stone fences, wrought-iron gates, and tantalising glimpses of creamy shutters and colonnaded porches'.⁹ The social hodgepodge of exiled aristocrats, entrepreneurs and their families that composed the early settlement of Hunters Hill suggests the patchwork nature of a certain elite French society in Sydney which soon, from the 1880s, centred around 'the French commercial world', as the *Sydney Morning Herald* put it: 'the most important part of the French among us'.¹⁰ This, by and large, meant wool buyers.

Before a telegraph line was opened between Europe and Australia in 1872, wool-buying firms from the north of France and Belgium sent lone buyers out to Australia, with power to act on their own authority and with hard cash in their luggage. As commerce increased and transport became easier, companies sent permanent representatives to live in Australia with their families. No longer transitory, they formed a relatively insular group whose social and professional worlds hinged on several French societies they either directly created or in which they played key roles.¹¹ The *Comptoir National d'Escompte de Paris* (the French bank) in Melbourne was created specifically to facilitate trade in wool between France and Australia.¹² The French Chamber of Commerce was created in 1899. Its first president, George Playoust, was a congenial, cigar-smoking

Frenchman, who indulged in what Norman Lindsay called 'the national prejudice in favour of whiskers'.[13] He had arrived with his young family and his brother ten years earlier from the northern French city of Tourcoing, settling first in Melbourne, then in Sydney, and became one of the de facto leaders of the small French community.[14] In 1898 a group of French notables acquired the *Courrier Australien*, a 'cosmopolitan' newspaper written in French which they transformed into the voice of the French Chamber of Commerce and the *Alliance Française*. Originally created by a Polish nobleman, the *Courrier Australien* purported to educate and edify a Francophile and Anglo-Saxon readership interested in politics, the arts, literature, commerce and fashion. In financial difficulty from the outset, despite French subsidies, the newspaper largely failed to fulfil its idealist goals or reach its intended readership, not least of all because of the language barrier. It faced a fiercely nationalist and at times jingoistic Australian competition. The transition of the *Courrier Australien* from an aspiring cosmopolitan newspaper to a more utilitarian publication is a watershed moment. It reveals a schism between, on the one hand, the fading strength of an older cosmopolitan vision of French culture that was meaningful and defined in part outside of France and, on the other, the material and cultural priorities of the geographically bound French nation and its overseas citizens.[15]

Supported by their own newspaper as well as by commercial and cultural institutions, the wool buyers divided their lives between the wool stores; the Wool Exchange on Macquarie Place; their houses in Mosman, Randwick or Hunters Hill; and frequent long trips back to France. Often civic-minded, they developed close bonds with the official representatives of the French government in Australia, with whom they worked closely, and the network of bankers and navigators who were the fulcrum of their commercial ventures.[16] In 1882, the opening of the Messageries Maritimes line, whose steamships could now avoid the long haul around the Cape by going through the recently opened Suez Canal, allowed the creation of a French-speaking world in

Sydney, and to a lesser extent Melbourne, directly connected to France and New Caledonia, a world-within-a-world that operated within and parallel to the greater routes of the British empire.[17]

A sprinkling of other professionals and artists of note completed this social set. There were men of passage – working at the Pasteur Institute or high-ranking officers of the Messageries Maritimes – and the ones who had moved to Australia permanently, such as the doctors Duret and Crivelli or civil servants such as Edmond Marin la Meslée, who would set up the Geographical Society of Australia and publish a popular social study of his adopted country in France, *L'Australie Nouvelle* (The New Australia).[18] Along with local French artists – the pianist Henry Kowalski, the violinist Henri Poussard or the singer and pianist Madame Charbonnet – these men and women and their families formed a self-selected elite among the French in Australia, the people Dr Crivelli thought 'worth knowing'.[19] Their social calendars were marked by charity balls, Bastille Day picnics and regattas regularly attended by prominent Australians in spite of international tensions, such as the premiers of New South Wales: George Reid, John See and the very Francophile William Holman.[20]

Within that world the idea of nationality – of being French – dovetailed in significant ways with the idea of honour, particularly male honour, and played an important role in defining individual as well as collective bourgeois identity. Being French could, for some, be more than a word on the page of a passport; it was a performance.[21] What it meant to be French was in fact not always straightforward, even in the small, intertwined French communities of Sydney and Melbourne. While the group of French notables in Sydney rallied in a show of force, demanding reparation after their collective honour was slighted by a blunder-prone colonial governor during the Dreyfus Affair, several of these same men were embroiled in a seemingly never-ending, internecine series of libel cases in Melbourne in which they questioned each other's nationality in the hope of swaying mystified Australian judges. Far from a singularly united migrant group, their Frenchness could serve to bring them together or pull them apart, drawing and redrawing the borders of an imagined state of belonging.

An indivisible people

The Dreyfus Affair (1894–1906) was a unique event in French history. It profoundly shook the body politic of the Third Republic and left an indelible mark on the nation and on many of its citizens. In 1894 the French state condemned the Jewish artillery officer Captain Alfred Dreyfus for high treason for allegedly selling military secrets to Germany. Dreyfus was demoted and deported to Devil's Island, off French Guiana, after a rigged and expedited first trial. Two years later, the Dreyfus Affair became a worldwide *cause célèbre* when his family, with the support of leading liberal and left-leaning intellectuals, denounced the real traitor and drew public attention to the state and army conspiracy that had wrongly accused and condemned Dreyfus.[22] For the French, in France and overseas, the affair forced heated debates about politics and society, about the perception of France's national decline, the body politic and anti-Semitism. It struck a nerve, affecting people in a personal as well as a public manner, deeply dividing families and friends between *Dreyfusards* and *anti-Dreyfusards*.[23]

This 'exceedingly complicated trial in a distant country' attracted vast commentary in Australia, as it did in Great Britain, all the more so because it pitted the French against one another.[24] The final condemnation of Dreyfus at his second trial in Rennes in August and September 1899 in particular unleashed waves upon waves of observations about the inferiority of the French, seen as a bigoted, belligerent and degenerate race. The rigged trials were seen as highlighting the failures of the French republican model, its institutions and its authoritarian army.[25] Across Australia, the affair kindled sectarian tensions. A rabbi summoned his flock in Perth in 1898 to hold forth on the rot of French anti-Semitism that had taken hold of the judicial process and demoted France 'to the last rung of civilised nations'.[26] A Protestant minister in Sydney enjoined his congregation to sign a letter of sympathy to Dreyfus and his wife. He recounted witnessing anti-Semitism himself during a stay 'at one of the continental towns, where a large military force was stationed', and among whom the 'gambling element was strongly in evidence'. As the money-lenders were Jewish, they became an object of hatred and scapegoats for the then penniless 'military dignitaries'.[27]

The *Courrier Australien* steered clear of pronouncing judgment on the ongoing trials, either trying to be a unifying force for the French community or diplomatically biding its time. But it denounced the 'revolting partiality' of British news arriving in Australia, which piled on the Francophobia *du jour* ad nauseam. And it condemned the 'simplicity' of the people in Australia who uncritically lapped it up.[28] The result of the wall-to-wall negative coverage 'had offended a great number of people' in the French community.[29] 'The main object' of the eruption in the press had seemed 'to be disagreeable to us'. At last, Dreyfus's pardon gave the editors a sense of relief, not for the man or for justice, but because the 'outburst' in the press would finally stop, even if Australian newspapers looked like 'a dog who has been robbed of a bone'.[30] But for the French colonists one incident particularly stung and stuck more than others, and it took place in a mining town, some 700 kilometres inland north-west of Sydney.

In mid-afternoon on Tuesday 26 September 1899, Lord Beauchamp, the last governor of the colony of New South Wales before Federation, disembarked from his private steam train onto the bunting-decorated platform at Cobar to be greeted by the sounds of the town's brass band and the cheering of hundreds of townspeople and school children. Beauchamp was stopping at the mining town for a brief visit of one afternoon and one evening on a whistle-stop tour of the colony. The spring air was dry, and if there was any wind at all it would have lifted clouds of dust off the dry, drought-stricken soil. Under the overbearing inland spring sun, Lord Beauchamp was promptly introduced to the 'leading citizens' awaiting him, was driven around, went down mine shafts, 'had a good look round underground', and speedily returned to the comforts of his 'state car' at the train station. He rested for a couple of hours with his party before making his way to a banquet thrown in his honour by the town. At the Masonic Hall, William Lygon, 7th Earl of Beauchamp, Knight Commander of the Most Distinguished Order of Saint Michael and Saint George, Governor and Commander in Chief of New South Wales and its dependencies, twenty-seven years old, blunder-prone and snooty, put his aristocratic foot in it, twice.[31]

Following the usual toasts to the queen and to himself, Beauchamp rose to respond, waiting for the 'prolonged applause' to subside. He turned to his host, the local mayor, and faced some seventy gentlemen, pastoralists and dignitaries, and some forty ladies parked in the galleries to get a glimpse of him, many of whom were seeing 'a real live governor fresh from home' for the first time. It had come to his attention, the Earl began, that none of the aldermen present, the mayor or any of his predecessors had embezzled any of the profits from the mines, 'and this indeed', he concluded, 'was a matter for congratulation'.[32]

From this first 'unpardonable thoughtlessness', Beauchamp then expressed his pleasure in the feelings of loyalty, respect and affection displayed for the Crown. Such feelings made him feel 'glad' that he was an Englishman, 'not a Frenchman'.[33] With a relatively narrow scope of topics available to him, constrained by his official position – and aided by 'a very little Cobar whisky', the *Bulletin* mused – Beauchamp went further down the road of 'loyalty to the mother country' rhetoric by expanding his arbitrary attack on France, to a point of no return.[34] Unprompted, he elaborated on his patriotic feelings: the Dreyfus trial was clearly 'a hideous travesty of justice'. It was well 'to speak of liberty, equality, and fraternity in France' but there is 'no freedom or equality, as the soldier was distinguished from the man, and fraternity excluded the Jew'.[35] The rest of the evening followed the usual course of more toasts to everybody's health, good wishes and applause. Beauchamp was escorted back to his state car and was off at eight o'clock the next morning for the rest of his tour of regional towns. He circled back to the New South Wales capital via Adelaide and Melbourne. But reports of his speech preceded him in Sydney.[36]

Unity in adversity

Australian colonists were already used to Beauchamp's gaffes. Before his arrival from Great Britain in May 1899, Beauchamp had sent forward a verse adapted from Kipling's *Songs of the Cities* that hit the bullseye of Australian convict origin straight on: 'Greetings! Your birthstain have you turned to good.' Largely out of his depth, almost a year later on his way to visit Norfolk Island, he confessed that he was still recovering from 'the shock of being offered the Governorship of N.S.W.', an offer he had almost refused, knowing next to nothing about the place, and 'so ridiculous did it appear to me'.[37] In Sydney, at a time of growing nationalism and egalitarian rhetoric, in a country on the verge of Federation, he came under fire for his attachment to etiquette, insisting that his rank should give him precedence over his female companions when climbing into carriages, and demanding that his own sister curtsey to him and leave the room walking backwards at public functions.[38]

The Cobar speech was not the French colonists' first experience of Beauchamp either, as the latter had consistently clashed with the consul general, George Biard d'Aunet. Their ongoing spat was duly made public in the *Courrier Australien*. Ironically, it is the things that made Beauchamp and Biard so similar that pitted them against one another. They repeatedly clashed over protocol, rank and precedence. The ice-cold relationship between the two men had diplomatic implications as Beauchamp twice declined to attend the foundation dinner of the French Chamber of Commerce in July 1899 at the Australia Hotel. He neither attended the 14 July celebrations nor sent the customary card for the occasion, while attending the celebrations of

American independence ten days earlier (which his predecessors had not done). Biard d'Aunet stopped going to government functions.[39]

Cobar had an added dimension. It was not about courtly etiquette or punctilio, nor could the speech be glossed over as another episode in the warfare between the two men. As the *Courrier Australien* put it 'there is no longer question here of Dreyfus, but a matter of national character'.[40] As historian Ivan Barko points out, at Cobar the Earl not only expressed a political opinion, but because he was speaking in an official capacity as governor, his comments carried the weight of the administration he represented, and were seen by the French as an enemy attack on the French Republic itself, its founding principles of liberty, equality and fraternity, and its army.[41] Beauchamp, probably realising he had gone too far, later offered some qualifiers to his speech (the press misrepresented what he had said; he had referred to the first trial, not the second) but fell short of an apology and stuck to his overall opinion.[42] This roused republican ardour in the expatriate community as well as anti-monarchic feelings. One 'very proud' French migrant, Eugène Languer, dismissed Beauchamp as a '*tartuffe*' – a fake, an imposter – through the pages of the *Courrier*. 'Notwithstanding your gross ignorance, your incapacity, and your madness, you have got the situation of Governor' in New South Wales. In France 'never such a thing would have occurred, as in my country favouritism and titles count for nothing'.[43] Unlike previous sectarian attacks in the press, Beauchamp's speech was an assault on the collective honour of French citizens in Australia.

The idea of honour, particularly male honour, played an important role in informing individual and group behaviour, in France and elsewhere. Historians have shown how 19th-century ideas in France about honour had their genealogy in gallant practices – such as the duel – of the *ancien régime*. These ideas held until at least the end of the First World War in various forms because they 'provided bourgeois men both with the basis for claims of individual distinction and a collective warrant for certifying the superiority and exclusiveness of their class'.[44]

The code served to regulate the social relations of men and settle disputes between them. Insults and slurs, attacks on one's honour, were central to defining group and individual behaviours because a slight on honour was a threat to social status. This is not to say that ideas about honour mattered only to Frenchmen; they mattered to Australian colonists as well, and in various ways across class, race and gender.[45] But here, Beauchamp's affront galvanised the need for collective action on the part of the French.

A few days after Beauchamp made his speech, on an otherwise cloudless Tuesday afternoon in Sydney in early October, a storm was brewing inside the French Chamber of Commerce on Bond Street.[46] Presided over by Georges Playoust, the most prominent notables of the French community met to draft an open letter of protest to the Earl, which they addressed to the consul Georges Biard d'Aunet, the defender of 'our national honour'. Dr Rougier (the director of the Pasteur Institute), Dr Laure, G Cochelet (the director of the Messageries Maritimes) and d'Orgeval (the director of the *Comptoir National D'Escompte*), along with sixty-six others, explained that though they had 'greatly suffered' from the recent malevolence of Australian newspapers, they had remained dignified and kept their own counsel. Hearing that the representative of the British government had denounced their 'primordial institutions' they could be silent no longer. 'Hurt in our innermost feelings, humiliated in our national pride', they said, 'we rise up and rally around our flag'.[47] Since Dreyfus had been found guilty twice, they rejected the idea that the French judicial system was corrupt. They defended the French army, 'this outstanding national institution' as the very embodiment of the ideals under attack, those of liberty, equality and fraternity, since 'all French families, rich or poor, are represented [there] regardless of their religious beliefs'.[48]

Reading the letter today is a strange exercise. Every argument they put forward to defend their republic has been disproved. The second condemnation of Dreyfus at Rennes was not proof of his guilt, nor a vindication of the French judicial system. It was a piece of political manoeuvring by a new, moderate republican government that was planning to pardon Dreyfus gradually while allowing the government and the army to save face.[49] The army, though it might elicit national pride, was neither democratic nor secular, but was in fact one of the last refuges of the Catholic aristocracy of the old order and of the Empire.[50] But the slight on the collective honour of the French community had been real, and to a point it erased the differences the Dreyfus Affair had elicited among them. To make matters worse, Lord Beauchamp dismissed the open letter when it appeared in the papers because it was addressed to the French consul rather than to him. But to the French, this was an official protest letter and could only, in due form, be presented to the official agent of the Ministry of Foreign Affairs.[51] This was another incident showing a cultural gulf between the parties and the peculiarity of meticulous French residents who ranked themselves orderly under the consul.

Australian newspapers largely sided with the French colonists. Some used the opportunity to herald their own national sentiment as Australian Britons pitted against an out-of-touch aristocrat. Many had not forgotten Beauchamp's first 'birthstain' insult and were not surprised that he was inflicting new ones. On the cusp of Federation, one nationalist commentator pointed out the irony of the Gallic tones of the noble surname – Lord *Beau champ* rather than *Fair field*.[52] The demonstration of the French did however also come across to some as needlessly florid, showing them to be overly sensitive and attached to points of detail that could be easily dismissed by a shrug of the shoulders. *The Bulletin* caricatured the French colonists as a genuflecting frog in a suit, taking off a top hat and apologising for asking a grumpy-looking governor to step off its toes – '*toujours la politesse*' ('politeness, always').[53] In the end, the Earl did get off their toes, albeit begrudgingly.

The apology came as an anticlimax to the show of force and unity of the French residents. Beauchamp was urged by the British Colonial Secretary to make a public apology. The Earl opted for a more conceited, private and half-baked reply to Lord Chamberlain expressing 'regret for any unwarranted impressions caused' and 'if feelings of French residents were wounded'.[54] Six months after the speech, the matter was finally laid to rest and the collective honour of the French notables restored. But while their Frenchness could bring them together in the face of adversity, it could also be wielded as a divisive tool to disrupt the orderly world they had created for themselves in these British colonies.

An indivisible people divided

'He would be a brave man who would propose gold mining ... to the French colony now', summarised the satirical Melbourne paper *Punch* in 1908.[55] Fifteen years earlier in 1893, about twenty French colonists had formed a mining syndicate – the French Prospecting Syndicate – 'to take up mining leases' in Western Australia. Most were Melbourne-based, except Georges Playoust and his brother, who relocated to Sydney in 1895, and moved in the same circles of wool buyers, bankers and entrepreneurs. Two of them, Léonce Cayron and Adolphe de la Cour Russell, were city merchants.[56] Through the syndicate, they purchased four mining leases near Coolgardie in Western Australia, known as the Liberty, the Liberty Extended, the Central and the *Polynésien* (named after the Messageries Maritimes ship).[57] The plan was simple: float the mines on the London stock exchange and make a fortune.

By the early 1890s, the gold rushes had moved westward after rich deposits were found around the remote towns of Coolgardie and Kalgoorlie in Western Australia. The boom was swift and big, and the population of Coolgardie rapidly reached half that of Perth, the capital, with most immigrants coming from the east.[58] Across the Australian colonies, the fever for gold was accompanied by a fever for speculation. Mines were daily being floated in London and colossal fortunes made overnight, whetting the appetite of bankers and farmers alike across the British empire. Anything Western Australian sold fast and well. In 1895, one mine, some 200 kilometres from Coolgardie, floated

100 000 shares at £1 each, which 'went off like smoke' and was subscribed for six times over.[59]

But things did not go according to plan, and instead of untold riches the French businessmen were left only with never-ending and expensive lawsuits fought among themselves. Each episode in the saga was widely publicised in the local press, which for seven years regaled Australian colonists with the tales of 'the mercurial Frenchmen' who 'were all certain that in a few days, or at least weeks or months, they would all be millionaires'. To Australian Britons who were taught to admire the British qualities of reserve and detachment, the fascination and amusement partly lay in the emotional exuberance and volatility of the Frenchmen. 'Although this little French group of citizens is small', *Punch* went on, they are 'continually on the boil', the histrionic characters 'seething' with 'gossip and quarrels'. This is the 'nature of the Frenchman … he screams when he gets angry. He weeps when he can no longer scream'.[60] Echoing down the cultural chasm that ripped open in the courtrooms, the laughter of Australian colonists also reveals how ideas about nationality and honour served to delineate the contours of respectability within this small, male, Gallic world.

A Dickensian affair

Once the mine leases were acquired, the French Prospecting Syndicate registered them under the name of Adolphe de la Cour Russell, and tasked Léonce Cayron with selling them on the Stock Exchange during a personal trip to London in early 1895. The City of London pumped capital through the extensive arteries of the British empire; opportunities abounded, but so did danger. As planned, Cayron found a contact, a Mr Coxon, who introduced him to a company named the Alliance Contracting Company. The parent company created the Liberty Consolidated Gold Mines, to which Cayron was to sell the leases that would then be floated for an enormous £225 000 (somewhere around 35 million Australian dollars today). The first telegrams between

Cayron and the French syndicate about the deal were enthusiastic and things were looking good. Unfortunately, the crew Cayron fell in with were, as the Melbourne *Age* later put it, 'the merest adventurers'. The Alliance Contracting Company was composed of five people: a father, his two sons, his two nephews and one other. 'The richest of them had nothing' and the others were felons with County Court judgments to their names. On the day of the sale, they each bought only £1 worth of shares, and the public £9100 worth, leaving a total wholly inadequate to pursue the enterprise (and develop the mines). Cayron in London and the syndicate in Melbourne became agitated 'at the absolute breakdown of all the arrangements'.[61] Left with nothing to show for his efforts, just before leaving the British capital, Cayron signed an agreement to sell the rest of the shares for £2000. By telegram, the French syndicate repudiated the deal and Russell and Cayron stopped talking to each other as the latter made his way back to Melbourne.[62]

For the better part of the following decade members of the French prospecting syndicate became embroiled in what the *Evening News* called a 'a stormy sea of litigations' that became the 'scarecrow suit' of Victorian courts. The length and intricacy of the cases recalled the fictitious Chancery suit of *Jarndyce v. Jarndyce* in Dickens' *Bleak House*, but with comic overtones. From August 1895, the 'prolonged incessant cut throat litigation', as the *Age* put it, moved back and forth between Victorian courts, the Privy Council and the Supreme Court with each case dredging up old material to inflict new wounds. When a final appeal was dismissed after seven years in 1902, three of the original defendants had died.[63] While the first lawsuits were straightforward enough, they quickly spiralled into a discordant series of moves and countermoves that lost meaning to the Australian courts as French tempers flared.

The first case was brought by Cayron who, upon his return, sued Russell and the others in the name of the two London companies for performance of the sale for £2000. The court found that he had neither the authority to sue on behalf of the companies, nor the authority to enter into the agreement in the first place without the assent of the other shareholders in Melbourne.[64] During proceedings, several of Cayron's erstwhile partners accused him of inventing the names of the London partners and drawing up fake contracts to pocket a commission as the middle man.[65] From this point, the following court cases were never just about the syndicate and the mines but became about libel and slander. Cayron felt gravely offended by the 'most audacious calumnies' said about him, which were gravely damaging, he thought, to his reputation and standing in the French community.[66] To defend himself he immediately sued Marcel Crivelli and the two Playoust brothers for defamation. This second trial took a year. On 3 July 1896, the Victorian court found in Cayron's favour, and ordered the defendants to pay £250 in compensation and to issue a formal apology.[67]

The 'little French colony' in Melbourne, just as in Sydney, was structured 'in order of strict social precedence' below its consul.[68] The apology took place at the Melbourne consulate, a couple of weeks after the judgment, in front of France's official representatives. Once delivered, matters seemed laid to rest and the four men went to celebrate with a drink.[69] But Cayron continued to harbour a deep-seated animosity towards Russell. His behaviour towards the man left no doubt as to his feelings, and was summarised by a Victorian court at a subsequent trial, to an amused audience. For months, at every meeting of the syndicate, 'the moment he set eyes on Russell [Cayron] charged at him'. He refused to allow Russell to chair meetings, 'demanding always the sacrifice of Russell before he would consent to discuss anything' and, on 27 January 1897, 'Cayron proposed to batter him with a flower pot'.[70] Outside the courtroom, Cayron was plotting his next move.

After the apparent reconciliation at the consulate he approached the consul, Léon Déjardin, to obtain a written statement summarising the exchange. The consul refused, believing Cayron could use it as evidence of the calumnious treatment he had received, in which his honour was slandered. Cayron then took the added step of writing directly to the Ministry of Foreign Affairs in Paris, going above

Déjardin and the orderly power structure of the French community in Melbourne. The letter he sent to the ministry grossly misrepresented the overall situation, talking of the 'rich veins of gold' he had been deprived of, whereas in court both plaintiff and defendants agreed they were barren.[71] Nothing came out of those efforts, but it does say something about the worldview of the French businessmen that Cayron attempted to resolve a colonial civil lawsuit in a British colony involving the London Stock Exchange by going to the French authorities both in Melbourne and France. Much as the businessmen had done with the protest letter to Lord Beauchamp, Cayron's appeals to the consul and the Ministry of Foreign Affairs reveal how much this male, Gallic world stood apart in the British colonies, their sense of honour and morality still defined by a country on the other side of the earth.

In the meantime, the mines in Western Australia were left untouched. The endless trials prevented the syndicate from pursuing its venture, and Cayron made sure they could not make a move without him. In a new trial, Cayron sued Russell and the syndicate to prevent a sale without his assent, and to have the syndicate dissolved. In the end, Cayron was found by the court, and during an appeal, not to have acted 'bona fide'. But of particular interest are the tactics he put in place to try to undermine Russell's credibility by attacking his Frenchness.[72]

Frenchness on trial

Accusations of corruption flew back and forth across the courtrooms, but they were lost in translation. In the witness box, Cayron was cross-examined by Russell's lawyer, Mr Topp, about his dealings in London some five years earlier. Specifically, Cayron was being accused of trying to bribe British newspapers to report favourably on the floating of the mines. The accusation rested on Cayron's use of the French word 'chantage', meaning 'to blackmail', when he wrote to Russell from London. Cayron disputed the accusation by explaining he only meant that it was a common practice for the specialised press to receive payment.⁷³ In turn, to force dissolution, Cayron also accused Russell of trying to bribe the man who wrote a report on the state and value of the mines. Here the debate in court revolved around whether the saying 'graisser la patte' ('to grease the palm') meant outright bribery or to offer a (legal) commission.⁷⁴ Local papers were quick to draw parallels between accusations of bribery and the 'Hooley revelations' in Great Britain. The revelations had been the most widely discussed case of fraudulent mine promotion of the time. The promoter *par excellence*, Ernest Hooley, had plummeted from the highest of social heights that money and prestige could buy to the shadowy depths of bankruptcy, social shame and, eventually, prison. The revelations had incriminated large sections of the financial press in London, which were accused of taking bribes from promoters.⁷⁵ But the comic twist in this Australian pastiche was that the two Frenchmen were accusing each other of the same misconduct, for a syndicate in which they were both shareholders, and that only held the promise of mounting legal fees. To the Australian judges and courtroom, beyond the opacity of meaning of translated words, the unintelligibility reached a crescendo when Cayron shifted his tactic to throw Russell into disrepute by questioning his nationality.

Backed into a corner after another attempt to accuse Russell of fraud was quickly dismissed by the court, Cayron proceeded to attack Russell's character directly. Russell was, Cayron said, 'the only man in our syndicate capable of doing such a thing' and 'the most immoral man in Australia'.⁷⁶ Whatever measure of success Cayron's new plea might have been building, whatever interest it generated in the presiding judge, it all came tumbling down when Cayron added 'but I am glad to say, although he pretends to be a Frenchman, he is not'. Cayron's attack fell apart as the courtroom burst out in laughter, and its weakest point was picked up by the defendant's lawyer: 'Well, I don't know much about it', he said, 'but it seems to me he has a strong French accent.' Here, Cayron's retort differs in various reports of the case. In one of them, he replied, 'Oh, no, pardon me. It is a Dutch accent' (which was met with more laughter from the courtroom). In another, he said that

Russell was French-Canadian. Pressed for clarification at a following sitting, he emphasised the point he was trying to make, which was simply: 'I do not consider him a Frenchman.'[77] Suggesting that Russell was of Dutch descent could have gone some way in discrediting him. Tensions between the British empire and Dutch-Afrikaners in South Africa would escalate into open conflict in the Boer War just one year later. But simply suggesting that Russell was untrustworthy because he was not a Frenchman not only fell flat as a strategy, it made Cayron look ridiculous in the eyes of British colonists, for whom France had been Britain's perennial 'sweet enemy', and who characterised the French by their volatile, histrionic and emotional temperament.

Cayron had to admit that the mines – which were worth next to nothing – and the syndicate had been the last things on his mind, that what he wanted was to restore his honour by attacking Russell, who had 'started the whole affair by his lies about me'.[78] Cooler tempers reined in the effusive passions of the preceding days, or indeed years. George Playoust took his turn in the witness box and dismissed all allegations of wrongdoing by either party, putting the numerous trials chiefly on Cayron's excitable character. He 'seemed to [be] wanting to make a quarrel', Playoust put to the court, but was not, in the end, a bad person – he never did throw the flower pot at Russell.[79] The court judge concurred with Playoust and found in favour of the defendants, but not without expressing sympathy for Cayron, who 'had been slandered in a very violent way, and the natural result, particularly in the case of a Frenchman, was to excite resentment'.[80]

To the Australian judges, lawyers and members of the public sitting on court benches and following the trials in local newspapers, the seemingly insignificant scuffle taking place publicly among French migrants took on comic overtones because of the cultural rift it laid bare. Lawsuits about personal honour were far from uncommon; they were a particularly bourgeois concern in settler colonies where social status was sometimes the only currency one possessed. But if the Frenchmen were seen as an amusing curiosity, it was the way they went about it that people found funny; the veneer rather than the substance. Calling each other's reputation as Frenchmen into question in a British dominion was probably not the safest route to take – and it did not win Cayron his case.

Léonce Cayron, Adolphe de la Cour Russell, George Playoust and other businessmen in Sydney and Melbourne were new migrants. Some in their circles did not stay in Australia. In the fight for control of the *Alliance Française* in Melbourne, the 'French' side was also composed of people who had only recently arrived in Australia and some who would go back to France or Europe, such as Paul Maistre and Irma Dreyfus. It is easy to understand how simple, how instinctive it might have been for these people to recreate a little world within a world that mirrored the social and gendered hierarchies of the *mère patrie* (mother country). Frenchness, for them, could be a tool for defining a personal and collective identity, delineating the boundaries of respectability, of social standing among themselves and in relation to their new home. But these communities disaggregated quickly in the course of the 20th century. For some, in this relatively well off and white migrant population, within two generations, processes of acculturation and adaptation changed the strength and meaning of their French connection.

CHAPTER 6
Fading family ties to France: Two diarists' views

Seventeen-year-old Lydia Delarue was sitting at the foot of the Pyrenees in the South of France in 1903 when she confided her frustration to her diary: 'I am an Australian, we are freer than anyone in France.'[1] Except that Lydia had grown up in Australia thinking that she *was* French. Her grandfather had migrated from the north of France in the 1850s, and she was the third generation – the second Australian-born generation – to proudly claim a French identity. It was not until her first trip to the country of her forebears and a six-month stay at a 'finishing school' in Pau that Lydia started scrutinising the accepted family creed. On this occasion, her thoughts about her nationality were prompted by her frustration at being denied the right to attend a local carnival because of her sex. As for many Australian women, her first encounter with the 'elsewhere' prompted both conscious and unconscious wrestling with big questions of self-identity and belonging.[2] What makes Lydia different from many Australian sojourners are her family ties to France, passed on by her Australian-born father, who also left a written record of his travels to their ancestral land.

In his small black notebook, Lydia's father Leopold Hyppolite Delarue had jotted down short daily entries throughout 1878. Leopold had gone to France to work at the Exposition Universelle with Jules Joubert, one of the founders of Hunters Hill. He helped with the everyday business of setting up the New South Wales stalls.

But he also used the opportunity to travel south. So some twenty-five years apart, through the same family connections, and perhaps luck, Lydia and her father trod some of the same paths, in London, Paris and the South of France, leaving us with a rare record of similar journeys to a place of origin, undertaken by members of the same family, yet their experiences were markedly different due to gender, time and age. Read alongside other Australian travel writings in the period, and the memoirs left by Lydia's sister Eugénie in her later years (recorded by her daughter), Leopold's and Lydia's diaries chart the changing and waning role France played in the Delarue family's story of origin. As each generation became more anchored in Australian soil the diaries also show the subtle process of assimilation for a white non-Anglo migrant family. And because they are private documents, they go beyond some of the clichéd ideas about France that attracted people such as HM Green or Norman Lindsay, people who rarely ventured beyond Paris. The Delarue family's diaries, memoirs and travel writing underscore the often-unrecognised importance of the French countryside in British views of France and the role it played in defining 19th-century ideas about tradition and civilisation. But first, let us meet the Delarues.

They used a bidet

From the mid-1870s, walking along Sydney's bustling George Street, passers-by would look up to number 396 to check the time and set their watches to the large clock adorning the entrance of the shop of 'H. F. Delarue' – clocksmith, importer and maker of silverwares and jewellery.[3] The clock was a city landmark: at street level, it saved people from having to crane their necks to look further up at the awkward and protruding clock of the new General Post Office (GPO), built two doors down. We can see the two clocks in an 1883 painting of George Street by the Communard artist Alfred Tischbauer, who had been exiled to New Caledonia and taught for a time at the Sydney Technical

College with Lucien Henry (see image 11). The Delarue clock would also have drawn people's attention to the window displays showcasing the award-winning creations of 'Old Delarue', and perhaps entice them to purchase a brooch, a watch, or a bracelet stamped with his maker's mark.

Hippolyte Felix Delarue migrated to Australia from Berck, near Calais, in the 1850s. He married British-born Lydia Knight (young Lydia's grandmother and namesake) in 1855 and they had three sons. His business, or 'The Business' as the family called it, prospered.[4] Like the landmark clock, Delarue's creations gained in renown and won national and international prizes. He exhibited at the *Exposition Universelle* in Paris in 1867, the Metropolitan Intercolonial Exhibition in Prince Alfred Park in 1870 and at the Sydney International Exhibition in 1879.[5] Much as Lucien Henry would do a few years later, Old Delarue incorporated native Australian flora and fauna into his elaborate designs. In Paris, he presented a miniature clock tower, shaped like 'a silver mounted emu's egg' heavily ornamented 'with frosted silver-grapes and leaves, kangaroos and emus, possums, flying squirrels, a laughing jackass and an Aboriginal surmounting a bouquet of wild bush flowers'.[6] Well established and respected, he also provided the gold trowel ceremoniously used in 1868 to lay the foundation stone of the new St Mary's Cathedral after the old building burnt down.[7] Yet despite his success and integration in the Sydney community, Hippolyte Felix Delarue was a proud Frenchman. And so were his Australian-born sons.

Old Delarue's eldest, Leopold Hippolyte Delarue, was born in Australia in 1855, but he did not really feel Australian. 'If you are born in a stable', he used to say, 'it doesn't make you a horse', or so the family story goes. He certainly worked to maintain the French connection: with his English-born wife Kate, the couple first settled in Hunters Hill, known by some as 'the French village', and called their house 'Berck' after his father's native town. Kate 'was often taken to be French herself' as if covered by a mantle of Frenchness by association.[8] From

Hunters Hill, Leopold left for Paris to help organise the New South Wales section at the International Exhibition in 1878. He accompanied Jules Joubert, who became a sort of international exhibition impresario from the mid-1870s and went on to organise multiple exhibitions across Australia, in France, and in India.[9]

Once in Paris, Jules Joubert had the more distinguished task of cajoling visiting royalty and dignitaries, himself pouring Australian wine for the Archduke of Austria, for instance, who politely compared it to Hungarian wines.[10] Leopold's duties were more mundane. He ran errands, swept the floor before the arrival of the Prince of Wales, and set up the displays of 'rough gems and gem sands' and minerals sent by Professor Archibald Liversidge of the University of Sydney.[11] The tedium of his activities might have left Leopold feeling uninspired; his diary entries then are succinct: 'Exhibition', 'Exhibition again', 'Exhibition again, nothing particular today'.[12] Yet the *Exposition Universelle* did provide him with a rare opportunity to visit Europe; he saw London, holidayed in Lisbon and went to the South of France to visit relatives. In August, during the European summer, he also stopped for some time in the Nouvelle-Aquitaine region, in the thermal cities of Eaux Bonnes and Eaux Chaudes, in the South-east of France, to tackle what he then called a 'little weakness' of the lungs.[13]

Back in Australia, Leopold's health gradually deteriorated. After the birth of Lydia Victorine, the eldest of the two Delarue daughters, the family left Hunters Hill for Bankstown on the medical advice that the warmer climate might help Leopold's health.[14] He probably had tuberculosis. The epidemic of 'consumption' caused millions of deaths through the 19th century. It was often called 'the white death' or 'the great white plague' because it produced a visible anaemic pallor, so warm weather was often prescribed as a palliative.[15] Whether it was TB or not, it claimed his life in 1891 when Lydia was about five years old. That same year, the clock on the new clock tower of the Sydney GPO was set in motion, visible from all surrounding streets, dwarfing in importance and usefulness the Delarue shop's clock. That clock was finally taken down in the 1920s, though long after The Business closed in around 1908.[16]

In the small municipality west of the city, though they had precious little time with their ailing father, Lydia and her sister Eugénie lived 'a happy and carefree childhood'.[17] They did not learn their grandfather's language, but after Leopold's death the family embraced other aspects of their French connection. On occasions, the Delarue girls would sing French songs they had learned by heart or dress up as Breton peasant girls at fancy dress balls. And to the dismay of their friends, they used a bidet.[18] Through these cultural quirks and family lore, the sisters grew up 'thinking of [themselves] as French', as Eugénie later recalled; it was an idea 'somewhat inaccurate but which made us a little "different"'.[19] In a colonial society that tried hard to indulge in an English fantasy, down to the 'frowsy carpets and heavy solid chairs of England's cold and foggy climate', the Delarues stood out.[20] During her journey to France, however, Lydia discovered she was neither really just French nor English.

Off to France

Australia's distance from Europe and America meant that throughout the 19th and much of the 20th centuries, the 'overseas trip' was, as historian Ros Pesman put it, 'a ritual event, a rite of passage, a convention in Australian middle-class social and cultural life'. Until the 1950s the convention for Australians of British heritage was to go to the heart of the British empire. Going 'Home' to Great Britain and London was an act 'culturally intelligible to family and friends', historian Angela Woollacott explains, which signified social, cultural and often financial affluence.[21] For many, the encounter with the fabled 'Home' was a turning point in their sense of self.[22] For the young, the trip was often undertaken as part of an education – and likely decided by someone else. Men were sent to England and women to the Continent, preferably France, to acquire the veneer of European refinement and culture that was still a hallmark of colonial female gentility. The practice, imported from Britain, was based on entrenched ideas of women's intellectual inferiority and their expected role as guardians of morality. It was well established in the elite Anglosphere at large: the English writer Dorothy Bussy and the Americans Natalie Barney and Eleanor Roosevelt all attended the same elite finishing school near Fontainebleau on the outskirts of Paris, called *Les Ruches* ('the beehives' – they were 'les abeilles', the bees).

Les Ruches is also where the Australians Margaret Isabella 'Daisy' White and her younger sister Dorothy were shipped off for two years between 1887 and 1889.[23] Daisy was convinced that she had been exiled by her stepmother to make way for her new family. But the decision is consistent with the class and status of a wealthy pastoralist family of the Upper Hunter Valley. The allure of a French aura still lingered one generation or so down the family tree. The author Patrick White, a distant cousin from a different White branch, talks of his parents' decision to name his sister Suzanne, pandering, he wrote, 'to the colonial nostalgia for what they believed to be French'.[24]

Though she initially felt punished and banished, Daisy's stay in France was a cultural whirlwind and she made the most of it. The school was of a high calibre and she became acquainted with the French literary canon, including Molière, Montaigne, Racine and Voltaire. She attended performances of some of the greatest plays in the French repertoire – *L'Avare*, *Ruy Blas*, *Le Cid* and many more. And there were also the much-anticipated visits to Paris, to the art galleries, to the Louvre, Notre Dame and the Pantheon. Her diary is sprinkled with many French phrases, Gallicisms and borrowings from the literary canon of the time, demonstrating her competence and her interest in the language and suggesting an already solid education in Australia. However, for Patrick White a few decades later French, due to its association with femininity, came with its share of trauma at an all-male Australian school: 'French was sissy; who needs French anyway?'[25]

Lydia's and Eugénie's stay in France for six months in 1902–1903 was, ostensibly, so they could be 'polished' as well. The trip could certainly signal financial ease and cultural standing in 'an Australia where class boundaries were insecure and status depended on adopted customs, behaviours and wealth more than breeding'.[26] But things were probably a bit more complex than that. In Pau, they attended a local school only as *externes* (day students) rather than *internes* (boarders) and lodged with Old Delarue's niece, Madame de Lostalot, along with their mother. Madame de Lostalot had moved back to France with her two children from New Caledonia after her husband's death (and they had stayed with the Delarues for six months on their way back).[27] And unlike Daisy's elite and rich experience, the Delarue girls seem to only have had thirty-odd simple language classes with their teacher, Mademoiselle Aubert.[28] Neither of the girls had ever had any formal schooling before the trip. The nearby state school was deemed 'unworthy' and their education was left in the hands of an impressive succession of 'governesses' (generally women who had themselves fallen on hard times and could, at best, teach the Delarue children to read and write).[29] The family had suffered financially since Leopold's death. Kate and her brother-in-law were not savvy managers and The Business declined year after year.[30] So maybe it was also just the right time for the three women to go away and regroup with their French relatives. And whatever the reason for the trip – prestige, escape, or a little bit of both – their Bankstown neighbours did not understand it. Such a trip was not intelligible in Bankstown the way it would have been to someone living in Hunters Hill or someone from Daisy's upper-middle-class background. One neighbour, in particular, thought it made sense for 'gentlefolks' to go 'Home' to England but could not fathom why three women would go alone 'gallivanting round a country as notoriously immoral as France, where they danced the can can, ate frogs and every man had three mistresses'. She was convinced the Delarues would be 'courting disaster' and 'fall into the hands of white slavers'.[31] But they left all the same.

The diaries

Diaries are best thought of as 'records of a life in process rather than finished narratives about a life', or what Paul Ricoeur calls a narrative identity. Ellipses, omissions, repetitions and genre are clues that help us make sense of the Delarue family story if we read the diaries together.[32]

Leopold's diary is the closest to what literary theorist Lynn Bloom calls a truly private diary: one whose scope, content and structure make it difficult for readers to understand. It was never intended to be published. The text has fewer symptoms of conscious crafting than diaries that show an awareness of a potential audience, present or future.[33] Leopold is quite factual. He is diligent; he writes daily, or nearly. He records dates; the time of day; distances; latitudes; heights of mountains; names of places. So his notebook is closer to older forms of diary-keeping (the ledger, the account book, gardening notebooks). His factual record seems at first to be an obtuse document that cannot reveal much of the inner workings of its author, unlike his daughter's, which shares much more explicitly.

Lydia's diary is closer to being written with an audience in mind. It belongs to two genres: that of the schoolgirl or premarital diary, and that of the travel journal, starting – and ending – with the overseas trip. By the mid-19th century, schoolgirls writing in diaries had their own literary canon of sorts, at least since the publication of the journal of Marie Bashkirtseff, a Russian artist who lived in Paris and died young. Lydia follows a pattern set by others, for instance, when she wishes her diary 'good night'. Daisy calls her diary 'my love'.[34] The style suggests intimacy and an unguarded flow of thoughts and desires, but also connects them to each other and to other young female diarists since the late 18th century, most of whom gave up the practice once they married. Certainly, Lydia engages in what historian Alan Atkinson calls 'the new game of introspection', asking questions about herself and her place in the world. However, as publication was at least a possibility we cannot just take the diary at face value. A potential readership –

family, future husband, children or even friends – is always lurking at the edges of the page.³⁵ We need to read beyond what Lydia writes.

Leopold's diary does give subtle clues as to how he felt about France. He does not explicitly tell us where 'home' is, but his sense of belonging, at least during this trip, is apparent. Australian colonists would often use the word 'Home' to refer to England. Even those born in Australia continued to do so long after Federation.³⁶ But looking at Irish–Australian correspondence in the 19th century, historian David Fitzpatrick cautions against seeing this use of the word as being imbued with romantic ideals about a place of belonging: an imagined Britain, France or Ireland. 'Home' or 'stopped at Home' for Leopold could mean Australia or his room in Paris.³⁷ But his attachment to France, a result of family history, education and self-identification, does come through. In London, he admired the architecture but did not recognise Westminster Abbey or the House of Parliament. After fourteen days, all he had to say was that the streets were 'very narrow'. On his first night in Paris he declared the French capital 'splendid'.³⁸ Lydia's experience was the opposite.

Lydia, Eugénie and their mother, Kate, travelled on a steamer called the *Suevic*. It took them first to England, before they went down to Paris and then on to Pau. As they reached port, Lydia wrote of 'the beautiful Cliffs of Dover'; she wrote about the 'beautiful (...) colour of the grass' and about the 'beautiful green hills'. Lydia's descriptions rely on repetitive language, and she sometimes confides her struggle to express her feelings. Historian Richard White has observed that first impressions are 'a crucial bridge between imagination and experience'.³⁹ Lydia's descriptions – her very inability to express herself, the use of repetitive adjectives – are similar to those of other Australians in the same period. They share a collective understanding that England, the heart of Empire, must constitute what White calls the 'ideal landscape'.⁴⁰ Leopold, for his part, simply noted: 'Saw the celebrated white Cliffs of Dover'.⁴¹ At Madame Tussaud's waxworks, the royal family and 'Our King' are, to Lydia, all 'beautiful'. These cues reveal 'the inadequacy of a colonial culture face to face with an imperial ideal' and mark Lydia as a product of that imperial culture.[42] Once in 'London Town', the little family's short visit reprised all the clichés of Australians in London. At alarming speed, all the sights and sites of their Britishness were consumed: Westminster Abbey, the Houses of Lords and Commons, the Chamber of Horrors, Kew Gardens, the Zoological Gardens, the Crystal Palace, the Tate Gallery and the Tower of London, where they walked 'up the very stairs where the little Princes were found' and 'walked over the same ground where poor Ann Boleyn was executed'.[43] Threading their way across London, the Delarues enacted a form of secular pilgrimage through the familiar maze of British history. In Paris, however, they were on unknown territory.

As soon as they arrived in the French capital, they were lost. 'We had a bit of a worry here, could not speak any more French than "Parlez-vous Anglais?"' Wherever they went they spoke English and were met with 'a shrug of the shoulders'. Though it was 'great fun', it left them stranded. Eventually they were rescued by a good Samaritan who pointed them in the direction of the St Petersburg Hotel, which their outdated Baedeker guide (maybe brought back by Leopold in 1878) described as 'respectable and conveniently situated'.[44] The Delarues were still in full tourist mode at that point. Lydia, like many other Australian or British visitors, loved to see people in Paris on the terraces of cafés and restaurants 'having tea or coffee outside'. She went to the Louvre, up and down the Boulevard des Capucines, to the 'Cathedral Saint Madaliene [sic]', the Tuileries and 'the Triumphal Arch'. Her descriptions are somewhat duller than those she wrote of London; less expressive. 'Lundi, today set out at 10 o'clock. Went around the town I am sure we have been down every street saw the two great arches St Dennis [sic]. Saw the shops, the place where all the marriages and papers are kept.'[45] But if these comments already show Lydia to be less familiar with Paris than she was with London, it is in Pau that her daily experience leads her to explicitly assert herself as an Australian Briton.

The countryside through Australian eyes

The education of 'the everyday Frenchwoman' is by and large the opposite of the British tradition, the *Argus* explained in 1899. 'The free and healthy life of English girls in the schoolgirl age is quite unknown in France.' Until 'mademoiselle is married ... they must be so brought up as to adorn the station in life in which they will marry'. French mothers were renowned for watching over their daughters 'as a trainer watches over a Derby winner'.[46] In the countryside in particular, British visitors were stunned to see that young ladies of the *petite* and *grande* bourgeoisie (the middle and upper classes) were always in the company of other, usually older, women: their mothers, governesses or even just a female servant.[47] In 1879, Lisbeth Seguin wrote a book titled *Life in a French Village*, where she despondently observed that French girls were guarded more closely than cows in a pasture.[48] Young French women, as late as 1900, had few opportunities to physically exercise (no archery practice like in England), were never left alone in the presence of men, and their education remained modest and prudish (unless a sympathetic servant sneaked in a novel by Zola). They were taught to fear and revere the authority of the church and priests. This was a culture shock for Lydia, as she vented to her diary. A girl 'is never allowed to walk by herself anywhere even in the Park'. She continued:

> As for speaking or walking with a young man in the street it would be considered shocking. The mother must be continually there. You must not even walk into a different room to take tea or anything as refreshment ... they must not go unless the mother or nurse went with her. How they get married is a wonder to me.[49]

Growing up in Australia, she and her sister were used to more direct and unsupervised interactions with their male contemporaries. On board the *Suevic*, from Cape Cod to London, the Delarues befriended a group of Canadian soldiers, who then accompanied them to Paris.

Both Lydia and Eugénie had an assigned 'beau'.[50] She was not prepared for life in the French country.

After several weeks of restrictions and confinement, Lydia's frustration was compounded when she was forbidden to attend a local carnival where 'girls or ladies must not go'. She writes, exasperated, 'Oh how I wish I were a man I could be free to the world, go where I liked, be my own master, how I wish.'[51] If we take Lydia's diary literally, this is a turning point in the way she thinks of herself. The gendered restrictions she experienced, which she found profoundly incapacitating, led her to reject her own previous identification with France: 'Well in France the poor girls are different in England we are free. I am an Australian, we are freer than anyone in France.'[52] Neither probably thought much about this, but in their diaries both Lydia and her father were looking at the French countryside through Australian eyes.

Pau, where the Delarues were staying, had attracted middle- and upper-class British visitors since the 1840s. British aristocrats and their children first stopped there during their exploration of the Pyrenees on the Grand Tour, on their way to or from Italy. The region's beneficial climate and its seemingly untamed wilderness gradually attracted more and more visitors from the British Isles.[53] Quickly the town adapted to its new clientele and British-style pubs opened alongside the traditional French taverns with names such as the *d'Angleterre*, the *Bristol* and the *Victoria*. By 1853 more than half the visitors in the winter season came from Britain.[54] Three years later Pau had a golf course.[55] But what British visitors came to experience was a state of nature they believed was still untainted by human interference and which seemed to be disappearing from England.

That was the experience British visitors sought in the South of France. By the late 19th century, the Industrial Revolution and increasing urbanisation had changed the British landscape considerably. People started to abandon the Lake District for rural France, which, in many parts, seemed to be spared the sweeping changes taking place in Great Britain, brought on by industrial modernity.[56] Looking out the window of the train taking her from Paris to Pau, Lydia avidly drank in the landscape. The bucolic autumnal colours drew her attention, 'all colours, small patches, red, brown, black, green, red, yellow, making the hills a magnificent picture'.[57] France industrialised later than Great Britain, and paradoxically perhaps, the country's focus on the discrete and specialised manufacturing of choice and luxury items by artisans helped to preserve what many saw as an Arcadian landscape. Lydia writes that 'France is the most beautiful place I have seen yet. London is grand and fine and old and antique buildings and all that, but France is so picturesque and quaint. There is brightness and life here the sun shines.'[58] At the same time as British consumers avidly purchased and used French luxury goods to show their sophistication, they sought refuge from modernity in the French countryside, a world that seemed unchanging, populated by peasants rooted in the land.

Between the middle of the 19th century and the Great War, two-thirds of the French population was rural. By the turn of the century, France only had fourteen cities of more than 100 000 people compared to England's forty-seven, and agriculture was more than half the national GDP. And it is only in the late 19th century that the Third Republic started turning 'peasants into Frenchmen' by extending the railway system, making military service compulsory as well as primary education (in French rather than in dialects or *patois*). Still, the slow pace of mechanisation and difficulties in transport entrenched differences between a closed-off entrepreneurial class and a self-sufficient, propertied peasantry.[59] To British visitors, however, those peasants were reminiscent of a bygone age, a simpler idealised past that found its truest expression in the landed country gentry. They embodied the admirable values of simplicity and austerity.[60]

In 1883 the American novelist Henry James, too, ventured out of Paris. By train and carriage, he travelled through many provinces – east, south and west – in search of 'the many good things in the *doux pays de France*'.[61] Ever the student of human character, James knew he could only scratch the surface ('the perception of surface') and write about clichés and the picturesque. One recurring set of characters were the washerwomen 'at little ponds or tanks', 'brown old crones' in traditional bonnets 'pounding and thumping a lump of saturated linen'.[62] Lydia noticed them as well. From her train in 1902, 'we see a peasant washing clothes in another river just as a picture'. Some months later in the depth of winter, again she writes of the 'very pretty picture' of the snow-covered country and 'to complete it, a woman … washing her clothes on a board at the river side'.[63] The peasant woman might have been freezing, dipping her hands in ice-cold water in the middle of winter, but Lydia, much as James, saw the surface, the symbol rather than the person.

In the late 19th century, peasants were showcased in made-up traditional 'villages' at International Exhibitions, like the one in 1867 where Old Delarue exhibited his ornamented miniature clock, or the one his son helped set up in Paris in 1878. Wearing traditional regional costumes, at those exhibitions peasants were meant to demonstrate the fast pace of change and progress, but also legitimise the power of nations by providing the impression of an unbroken link to the past.[64] This image of the peasant was then reproduced in public and private representations. In 1903 in Melbourne the Scandinavian consulate threw a masked ball around the theme of 'National or peasant dress of various countries'.[65] Growing up in Bankstown, the Delarue girls dressed up as 'Breton peasant girls' at parties, and again for a party on board the ship taking them to France.[66] But while they were in France, Lydia and her father wrote about the countryside and peasants in a different way. To the Delarues they were actually agents of civilisation.

As they travelled, the Delarues both keenly noted signs of development. As soon as he arrived in France from London, Leopold's first thoughts went to agriculture: 'took train to Paris. The country through which we passed is finer than that of England, every available spot is cultivated'.[67] When he travelled through the Landes region, from Bordeaux to Dax, Leopold found the landscape monotonous, stretching for miles on end with pine trees and 'not cultivated'. But once his train departed Dax in the direction of Pau, through the same landscape his daughter would gaze at twenty-five years later, his mood picked up and he used a rare adjective: 'the country is beautiful, well cultivated'.[68] Lydia, too, was continually amazed at the work of French peasants, the 'greatest workers I ever saw' in a country where 'not a piece of land is not cultivated'. She talks of 'the most beautifully cultivated land I ever saw miles at a stretch' as she continues through the autumnal landscape 'out on the flatter country'; she passes 'more hayfields', the land is 'still cultivated, not an inch wasted'. She ends with 'Grand!'[69]

This view of French arable land reveals the Delarues' mental furniture as colonial Australians. Agriculture, or land exploitation more generally, had become a litmus test of civilisation since the scientific revolution of the 17th century. The idea that 'unimproved land was indicative of sloth and mismanagement' was well established.[70] This idea served potently to legitimise ownership of the land and the dispossession of Indigenous populations in settler colonies.[71] Some colonial Australians used this logic well into the late 19th century, and even the early 20th century, to demand a British-backed Australian takeover of New Caledonia from the French, because they were perceived as failing in effectively exploiting the natural resources of the islands.[72] During the First World War, some fifteen years after Lydia went back to Australia, the journalist and war historian Charles Bean was travelling through France with the Australian Imperial Force as a war correspondent. He lauded French peasants as the salt of the earth and the soul of the nation: 'Whatever the jabber of the world outside', he mused, 'whatever may be the case with Paris, these country people of France are one of the freshest and strongest nations on earth.'[73] Bean was in awe: '[t]he country was almost all cultivated land, one vast farming industry'. The prowess was all the more noteworthy because women had been doing the work in the absence of men during the war, 'they had managed to get through the whole year's work exactly as if the men were there. As far as we could see every field was ploughed, every green crop springing. It is a wonderful performance.'[74]

French peasants, in these descriptions, do not just embody a remedy to the cultural and social changes of the 19th century, but also served to measure the prowess and civilisation of the French nation. The continuity between the Delarues' observations make clear that whatever they were telling themselves and their diaries, they were both partly products of a colonial British culture, both seeing France through Australian eyes.

For Lydia and her father, their Frenchness was an explicit marker of their personal identity deeply rooted in their family history but it did not withstand the test of time. The place of belonging that in part shaped their view of the world was the one they grew up in, though neither was probably taught to call it 'Home'. For Lydia, a young woman who experienced the oppressive gender order of rural France, her self-identification with the country of her forebears underwent a transformation during her sojourn. As each generation became more rooted in Australia, the Delarue family's connection to France faded and took on a different, more romantic hue than the strong nationalist sentiments that animated the French settlers in the preceding chapter. When she started the long voyage back to Australia, Lydia 'felt parted from France and all its pleasures & dislikes forever'. Still, she confided in her diary in broken French that she would like to go back for her honeymoon. She married later in life, in 1924, at St Paul's Church in Sydney, and never had children. It is unknown if she did find her way back to France after her wedding. As for her sister Eugénie, her own daughter, Eugénie Crawford (née McNeil), who diligently wrote down her mother's memoirs with her, still claimed in the 1980s to know the streets of Paris as well as those of the Australian capital cities. A French accent was preserved in her name, although she confessed herself 'a poor linguist'.[75]

Epilogue: France and ideas of the 'feminine' in 20th-century Australia

Before the global pandemic that brought us to a standstill in 2020, an estimated 1.2 million Australian tourists visited France every year.[1] Many also tried to live in France, to try out the French way of life – and many wrote about it. The number of Australian memoirs of life in France, such as Sarah Turnbull's immensely popular *Almost French*, have skyrocketed.[2] There have been more than forty such books published in the past twenty years compared to one in the 1990s. The distinctiveness of this pervasive Australian genre, compared to similar memoirs published in America or Great Britain, is that they are nearly all written by women, and heavily marketed to an eager female readership.[3] Intercultural scholar Juliana de Nooy explains that haute couture and haute cuisine are part of the attraction of life in France (or reading about it), as are ideas about prestige, femininity and distinction. To the majority of these authors, spending extended periods of time living in France, and often Paris, allows them to weigh up, embody, try out for themselves and sometimes reject 'postfeminist ideals of elegance, romance and luxury domesticity'.[4] For the handful of Australian male writers who have written memoirs of living in France in the 20th and 21st centuries, France is more likely to be attached to ideas of epicurean and nostalgic food experiences. It is a more rural space, mythologised for its slower and more authentic life. Unlike Lindsay and Green in the 19th century, however, they rarely question their assumptions about rugged Australian masculinity (what it means to be a *real* man) or seek to emulate a less than hyper-masculine French ideal of manhood.[5]

I have taught French Language and Culture subjects at several universities across Australia for the better part of the last decade. I have no doubt that many colleagues would agree with me that the vast majority of our students are women. While this phenomenon might not be unique to Australia, it is definitely very pronounced here. It might find its roots in the 19th century and the feminisation of the perception of French culture over time, but it is also a more direct result of a cultural *rapprochement* between France and Australia that took place from the beginning of the First World War.

The AIF and the women of Paris

The Bastille Day celebrations in Melbourne in 1915 reached a zenith of pomp and popularity never before seen in Australia. In the early hours of the morning on that 14 July, an 'army' of hundreds of women spilled onto the streets of the Victorian capital, selling flowers and 'cockades and flags in the colours of France', explained the *Argus*. By noon a pageant of the heroes and heroines of the French nation glided down the streets to festive music, some on ox-drawn carts, on horseback or on foot. Vercingetorix – the valiant chieftain who united the Gauls against the Romans – waved from atop his throne at the 'compact and enthusiastic crowd'. Henri of Navarre followed, then Charlemagne and Joan of Arc. Louis XIV, flanked by several of his mistresses, trailed behind the red cloak of Cardinal Mazarin. Had Eugène Lucciardi still been in Australia, the disillusioned French acting vice-consul might well have thought the ignorant school pupils who caused him such anguish in 1906 had grown into fine men and women. At noon, the Marseillaise was blaring from more than twenty 'café chantants', where patrons were encouraged to donate to the French Red Cross and the war effort. In the evening, high dignitaries of the state and representatives of friendly nations met at a great concert of French music at the Town Hall. Jules Homéry, the newly arrived French vice-consul in Melbourne, was moved by the 'extraordinary devotion' of so many men and women, whose evident 'friendship for France and their admiration' reflected their 'gratitude for everything She is accomplishing' for '[her] own protection and for the good of humanity and the salvation of the world'.[6]

The First World War brought France and Australia into a closer and less suspicious embrace. Australian soldiers first fought side by side with the French at Gallipoli, and between 1916 and 1918 more than 300 000 AIF were stationed in France in support of the British empire.[7] Baptised in blood, the Australian nation suffered heavy losses of life, which made Australians look to France as a site of devastation and mourning but also pride.[8] Along the figure of the digger, names such as Villers-Bretonneux, Pozières and Fromelles gained a mythical dimension echoing with national narratives of patriotic fervour and sacrifice that have turned France in the Australian imaginary into a validating mirror, reflecting Australia's bravery and courage.[9]

In the 21st century, ever more lavish celebrations of Franco-Australian friendship brought on by the commemorative frenzy of the centenary years have obscured a more complex past. Before the First World War, the relationship between Australia and France, and between Australians and the French, reflected a time when the recent settlers of this continent looked to the outside world, and not just Britain, with friendship and for inspiration, but also with envy, suspicion and fear.

France and French culture were many things to many people. A gauge of taste and refinement to some, it was also seen as a repository of tradition, a herald of modernity or a cautionary tale of moral decadence. At the time of Federation, discussions about French culture mattered a great deal because they facilitated conversations among Australians about the place they wanted to occupy on the global stage. As the French empire expanded in the Pacific, as its convicts nagged at the Australian colonies' own sense of propriety and respectability,

Frenchness remained a largely unchanged tool of social mobility that played on ongoing images of luxury, taste and aristocratic refinement. These ideas endured even if the majority of the very small numbers of French migrants coming to Australia in the 19th century were of low socio-economic backgrounds: peasants, farmers and professionals. They endured because of what they allowed Australians to say about themselves, and because they played a role in the games of distinction in a culture that was still predominantly defined by its relationship to Great Britain.

By the time diggers set off for Gallipoli and the Western Front, the *bagne* in New Caledonia had been closed for almost twenty years. It remained an object of fascination for some Australian travellers, attracted by the remnants of a colonial experiment that validated their own story of progress and political maturity.[10] But New Caledonia gradually shifted in Australian minds into a more exotic tourist site; that is, if they thought about it at all.[11] On the ground in 1940 after the overthrow of the pro-Vichy administration, a young Australian journalist from Gippsland, Wilfred Burchett, reflected on Australia's ignorance of New Caledonia, which he put down to his country's 'parochialism'. He believed the pace of world events and the Second World War would make Australia embrace New Caledonia. 'Whatever the fate of the French Empire, it is certain that relations between New Caledonia and its Pacific neighbours will become ever closer, and it's high time that all we Pacific neighbours began to know each other a little better.'[12] And yet today, some eighty years after he penned these words, New Caledonia, in the midst of an ongoing process of decolonisation, barely registers a mention in Australian newspapers. Much as they do now, 20th-century Australians continued to look for Frenchness in France, not in its empire.

In the trenches on the Western Front, the AIF found an escape from the mud, the filth and the cold by dreaming about their four or five days of leave in Paris.[13] But the short trips of 'leave-making in Paris' were not just about relief from the horrors of war, they were also reminders of the beauty of life. When they finally arrived in the French capital, it was often plunged in the dark, the Eiffel Tower reduced to a radio antenna. And yet to the AIF it was all still there, as they had been imagining it: the charm, the sophistication and the indulgence. Less than ten years after HM Green tried to put his finger on the pulse of the city, Harry Buckie, a draughtsman from Victoria, talked about the elusive 'atmosphere' which 'seems to sweep you off your feet'.[14] The air was so light people seemed like 'butterflies' and he felt like one himself.[15] 'All I have to write about is Paris', confided another AIF, Cyril Lawrence, in a letter back home. 'First of all until you have seen it there are two subjects you know nothing about – cities and women. In both it surely stands without equal.'[16] And both came hand in hand, as contact with *les Parisiennes* was first made on the boulevards, then at the Folies-Bergère and other cafés-concert.

But for some, the socially sanctioned, sensuous hedonism of life on the boulevards and its cafés was not enough. One soldier, George Rose, hired a former Thomas Cook guide to take him to the *bas-fonds*, the seedier side of the more respectable entertainment venues. The deeper Rose went the more horrified he became. The first 'dirty shop' had a couple of near-naked women 'flitting about in it' wearing only 'shoes, stockings and a flimsy silk scarf'. In the second establishment the women wore more clothing but 'they went on with some disgusting dances and foolery'. As historian James Curran explains, the third and last stop filled him with disgust and a sense of betrayal. 'It was an exhibition such as might grace a back street in Cairo, but something that I did not believe could be seen in Paris.'[17]

Rose's misadventures point to the enduring legacy of particular images of sensuality and femininity associated with Paris and Parisian women, but also to his need for those images to remain unchanged. While more Australians than ever before gained first-hand experience of France during the war, with some diggers bringing back French brides, the association of Frenchness with taste, refinement and femininity never subsided. This, in the post-war years, was particularly true in cooking and fashion, which contributed to the further association of French culture with femininity in Australia.

Oh, for a French wife!

In the second half of the 20th century, Australians went crazy for French cuisine. The French, still low in numbers, were not one of the post-war migratory waves that saw Yugoslav, Italian, German and Greek communities and networks contribute new labour, entrepreneurial skills and different tastes to the reconstruction period and the fabric of modern Australia. And yet during the 'epicurean outburst' that started in the late 1950s Don Dunstan, the gourmet premier of South Australia, even talked about what he perceived to be the 'average Hungarian chef's idea of the French cuisine'.[18] 'French' had been a marker of refinement in cooking for centuries. We saw this in Sydney and Melbourne in the 19th century, and it is still apparent today. French restaurants are more likely to be fine dining and be more expensive, although it does bear saying that the food might not necessarily be prepared by a French chef nor be haute cuisine (*glace à la vanille* is still just vanilla ice cream).[19]

In 1953, two Sydney-based advertising men, Ted Moloney and Deke Coleman, published a cookbook called *Oh, for a French Wife!* It was humorously illustrated by George Molnar and contained recipes from four prominent French women in Sydney: Henriette Lamotte (the Countess d'Espinay, a renowned milliner); Jean Strauss, the wife of the French consul general; Louise Coleman, the Belgian-born wife of Loyd (Deke) Coleman; and Paulette Pellier, a sought-after dressmaker. The front-cover cartoon was of a young 'French wife' in a state of undress strategically covered in vine leaves, with flowers in her hair, standing in a garden in front of an apple tree under the watchful gaze of a biblical serpent. We see her tempting a grubby, hirsute, ogre-like man with what can only be *une tarte à la pomme*, or an apple pie. The caption reads 'Gown by Pellier, Hat by Lamotte'. The cartoon hints at popular ideas about the sinful yet civilising effects of French (food)ways – the same duality that enticed Edwardian intellectuals like HM Green and Norman Lindsay to flirt with France as an alternative to their colonial Britishness. By 1980 the cookbook had been reprinted eighteen times and in three editions.

In the thirty-year period following the first edition, France also became more associated with technological modernity, as part of France's efforts and stated aim to become a medium-sized world power.[20] But it also came under fire and alienated large swathes of the Australian population because of its ongoing nuclear tests in the Pacific, and the bombing of Greenpeace's *Rainbow Warrior* in Auckland Harbour. When plans were afoot to begin testing again at Moruroa, Prime Minister Paul Keating reminded French readers of *Le Monde* in 1995 how significant 'French culture' had been in shaping 'our own cultural development'. He underscored that Australia's hostility towards the resumption of testing was not directed to 'the French people or the French nation' but rather was 'specific to the French Government's decision to resume testing in the Pacific'.[21] One opinion poll showed 95 per cent of Australians opposed the testing. Arsonists destroyed the French consulate in Perth. And while some for a time boycotted French products and restaurants, this same period saw a surge in interest in French cookery, food writing and French fashion, underscoring an ongoing divide between the idea of France as a geopolitical presence in the region, and Frenchness as an enduring instrument of social distinction.[22]

From the mid-1960s, propelled by cheap flights, new affluence and a desire to compensate for the restrictions of the war years, the number of Australians going overseas, and to Europe, grew by tens of thousands every year. On this 20th-century Grand Tour they tasted cheap but delicious Médoc wines, discovered small Italian villages and bakeries selling crusty, flour-dusted bread and trekked through the vineyards of Bordeaux and Bourgogne. Upon their return they started looking down on the ubiquitous steak and eggs. Fine dining, or its approximation, became an upper-middle-class affair and French cooking moved from restaurants into the homes of Australians.[23]

Embodying French femininity

To this day many associate French fine dining with male chefs (one thinks, for instance, of the omnipresent TV-star chef Manu Feildel, who appears on shows like *Plate of Origin* and *My France*). But it was aspirational middle- and upper-class women who turned to French cooking in the second half of the 20th century in search of something a little different. And this desire for the foreign and sophisticated continued to sell. In the mid-1950s the *Australian Women's Weekly* sponsored the Le Cordon Bleu trained chef Dione Lucas to come to Australia on three occasions to give demonstrations of French cooking at department stores. Not only were the demonstrations popular, but so were the magazine issues in which her recipes were printed.[24] In Sydney, The Bistro, perhaps the first informal French eatery in the city, opened in 1957 in the basement of the Royal Exchange building. It became a regular haunt of the wool brokers who worked in the building and their network of bankers, lawyers and professionals. But it also offered cooking lessons and these attracted not men but women, well-to-do women of the Eastern Suburbs and the North Shore who came to learn about French foodways and more mysteriously 'to see how they should enrich their lives'.[25]

In Melbourne, Belgian-born Wivine de Stoop, the wife of a prominent industrialist, gave cooking lessons from her luxury homes in the exclusive suburbs of Toorak and Blackburn until the 1980s. Diane Holuigue, who was Le Cordon Bleu trained, taught an estimated 64 000 students at her cookery school The French Kitchen, a Melbourne institution for over forty years. Historians Donna Brien and Alison Vincent suggest that these influential women, and many others, offered more than their skills. They 'personified the justification of a domestic role for women that was becoming increasingly unfashionable'. They made domesticity glamorous because of 'their exotic foreign names, attractive lifestyles and aura of confidence and knowledge'.[26]

The women who contributed their recipes to *Oh, for a French Wife!* formed part of a subset of *le tout* Sydney. They were often featured in the social pages of newspapers and magazines along with the women of the by then well-established and prominent wool-buying families, such as the Playousts, the Lamérands, the Droulers or the Dekyvères.[27] The importance of the wool buyers and their network on Australian perceptions of French culture in the post-war period should not be underestimated. They might have been a small network but they were influential. The women, wives and daughters of these dynasties, set the tone for Parisian elegance in fashion in Sydney until the 1970s, when popular taste shifted towards the more casual.[28]

In addition to local couture salons run by Pellier and Lamotte in Sydney or Le Louvre on the 'Paris end' of Collins Street in Melbourne, the more upmarket and exclusive department stores such as Farmers or David Jones became purveyors of French couture, whether imported or locally copied.[29] From 1946 several French fashion shows were staged in Australia, with French models flown in. Department store owners Charles Lloyd Jones and Norman Myer teamed up with the Australian Consolidated Press and the *Australian Women's Weekly* to bring Parisian haute couture parades to Australia. Mary Hordern, the fashion editor, flew to Paris to recruit six French models and select the gowns, the whole process once again being documented to increase magazine sales. The models, with their 'French femininity' and their impossibly small waists, were treated like celebrities, and were given an inordinate amount of coverage in newspapers, newsreels and the radio.[30] In 1947 David Jones secured a franchise agreement with the House of Dior for a *Paris Fashion for All Parade* that showcased Dior's model garments alongside Australian adaptations. According to fashion historian Margot Riley, Dior himself was well aware that in the austerity period following the war, Australia was his third largest market after Paris and New York, and that Australian women spent more on fashion – relative to income – than women anywhere else in the world.[31] One year later Jones negotiated directly with Christian Dior to stage a 'world fashion coup': the first Dior-only fashion show outside of Paris. The association of David Jones with the House of Dior endures to this day in the department store's logo, the classic Dior black-and-white houndstooth check.[32]

Australians may have to become armchair travellers for some time longer as the ripple effects of the global pandemic continue to be felt throughout the world. Travel was also the domain of a privileged minority a century ago. But while few Australians had the opportunity to travel as far as France, let alone live there, a French connection carried meaning for many, including those bound by our newly felt geographic insularity. It held meaning because it said something about them, as British subjects but also as independent Australians. As in the stories recounted in this book, today France and French culture continue to be a mirror that reflect our own Australianness, and perhaps offer tempting glimpses of how else to exist in the world. Small acts of consumption and cultural embodiment are not anodyne. Going to the *Alliance Française* Film Festival, or to the Melbourne Bastille Day festival to sample the obligatory crêpe, or take a masterclass on how to 'French Up Your Style' or on 'The Cosmopolitan Origins of Bordeaux Wines', tell a story about who we are, or aspire to be. What will this story be in the 21st century?

Appendix

Introduction: Frenchness in Australia

Page 1   un accident d'automobile traduit textuellement

1 A glittering, raucous ritual : French cafés and culture

Page 16   l'art vestimentaire féminin

2 A battle for control : *Alliance* and misalliance

Page 38   de couleur

          en raison de la haute estime où le tiennent nos compatriotes, et du goût qu'il montre pour la langue et la littérature française

Page 43   sociétés mondaines australiennes où, sous prétexte d'arts et de belles-lettres, on s'occupe autant de « thès », de « soirées amusantes » et de bals

          une pâle copie de l'Austral Salon

Page 44   nos examens sont sérieux et qu'il est parfaitement inutile d'envoyer ceux de leurs élèves qui en sont encore aux quatre conjugaisons

Page 46   ma famille n'est alliée, ni de près, ni de loin, à celle de cet homme

mais lorsqu'on me demandera si nous avons organisé des cours de notre langue, les réunions mensuelles de notre section de Melbourne qui, par la force des choses ne concernent qu'une classe de la société, et la classe la moins nombreuse, pourront paraître une substitution insuffisante. Je défendrai ces réunions qui ont du bon, beaucoup de bon, mais qui, chacun en convient, je crois, ne peuvent faire, et ne font réellement que bien peu pour la propagation de la langue

Page 50   Les Crivelli se plaignaient de ce qu'on avait fait entrer des perruquiers comme membres du comité, des corsetières et que sais-je encore ! Et que ce voyant, la femme du Gouverneur qui devait assister à la réunion, y a envoyé sa femme de chambre, la trouvant plus à sa place qu'elle

Page 51   le Comité ne peut que dire, si dans les séances il y a eu des omissions ou s'il n'a pas observé strictement le réglement [sic], tous ont cherché toujours l'avancement de la Société

Page 52   cette habitude des affaires, ce jugement reposé et cet esprit de logique qui ne sont pas, en général, l'apanage du beau sexe

Appendix

et, comme jusqu'à présent tout ce qu'elle a fait semble être plutôt dirigé contre l'Université, celle-ci naturellement ne peut que lui être hostile

tous ceux qui étudient notre langue et notre littérature, sans distinction d'âge ou de condition sociale, et qu'elles instruisent en amusant

Page 57   je vous invite, en conséquence, à faire vos préparatifs pour rentrer en France

3 The scum of France : A reckoning with Australia's convict past

Page 59   Les colonies australiennes sont peu cordiales, il est vrai : et le sentiment d'une amicale réciprocité envers la France n'est point encore née chez elles. Elles sont même injustes à l'égard de notre pays, je n'en ai fait que trop fréquemment la pénible constatation

Page 60   des pieds à la tête

Page 69   L'on ne connaît pas de papiers la conduite est la seule chose qui fait preuve de ce que tu es.

ils ont horreur des Calédoniens. Si tu voulais te faire prendre en arrivant tu n'aurais qu'à dire que tu en viens.

Page 70   Ah! Il y en a des Anglaises et des belles, il y en a ... où je travaille et qui ont de jolis yeux

>J'ai toujours dans la tête d'aller dans mon pays de prédilection l'Amérique mais j'attends et veut goûter un peu de la vie Austral.

Page 73   ici c'est la liberté

Page 77   Sur le chapitre des criminels, tous les partis sont d'accord, la législation n'hésite que devant les indigènes et les asiatiques

> Les exagérations mensongères [sur le] danger de contamination morale … à la vertueuse population victorienne

4   French migrants : The 'crème de la crème'

Page 82   Comme négociants sérieux, des étrangers ; comme Français, l'éternel coiffeur, la marchande de gants, l'ancien failli qui s'est établi photographe, ou qui tient un café,… et des nuées de fonctionnaires

Page 83   Le Français ne s'expatrie qu'à son corps défendant, et tel jeune capable de se faire une position indépendante et lucrative de l'autre côté de l'océan préfère mener une existence de privations dans la ville qui l'a vu naître, en lutte souvent avec les besoins les plus matériels de la vie

> les rigueurs de l'hiver

Page 88   Mon amour pour la vie plus large des colonies anglaises m'a fait jeter mon dévolu sur l'Australie, dont je connais les progrès immenses

Appendix

brevet de capacité

Si vous ne pouvez me donner tous ces renseignements, auprès de qui pourrai-je les recueillir?

Page 89 quitter Paris, c'est quitter le monde

Les personnes mal payées ou mal nourries

Le manger en Australie coûte la moitié de ce qu'il vous coûte ici, les gages sont le double de ce que vous recevez, les heures de travail sont moins longues

Partons-nous pour l'Australie?

Pourquoi pas?

Si l'on apprend qu'il y a des riches qui ne demandent pas mieux que d'encourager l'installation des fabricants, des vignerons, des artistes et des professeurs étrangers

on laisse de côté les sauvages et les forçats, et l'on songe à ce que l'on pourrait avoir de profit à s'expatrier

Page 93 existe encore

Page 94 les conditions de travail étant absolument contraires à tout ce qui m'avait été promis, je quittai cette place et fut à Sydney 2 ans et demie

à doubler et faire des fourrures

tant qu'à faire la misère, j'aime mieux la faire dans mon pays

Je suis toute prête à partir, l'Australie est un beau pays, mais la misère y est bien dure

dans ce pays ici, à Melbourne, je gagne ma vie très misérablement dans un hôtel, avec 12 shillings par semaine et cela ne me suffit pas pour tous mes besoins, et je n'ai point d'amis ni de connaissance

Page 95   m'empresse … pour vous dissuader, si possible, de venir chercher, je ne dirai pas la fortune, mais une modeste aisance, en Australie

les professeurs de français sont, malheureusement pour vous, déjà trop nombreux dans ce pays, où pour arriver à subsister, ils se voient réduits à donner des leçons à des prix dérisoires

une crize assez aiguë qui n'est pas faite pour faciliter votre placement dans un pays ou les étrangers ne sont pas vu d'un bon oeil par la population ouvrière très hostile à l'immigration

Page 96   Ignorant complétement la langue, les mœurs, les usages du pays, et par conséquent, obligés d'accepter n'importe quelles offres, ils sont, en général, consciencieusement exploités jusqu'au jour ou, leurs employeurs australiens, ayant amplement profité de leurs connaissances particulières et de leur main d'œuvre expérimentée, ils se voient remerciés et s'aperçoivent qu'ils ont lâché la proie pour l'ombre, et peiné pour les autres

Son amour des voyages et principalement pour les pays lointains me fait supposer qu'il pourrait bien s'être réfugié à [sic] l'Australie

séparée de corps et de bien

Page 97   j'ai l'honneur de vous prier de l'informer que je suis bien où je suis, pour mon repos que je l'engage à respecter toujours

vous êtes l'auteur de ma ruine

ni elle ni son mari ne voulaient plus entendre parler de leur fils, qu'ils ne voulaient plus rien faire pour lui et ne désirait pas le moins du monde son retour en France

Page 98   Citons encore des déserteurs, quelques coiffeurs et cuisiniers, et c'est tout!

5 A matter of honour : Frenchness on trial

Page 105 la France est tombée au dernier rang des nations civilisées

Page 109 nos institutions primodiales

Sous la blessure de nos sentiments intimes outragés, de notre fierté nationale humiliée, nous nous redressons et nous courons au drapeau afin de nous y rallier

cette belle institution nationale dans laquelle toutes les familles françaises, riches et pauvres, sans distinction de foi religieuse, ont leur représentant

Page 114   les calomnies les plus odieuses

Page 115   de riches filons d'or

Epilogue: France and ideas of the 'feminine' in 20th-century Australia

Page 137   leur amitié pour la France, et leur admiration et leur reconnaissance pour tout ce qu'Elle est en train d'accomplir, au prix de quels sacrifices, en même temps que pour sa protection, pour le bien de l'humanité et le salut du monde

Select bibliography

This book draws on extensive archival material in Australia and in France. In France I consulted the Archives of the Ministry of Foreign Affairs: the Série Océanie, the French Embassy in London (378PO/CH and 378PO/K), the Archives of the Melbourne and Sydney French consulates (respectively 428PO and 662PO), and the Political and Commercial correspondence of the Ministry (2CPC and 139CPCOM). Collections consulted in Australia include documents held at the Mitchell Library, the National Archives of Australia, the National Library of Australia, the State Library of Victoria and the State Records of New South Wales, particularly the Colonial Secretary's Correspondence (NRS 906). Trove, the digitised database of newspapers held by the National Library of Australia, is the envy of scholars overseas, and has been an invaluable resource. Newspaper titles can be found in the endnotes for each chapter. The same goes for the invaluable online *Australian Dictionary of Biography* published by the National Centre for Biography at the Australian National University.

The starting point for this book has been the incredible wealth of secondary material written by members of the Institute for the Study of French–Australian Relations over the past thirty-five years and, increasingly, ISFAR's online *French–Australian Dictionary of Biography*.

Published primary sources
Austen, Jane. *Pride and Prejudice*. Irwin: Saddleback Educational Pub, 2010.
Baedeker, Karl. *Paris and Its Environs with Routes from London to Paris, and from Paris to the Rhine and Switzerland*. Leipsig: K. Baedeker, 1878.
Bean, Charles EW. *Letters from France*. London, New York: Cassell and Company Ltd, 1917.
Brodsky, Isadore. *Sydney Looks Back*. Sydney: Angus and Robertson, 1957.

Catalogue of the Natural and Industrial Products of New South Wales Forwarded to the Paris Universal Exhibition of 1867 by the New South Wales Exhibition Commissioners. Sydney, 1867.
Chabrillan de, Céleste. *The French Consul's Wife: Mémoirs of Céleste de Chabrillan in Gold-Rush Australia.* Translated by Patricia Clancy and Jeanne Allen. Melbourne: The Miegunyah Press, 1998.
Chisholm, AR. *Men Were My Milestones: Australian Portraits and Sketches.* Melbourne: Melbourne University Press, 1958.
——. *The Familiar Presence and Other Reminiscences.* Melbourne: Melbourne University Press, 1966.
Clarke, Marcus. *For the Term of His Natural Life.* Sydney: New Holland, 2008.
Comettant, Oscar. *Au Pays des Kangourous et des Mines d'Or.* Paris: Fischbacher, 1890.
Crawford, Eugénie. *A Bunyip Close Behind Me.* Melbourne: Hawthorn Press, 1972.
——. *Ladies Didn't. Recollections of an Edwardian Girlhood.* Melbourne: Penguin Books, 1984.
Crivelli, Georges M and Pierre Louvet. *L'Australie et le Pacifique.* Paris: G. Cres et Cie, 1923.
Dreyfus, Irma. *Lectures on French Literature.* London: Longmans, Green, and Co, 1896.
Dumas, Alexandre. *The Journal of Madame Giovanni.* London: Liveright Publishing Corporation, 1944.
Fauchery, Antoine. *Letters from a Miner in Australia.* Translated by AR Chisholm. Melbourne: Georgian House, 1965.
Flaubert, Gustave. *Dictionary of Accepted Ideas.* Translated by Jacques Barzun. New Directions Publishing, 1968.
Gamas, Citizen. *The First 'Australian' Play: Les Émigrés aux Terres Australes (1792).* Edited and translated by Patricia Clancy. Melbourne: Monash University, 1984.
James, George Payne Rainsford. *The Desultory Man.* Vol. 2. London: Saunders and Otley, 1836.
James, Henry. *A Little Tour in France.* Penguin Books, 1984.
——. *The American.* London: Harper Press, 2013.
Jaurès, Jean. 'Discours pour l'Alliance Française à Albi en 1884', in Raoul Girardet, *Le Nationalisme Français 1871–1914.* Paris : Armand Colin, 1966, 94–96.
La Meslée, Edmond Marin. *The New Australia.* Translated by Russel Ward. London: Heinemann Educational, 1979.
Lindsay, Norman. *Letters of Norman Lindsay.* Edited by RG Howarth and AW Barker. London: A. & R., 1979.
——. *My Mask: For What Little I Know of the Man Behind It: An Autobiography.* Sydney: Angus and Robertson, 1970.
Maistre, Paul. *Dans la Brousse Australienne: Scènes de Chasse.* Paris: Montgredien, 1901.
Marion, Horace. *Il Faut Sauver la France: La Décadence, Ses Causes, Remèdes et Moyens.* Paris: J. Jeannin (Trévoux), 1910.
Maurier, George de. *Trilby.* New York: Harper, 1894.
McKenna, Mark. *The Captive Republic: A History of Republicanism in Australia 1788–1996.* Cambridge: Cambridge University Press, 1999.
Murger, Henri. *Scènes de La Vie de Bohème.* Paris: Librairie Garnier, 1914.
Official Catalogue of the Natural and Industrial Products of New South Wales Forwarded to the Universal Exhibition of 1878 at Paris, 1878.
Parkes, Henry. *Fifty Years in the Making of Australian History*, Vol. I (London: Longmans, Green, and Co., 1892).

Select bibliography

Pearson, Charles H. 'L'Australie dans ses Rapports avec la France et l'Allemagne'. *Revue Coloniale Internationale* 1, no. 5 (1885): 337–44.
Poiré, Eugène. *L'Émigration Française aux Colonies*. Paris: Plon, 1897.
Pratz, Clair de. *France from Within*. London: Hodder and Stoughton, 1912.
Rochefort, Henri. *Retour de la Nouvelle-Calédonie: De Nouméa en Europe*. Paris: Ancienne Librairie Martinon, 1877.
Royal Commission on the University of Melbourne: Minutes of Evidence on Administration, Teaching Work, and Government of the University of Melbourne. Melbourne: Robt. S. Brain, Government Printer, 1903.
Schoell, Franck L. *La Langue Française dans le Monde*. Paris: Bibliothèque du Français Moderne, 1936.
Stead, Christina. *A Web of Friendship. Selected Letters (1928–1973)*. Edited by RG Geering. Angus & Robertson, 1992.
Stephens, Alfred G. 'Paul Wenz', in *AG Stephens, His Life and Works*. Edited by Vance Palmer, Melbourne: Robertson & Mullens Ltd, 1941.
Turnbull, Sarah. *Almost French*. Penguin, 2002.
Twopeny, Richard. *Town Life in Australia*. Melbourne: The Dominion Press, 1976.
Vazelhes, Etienne de. *Étude sur l'Extradition: Suivie du Texte de Traités Franco-Belge de 1874 et Franco-Anglais de 1843 et 1876*. Paris: P. Pichon, 1876.
Verne, Jules. *A Voyage Round the World: In Search of the Castaways*. Philadelphia: Lippincott, 1873.
Verschuur, G. *Aux Antipodes: Voyage en Australie, la Nouvelle-Zélande, aux Fidji, à la Nouvelle-Calédonie, aux Nouvelles-Hébrides et dans l'Amérique du Sud, 1888–1889*. Paris: Librairie Hachette et Cie., 1891.
White, Daisy. *Daisy in Exile: The Diary of an Australian Schoolgirl in France (1887–1889), Introduced and Annotated by Marc Serge Rivière*. Canberra: National Library of Australia, 2003.
White, Patrick. *Flaws in the Glass, a Self-Portrait*. London: Penguin Books, 1983.

Secondary articles and books

Ageron, Charles-Robert. *France Coloniale ou Parti Colonial?* Paris: Presses Universitaires de France, 1978.
Agulhon, Maurice. *The French Republic, 1879–1992*. English ed. Oxford: B. Blackwell, 1993.
Aldrich, Robert. *The French Presence in the South Pacific, 1842–1940*. London: Macmillan, 1990.
Ariès, Philippe. *Histoire des Populations Françaises et de Leurs Attitudes Devant la Vie Depuis le XVIIIe Siècle*. Paris: Éditions du Seuil, 1971.
Arthur, Paul. 'Antipodean Myths Transformed: The Evolution of Australian Identity'. *History Compass* 5, no. 6 (2007): 1862–1878.
Atkinson, Alan. *The Europeans in Australia: A History*. Vol. 3. Sydney: NewSouth Publishing, 2014.
Barko, Ivan. 'Felicite Cochard and the Foundation of the Sydney French Benevolent Society'. *Explorations* 44 (June 2008).
——. 'Georges Biard d'Aunet: The Life and Career of a Consul General'. *Australian Journal of French Studies* 39, no. 2 (August 2002): 271–91.
——. 'La Fondation et les Débuts de l'Alliance Française – Part 1'. *Explorations*, no. 26 (2010): 3–25.

———. 'The Cobar Incident, Its Antecedents and Sequels 1899–1900'. *JRAHS* 86, no. 2 (2000): 134–58.
———. *Vive la Différence! The French in NSW, Catalogue of the Exhibition*. Sydney: State Library of New South Wales, 2004.
Bergantz, Alexis. 'French Connection: The Culture and Politics of Frenchness in Australia, 1890–1914'. PhD Thesis, The Australian National University, 2016.
———. 'Mapping the Consul's Treasure: A Discussion and Guide to French Consular Archives'. *The French Australian Review*, 61 (Australian Summer 2016–2017): 40–46.
———. '"Remembering *Australasie*: Trans-Imperial Thinking and Migrant-Settler Legitimacy in *Le Courrier Australien* (1892–1896)'. In *Voices of Challenge in Australia's Migrant and Minority Press*, edited by Catherine Dewhirst and Richard Scully. Palgrave, forthcoming.
Bhabha, Homi K. *The Location of Culture*, Routledge Classics. London; New York: Routledge, 1994.
Bloom, Lynn Z. '"I Write for Myself and Strangers": Private Diaries as Public Documents'. In *Inscribing the Daily: Critical Essays on Women's Diaries*, 23–37. Massachusets: University of Massachusetts Press, 1996.
Bong, Jin Guan. 'Alice Ellen Charbonnet: A French Musician in Nineteenth-Century Australia'. Masters Research Thesis, Faculty of Music, University of Melbourne, 2006.
Bongiorno, Frank. '"Every Woman a Mother": Radical Intellectuals, Sex Reform and the "Woman Question" in Australia, 1890–1918'. *Hecate* 27, no. 1 (2001): 44–64.
———. *The Sex Lives of Australians: A History*. Melbourne: Black Inc, 2012.
Bourdieu, Pierre. *Distinction: A Social Critique of the Judgement of Taste*. London: Routledge & Kegan Paul, 1984.
Brien, Donna Lee and Alison Vincent. 'Oh, for a French Wife?: Australian Women and Culinary Francophilia in Post-War Australia'. *Lilith: A Feminist History Journal*, no. 22 (2016): 78.
Bullard, Alice. *Exile to Paradise: Savagery and Civilization in Paris and the South Pacific, 1790–1900*. Stanford: Stanford University Press, 2000.
Bunkers, Suzanne L and Cynthia A Huff. 'Issues in Studying Women's Diaries: A Theoretical and Critical Introduction'. In *Inscribing the Daily: Critical Essays on Women's Diaries*, edited by Suzanne L Bunkers and Cynthia A Huff, 1–22. Amherst: University of Massachusetts Press, 1996.
Burchett, Wilfred. *Pacific Treasure Island: New Caledonia; Voyage through Its Land and Wealth, the Story of Its People and Past*. Melbourne: Cheshire, 1941.
Burke, Anthony. *In Fear of Security: Australia's Invasion Anxiety*. Sydney: Pluto Press, 2001.
Campos, Christopher. *The View of France: From Arnold to Bloomsbury*. London: Oxford University Press, 1965.
Certeau, Michel de. *The Practice of Everyday Life*. Berkeley: University of California Press, 1984.
Charle, Christophe. *Paris Fin de Siècle*. Paris: Editions du Seuil, 1998.
Chartier, Roger. *Au Bord de la Falaise: L'Histoire Entre Certitudes et Inquiétude*. Paris: Albin Michel, 1998.
Chevalier, Louis. 'L'Émigration Française au XIX Siècle'. *Études d'Histoire Moderne et Contemporaine* 1 (1947): 127–71.
Clarke, Patricia. *Tasma: The Life of Jessie Couvreur*. Sydney: Allen & Unwin, 1994.
Cochrane, Peter. *Colonial Ambition: Foundations of Australian Democracy*. Melbourne: Melbourne University Press, 2006.

Select bibliography

Cohen, Michèle. *Fashioning Masculinity: National Identity and Language in the Eighteenth Century*. London; New York: Routledge, 1996.
Colley, Linda. *Britons: Forging the Nation, 1707–1837*. New Haven: Yale University Press, 1992.
Cornick, Martyn. 'La Réception de l'Affaire en Grande-Bretagne'. In *L'Affaire Dreyfus de A à Z. Histoire et Dictionnaire*, edited by Michel Drouin, 441–47. Paris: Flammarion, 1994.
Davison, Graeme. 'Rethinking the Australian Legend'. *Australian Historical Studies* 43, no. 3 (2012): 429–51.
——. *The Rise and Fall of Marvellous Melbourne*. Melbourne: Melbourne University Press, 1988.
Davison, Graeme, John Hirst and Stuart Macintyre (eds). *The Oxford Companion to Australian History*. Oxford University Press, 1999.
Docker, John. *The Nervous Nineties: Australian Cultural Life in the 1890s*. Melbourne: Oxford University Press, 1991.
Donegan, Jacqui. 'Banned in Boston. A Biography of Annette Kellerman (1886–1975)'. Bachelor of Arts with Honours, Thesis, University of Queensland, 2001.
Donohoo, Jill. 'NSW Premier William Holman and the "Inexhaustible Interest of French Literature and Affairs"'. *The French Australian Review*, 61 (Australian Summer 2016–2017).
Drury, John. 'Berthe Mouchette (1846–1928), Artist and Founder of the First Alliance Française in Australia, and Marie Lion (1855–1922), Artist and Writer'. In *French Lives in Australia*, edited by Ivan Barko and Eric Berti, 129–45. Melbourne: Australian Scholarly Publishing, 2015.
Duché, Véronique, and Diane de Saint Léger. 'Aussie, Code-Switching in an Australian Soldier's Magazine – an Overview'. In *Languages and the First World War: Representation and Memory*, edited by Julian Walker and Christophe Declercq, 75–93. London: Palgrave, 2016.
Duclert, Vincent. *L'Affaire Dreyfus*. Paris: La Découverte, 2012.
Dutton, David. *One of Us?: A Century of Australian Citizenship*. Sydney: University of New South Wales Press, 2002.
Dwyer, Jacqueline. *Flanders in Australia: A Personal History of Wool and War*. Sydney: Kangaroo Press, 1998.
Eagles, Robin. *Francophilia in English Society, 1748–1815*. New York: St. Martin's Press, 2000.
Elias, Norbert. *The Civilizing Process*. Oxford: Blackwell, 1978.
Emery, Linda. *Hunters Hill: Pictorial History*. Alexandria, NSW: Kingsclear Books, 2011.
Faivre, Jean-Paul. *L'Expansion Française dans le Pacifique de 1800 à 1842*. Paris: Nouvelles Éditions Latines, 1953.
Fathi, Romain. *Our Corner of the Somme: Australia at Villers-Bretonneux*. Cambridge: Cambridge University Press, 2019.
Fayaud, Viviane. 'Le Temps du Rêve Français: L'Australie dans l'Iconographie au XIXe Siècle'. *Le Journal de la Société des Océanistes*, no. 129 (2009): 219–29.
Febvre, Lucien. 'Civilisation: Evolution of a Word and a Group of Ideas'. In *A New Kind of History: From the Writings of Febvre*, edited by Peter Burke, translated by K Folca, 219–57. London: Routledge & Kegan Paul, 1973.
Firth, John. 'History of Tuberculosis. Part 1 – Phthisis, Consumption and the White Plague'. *Journal of Military and Veterans' Health* 22, no. 2 (June 2014).

Fitzpatrick, David. *Oceans of Consolation: Personal Accounts of Irish Migration to Australia*. Melbourne: Melbourne University Press, 1995.

Forster, Colin. *France and Botany Bay: The Lure of a Penal Colony*. Melbourne: Melbourne University Press, 1996.

Forth, Christopher E. *The Dreyfus Affair and the Crisis of French Manhood*. Baltimore: Johns Hopkins University Press, 2004.

Foucrier, Annick. *Le Rêve Californien: Migrants Français sur la Côte Pacifique, XVIIIe–XXe Siècles*. Paris: Belin, 1999.

Fraser, Corille. *Come to Dazzle: Sarah Bernhardt's Australian Tour*. Sydney: Currency Press in association with National Library of Australia, 1998.

Fumaroli, Marc. *Quand l'Europe Parlait Français*. Paris: de Fallois, 2001.

Gammage, Bill. *The Biggest Estate on Earth: How Aborigines Made Australia*. Sydney: Allen & Unwin, 2012.

Gascoigne, John. *The Enlightenment and the Origins of European Australia*. Cambridge: Cambridge University Press, 2005.

Genion, Jennifer. 'The Adventure Playground: Australia in the Popular Literature of Nineteenth-Century France'. PhD Thesis, University of Sydney, 2007.

——. 'The Classroom on the Other Side of the World: The Redemption Narrative in Nineteenth-Century French Popular Literature Set in Australia'. *Explorations* 38 (June 2005): 29–60.

Gigante, Denise. *Taste: A Literary History*. New Haven: Yale University Press, 2005.

Girardet, Raoul. *L'Idée Coloniale en France de 1871 à 1962*. Paris: La Table Ronde, 1972.

Gray, Anne. 'Art and the Environment: New Visions from Old'. In *Australia's Empire*, edited by Deryck M Schreuder and Stuart Ward, 103–39. Oxford: Oxford University Press, 2008.

Green, Nancy. *Repenser les Migrations*. Paris: PUF, 2002.

——. 'Classe et Ethnicité, des Catégories Caduques de l'Histoire Sociale?' In *Les Formes de l'Expérience: Une Autre Histoire Sociale*, edited by Bernard Lepetit, 165–86. Paris: Albin Michel, 1995.

Griffiths, Tom. 'Past Silences: Aborigines and Convicts in Our History-Making'. *Australian Cultural History* 6 (1986): 18–32.

Halter, Nicholas. '"Cannibals and Convicts": Australian Travel Writing About New Caledonia'. In *The Palgrave Handbook of Prison Tourism*, edited by Jacqueline Z Wilson, Sarah Hodgkinson, Justin Piché and Kevin Walby, 867–84. Basingstoke: Palgrave, 2017.

Hassam, Andrew. *Through Australian Eyes: Colonial Perceptions of Imperial Britain*. Melbourne: Melbourne University Press, 2000.

Hawkins, John Bernard. *19th Century Australian Silver*. Woodbridge, Suffolk, England: Antique Collectors Club, 1990.

Heath, Deana. 'Literary Censorship, Imperialism and the White Australia Policy'. In *A History of the Book in Australia 1891–1945. A National Culture in a Colonised Market*, edited by Martyn Lyons and John Arnold, 69–82. Brisbane: University of Queensland Press, 2001.

Helbich, Wolfgang and Walter D Kamphoefner. 'How Representative Are Emigrant Letters? An Exploration of the German Case'. In *Letters Across Borders: The Epistolary Practices of International Migrants*, edited by Bruce S Elliott, David A Gerber and Suzanne M Sinke, 29–55. Basingstoke: Palgrave Macmillan, 2006.

Select bibliography

Hutchison, Margaret. *Painting War: A History of Australia's First World War Art Scheme*. Melbourne: Cambridge University Press, 2018.
Inglis, Kenneth S. 'Going Home: Australians in England, 1870–1900'. In *Home or Away?: Immigrants in Colonial Australia: Visible Immigrants*, edited by David Fitzpatrick. Canberra, 1992.
Irving, TH and Rowan J Cahill. *Radical Sydney: Places, Portraits and Unruly Episodes*. Sydney: University of New South Wales Press, 2010.
Jones, Colin. *Paris. Biography of a City*. London: Penguin, 2006.
Kalifa, Dominique. *Paris, Une Histoire Érotique, d'Offenbach aux Sixties*. Paris: Payot, 2018.
Kelly, Max. *Faces of the Street: William Street, Sydney 1916*. Sydney: Doak Press, 1982.
———, ed. *Nineteenth-Century Sydney: Essays in Urban History*. Sydney: Sydney University Press, 1978.
Kirkpatrick, Peter. *The Sea Coast of Bohemia. Literary Life in Sydney's Roaring Twenties*. Brisbane: University of Queensland Press, 1992.
Kynaston, David. *City of London: The History*. London: Random House, 2012.
Lack, C. 'The Problem of the French Escapees from New Caledonia'. *Journal of the Royal Historical Society of Queensland* 5 (1955).
Lake, Marilyn. '"Essentially Teutonic": E. A. Freeman, Liberal Race Historian. A Transnational Perspective'. In *Race, Nation and Empire: Making Histories, 1750 to the Present*, edited by Catherine Hall and Keith McClelland, 56–73. Manchester: Manchester University Press, 2010.
———. *Progressive New World: How Settler Colonialism and Transpacific Exchange Shaped American Reform*. Cambridge, Mass: Harvard University Press, 2019.
———. 'The Australian Dream of an Island Empire: Race, Reputation and Resistance'. *Australian Historical Studies* 46, no. 3 (2015): 410–24.
———. 'The Politics of Respectability: Identifying the Masculinist Context'. *Australian Historical Studies* 22, no. 86 (1986): 116–31.
———. 'White Man's Country: The Trans-national History of a National Project'. *Australian Historical Studies* 34, no. 122 (2003): 346–63.
Lancaster, Rosemary. *Je Suis Australienne: Remarkable Women in France, 1880–1945*. Perth: UWA Press, 2008.
Lassus, Geoffrey de. *The History of BNP Paribas in Australia and New Zealand 1881–2011*. BNP Paribas Australia & New Zealand in collaboration with Group Heritage and Historical Archives of BNP Paribas and BNP Paribas Historical Association, 2011.
Lawson, Sylvia. *The Archibald Paradox: A Strange Case of Authorship*. Melbourne: The Miegunyah Press, 2006.
Lejeune, Dominique. *La France de la Belle Époque, 1896–1914*. Paris: Armand Colin, 2011.
———. *Les Sociétés de Géographie en France et l'Expansion Coloniale au XIX Siècle*. Paris: Albin Michel, 1993.
Lejeune, Philippe. 'The "Journal de Jeune Fille" in Nineteenth-Century France'. In *On Diary*, edited by Jeremy D Popkin and Julie Rak, 129–46. Honolulu: University of Hawai'i Press, 2009.
Lockley, Tom. 'Maurice Guillaux: France's Forgotten Pioneer Airman in Australia'. *The French Australian Review*, no. 56 (Winter 2014): 4–25.
Lyng, Jens. *Non-Britishers in Australia: Influence on Population and Progress*. Melbourne: Melbourne University Press, 1935.
Macintyre, Stuart. *A Concise History of Australia*. Melbourne: Cambridge University Press, 2009.

Maclellan, Nic and Jean Chesneaux. *After Mururoa: France in the South Pacific*. Melbourne: Ocean Press, 1998.

Marandon, Sylvaine. *L'Image de La France dans l'Angleterre Victorienne, 1848–1900*. Paris: Armand Colin, 1967.

Marchant, Leslie R. *France Australe: A Study of French Explorations and Attempts to Found a Penal Colony and Strategic Base in South Western Australia 1503–1826*. Perth: Artlook, 1982.

Mars, Valérie. 'Experiencing French Cookery in Nineteenth-Century London'. In *A History of the French in London: Liberty, Equality, Opportunity*, edited by Debra Kelly and Martyn Cornick, 217–40. London: Institute of Historical Research, 2013.

Maynard, Margaret. 'Fashion Modelling in Australia'. In *Fashioning Models: Image, Text and Industry*, 145–54. New York: Berg Publishers, 2012.

McIntyre, Julie. *First Vintage: Wine in Colonial New South Wales*. Sydney: NewSouth Publishing, 2012.

McPherson, Bernice. 'A Colonial Feminine Ideal: Femininity and Representation'. *Journal of Australian Studies* 18, no. 42 (1994): 5–17.

Meany, Neville. *The Search for Security in the Pacific; 1901–14: A History of Australian Defence and Foreign Policy 1901–23, Volume 1*. Sydney: Sydney University Press, 1976.

Merle, Isabelle. 'Drawing Settlers to New Caledonia: French Colonial Propaganda in the Late Nineteenth Century'. In *Promoting the Colonial Idea: Propaganda and Visions of Empire in France*, edited by Tony Chafer and Amanda Sackur, 40–52. Houndmills, Basingstoke, Hampshire; New York: Palgrave, 2002.

———. *Expériences Coloniales: La Nouvelle-Calédonie 1853–1920*. Paris: Belin, 1995.

Meyzie, Philippe. 'La Construction de la Renommée des Produits des Terroirs: Acteurs et Enjeux d'un Marché de la Gourmandise en France (XVIIe – Début XIXe Siècle)'. *French Historical Studies* 38, no. 2 (2015): 225–51.

Mirmohamadi, Kylie. 'Melbourne's Sites of Reading: Putting the Colonial Woman Reader in Her Place'. *History Australia* 6, no. 2 (2010): 1–18.

Moore, Tony. *Dancing With Empty Pockets: Australia's Bohemians Since 1860*. Sydney: Pier 9, 2012.

Neilson, Briony. 'Settling Scores in New Caledonia and Australia: French Convictism and Settler Legitimacy'. *Australian Journal of Politics & History* 64, no. 3 (2018): 391–406.

———. 'The Paradox of Penal Colonization: Debates on Convict Transportation at the International Prison Congresses 1872–1895'. *French History and Civilization: Papers from the George Rudé Seminar* 6 (2015): 198–211.

Nettlebeck, Colin. 'The Consul's Treasure'. *Explorations* 7 (1988): 18–23.

Newman, Gerald. *The Rise of English Nationalism: A Cultural History, 1740–1830*. New York: St. Martin's Press, 1987.

Nile, Richard, ed. *The Australian Legend and Its Discontents*. Brisbane: University of Queensland Press, 2000.

Nooy, Juliana de. *What's France Got to Do with It?* Canberra: ANU Press, 2020.

Nye, Robert. *Masculinity and Male Codes of Honor in Modern France, Studies in the History of Sexuality*. New York: Oxford University Press, 1993.

Ory, Pascal and Jean-François Sirinelli. *Les Intellectuels en France: De l'Affaire Dreyfus à Nos Jours*. Paris: A. Colin, 2002.

Paulle, Bowen, Bart Heerikhuizen, von, and Mustafa Emirbayer. 'Elias and Bourdieu'. In *The Legacy of Pierre Bourdieu: Critical Essays*, edited by Simon Susen and Bryan S. Turner, 145–72. London; New York: Anthem Press, 2011.

Select bibliography

Pesman, Ros. *Duty Free: Australian Women Abroad*. Oxford: Oxford University Press, 1996.

Pesman, Ros, David Walker and Richard White. *The Oxford Book of Australian Travel Writing*. Melbourne: Oxford University Press, 1996.

Petrow, Stefan. '"Convict-Phobia": Combating Vandiemonian Convicts in 1850s and 1860s Victoria'. *Journal of Australian Colonial History* 14 (2012): 260–71.

Potter, Simon James. *News and the British World: The Emergence of an Imperial Press System, 1876–1922*. Oxford: Oxford University Press, 2003.

Rak, Julie. 'Dialogue with the Future: Philippe Lejeune's Method and Theory of Diary'. In *On Diary*, edited by Jeremy D Popkin and Rak, 16–28. Honolulu: University of Hawai'i Press, 2009.

Ramsland, John and Marie Ramsland. 'Visitors with "An Unusual Charm": French Celebrities at the Australia Hotel, 1891–1932'. *Explorations* 34 (June 2003): 3–12.

Rapoport, Michel. 'The London French from the Belle Epoque to the End of the Inter-War Period (1880–1939)'. In *A History of the French in London: Liberty, Equality, Opportunity*, edited by Debra Kelly and Martyn Cornick, 241–79. London: Institute of Historical Research, 2013.

Rasmussen, David. 'Rethinking Subjectivity: Narrative Identity and the Self'. *Philosophy and Social Criticism* 21, no. 5 (1995): 159–72.

Rearick, Charles. *Paris Dreams, Paris Memories: The City and Its Mystique*. Stanford: Stanford University Press, 2011.

Rees, Anne. 'Reading Australian Modernity: Unsettled Settlers and Cultures of Mobility'. *History Compass* 15, no. 11 (2017): e12429.

Reps, John William. *Canberra 1912: Plans and Planners of the Australian Capital Competition*. Melbourne: Melbourne University Press, 1997.

Reynolds, Sian. *Paris–Edinburgh: Cultural Connections in the Belle Epoque*. England: Ashgate, 2007.

Rickard, John. *Australia: A Cultural History*. London; New York: Longman, 1996.

Riley, Margot. 'Fashioned from Fleece: Australian Wool and French Haute Couture'. *Explorations* 46 (June 2010): 21–42.

Rioux, Jean-Pierre. *La France de 1900*. Paris: Éditions du Seuil, 2012.

Robb, George. *White-Collar Crime in Modern England: Financial Fraud and Business Morality, 1845–1929*. Cambridge: Cambridge University Press, 2002.

Roberts, David. 'Beyond "The Stain": Rethinking the Nature and Impact of the Anti-Transportation Movement'. *Journal of Australian Colonial History*, vol. 14, 2012.

Rosemberg, John. 'A Steady Ethnic Group: The Role of the French in Australia'. *Ethnic Studies* 2, no. 3 (1978): 52–57.

Russell, Penny. *A Wish of Distinction: Colonial Gentility and Femininity*. Melbourne: Melbourne University Press, 1994.

——. 'Cultures of Distinction'. In *Cultural History in Australia*, edited by Richard White and Hsu-Ming Teo, 158–71. Sydney: University of New South Wales Press, 2003.

——. *Savage or Civilised? Manners in Colonial Australia*. Sydney: University of New South Wales Press, 2010.

Salon, Albert. *L'Action Culturelle de la France dans le Monde*. Paris: Nathan, 1983.

Serle, Geoffrey. 'The Victorian Government's Campaign for Federation, 1883–1889'. In *Essays in Australian Federation*, edited by AW Martin, 1–56. Melbourne: Melbourne University Press, 1969.

Sherry, Beverley. *Hunter's Hill, Australia's Oldest Garden Suburb*. Sydney: David Ell Press, 1989.

Smith, Bernard. *European Vision and the South Pacific*. Melbourne: Oxford University Press, 1989.
Sowerwine, Charles, and Gabrielle Wolf. 'Echoes of Paris in the Antipodes: French Theatre and Opera in Melbourne (1850–1914).' *Australian Journal of French Studies* 45, no. 1 (2008): 81–98.
Speedy, Karin. '"Arab Castaways/French Escapees": Mobilities, Border Protection and White Australia'. *Law, Crime and History*, no. 2 (2016): 15–30.
Stephen, Ann (ed.). *Visions of a Republic: The Work of Lucien Henry – Paris – Noumea – Sydney*. Sydney: Powerhouse Publishing, 2001.
Stewart, Ken. 'The Colonial Literati in Sydney and Melbourne'. In *Nellie Melba, Ginger Meggs and Friends: Essays in Australian Cultural History*, edited by Susan Dermody, Drusilla Modjeska and John Docker, 176–91. Melbourne: Kibble Books, 1982.
Stuer, Anny. *The French in Australia*. Canberra: Australian National University, 1982.
Symons, Michael. *One Continuous Picnic: A History of Eating in Australia*. Adelaide: Duck Press, 1982.
Teo, Hsu-Ming. 'Multiculturalism and the Problem of Multicultural Histories: An Overview of Ethnic Historiography'. In *Cultural History in Australia*, edited by Richard White and Hsu-Ming Teo, 142–58. Sydney: University of New South Wales Press, 2003.
The Hunter's Hill Trust. *Heritage of Hunter's Hill*. Sydney: The Hunter's Hill Trust, 2002.
Thiesse, Anne-Marie. *La Création des Identités Nationales, Europe XVIII–XIX Siècles*. Paris: Seuil, 2001.
Thompson, Patricia. *Hunter's Hill Sketchbook*. Adelaide: Rigby, 1973.
Thornton-Smith, Colin. 'Paul Maistre, Vice-Consul and Later Consul for France in Victoria, 1886–1898, 1901–1908 Part 1'. *Explorations*, no. 17 (1994): 3–25.
Tombs, Robert. 'La Nouvelle Arcadie ou l'Evolution des Représentations Britanniques de la France Rurale au XIXe Siècle'. In *Gallomanie et Gallophobie, Le Mythe Français en Europe au XIX Siècle*, edited by Laura Fournier-Finocchiaro and Tanja-Isabel Habicht, translated by Jacqueline Odin, 19–38. Rennes: Presses Universitaires de Rennes, 2012.
Torpey, John. *The Invention of the Passport: Surveillance, Citizenship and the State*. Cambridge: Cambridge University Press, 2000.
Tremewan, Peter. 'La France Australe: From Dream Through Failure to Compromise'. *Australian Journal of French Studies* 50, no. 1 (April 2013): 100–114.
Tucoo-Chala, Pierre. *Pau, Ville Anglaise*. Orthez: Editions Gascogne, 2013.
Varouxakis, Georgios. *Victorian Political Thought on France and the French*. New York: Palgrave, 2002.
Walton, Whitney. *France at the Crystal Palace: Bourgeois Taste and Artisan Manufacture in the Nineteenth Century*. Berkeley: University of California Press, 1992.
Ward, Russel. *The Australian Legend*. Melbourne: Oxford University Press, 1966.
Ward, Stuart. *Australia and the British Embrace: The Demise of the Imperial Ideal*. Melbourne: Melbourne University Press, 2001.
——. 'Security: Defending Australia's Empire'. In *Australia's Empire*, edited by Stuart Ward and Deryck M Schreuder, 232–58. Oxford: Oxford University Press, 2008.
Weber, Eugen. *Peasants into Frenchmen: The Modernization of Rural France, 1870–1914*. Stanford: Stanford University Press, 1976.
White, Richard. 'Bluebells and Fogtown: Australians' First Impressions of England 1860–1940'. *Australian Cultural History*, 1986, 44–59.
——. *Inventing Australia: Images and Identity, 1688–1980*. Sydney: Allen & Unwin Australia, 1981.

Select bibliography

———. *On Holidays: A History of Getting Away in Australia*. Melbourne: Pluto Press Australia, 2005.
Williams, John Frank. *The Quarantined Culture: Australian Reactions to Modernism 1913–1939*. Cambridge: Cambridge University Press, 1995.
Williams, Raymond. *Keywords: A Vocabulary of Culture and Society*. New York: Oxford University Press, 1985.
Winock, Michel. *Le Siècle des Intellectuels*. Paris: Seuil, 1997.
Woollacott, Angela. *To Try Her Fortune in London. Australian Women, Colonialism, and Modernity*. Oxford: Oxford University Press, 2001.
Zaidman, Pierre-Henri. 'Les condamnés de Nouvelle-Calédonie en Australie et en Nouvelle-Zélande'. *Criminocorpus, Revue Hypermédia. Histoire de la Justice, des Crimes et des Peines*, 1 January 2010. <criminocorpus.revues.org/176>
Zeldin, Theodore. *Histoire des Passions Françaises 1848–1945*. Translated by Denise Demoy. Vol. 1. Oxford: Oxford University Press, 1978.

Abbreviations

ADB	Australian Dictionary of Biography
2CPC	Correspondance Politique et Commerciale (Political and Commercial Correspondence)
139CPCOM	Correspondance Politique et Commerciale, Nouvelle Série (Political and Commercial Correspondence, New Series)
CA	*Courrier Australien*
428PO	Archives of the French Consulate in Melbourne
662PO	Archives of the French Consulate in Sydney
378PO/CH	Archives of the French Embassy in London (Fonds CH)
378PO/K	Archives of the French Embassy in London (Fonds K)
MAE	Ministère des Affaires Etrangères (Ministry of Foreign Affairs)
ML	Mitchell Library
NAA	National Archives of Australia
NLA	National Library of Australia
SLNSW	State Library of New South Wales
SRNSW	State Records of New South Wales
SLV	State Library of Victoria
SMH	*Sydney Morning Herald*

Notes

Note: An asterisk (*) following an author's name indicates a quotation that was originally in French.

Introduction: Frenchness in Australia
1. Lucciardi* to MAE, 11 September 1906, MAE, 428PO/1/69; *Argus*, 4 September 1906, 6; *Raleigh Sun*, 14 September 1906, 7.
2. Marc Fumaroli, *Quand l'Europe Parlait Français* (Paris: de Fallois, 2001).
3. Christina Stead, Letter to Nellie Molyneux, 1 March 1929, in RG Geering (ed.), *A Web of Friendship: Selected Letters (1928–1973)* (Angus & Robertson, 1992), 12; on Christina Stead's Paris see Rosemary Lancaster, *Je Suis Australienne: Remarkable Women in France, 1880–1945* (Crawley: UWA Press, 2008), 124–50.
4. *Age*, 29 August 1907, 6; Weston Bate, 'Bent, Sir Thomas (1838–1909)', in *Australian Dictionary of Biography* (Canberra: National Centre of Biography, Australian National University), <adb.anu.edu.au/biography/bent-sir-thomas-2978>.
5. Linda Colley, *Britons: Forging the Nation, 1707–1837* (New Haven: Yale University Press, 1992), 5.
6. Michèle Cohen, *Fashioning Masculinity: National Identity and Language in the Eighteenth Century* (London; New York: Routledge, 1996).
7. Gerald Newman, *The Rise of English Nationalism: A Cultural History, 1740–1830* (New York: St. Martin's Press, 1987); Robin Eagles, *Francophilia in English Society, 1748–1815* (New York: St. Martin's Press, 2000).
8. Homi K Bhabha, *The Location of Culture*, Routledge Classics (London; New York: Routledge, 2004), 9.
9. Eugen Weber, *Peasants into Frenchmen: The Modernization of Rural France, 1870–1914* (Stanford: Stanford University Press, 1976).
10. A 'juste milieu' proposed by Robert Tombs, 'La Nouvelle Arcadie ou l'évolution des Représentations Britanniques de la France Rurale au XIXe siècle', in Fournier-Finocchiaro and Habicht, eds., *Gallomanie et Gallophobie, Le Mythe Français en Europe au XIX Siècle*, 21. The historiography in this field is vast. For a list of recent titles see Alexis Bergantz, 'French Connection: The Culture and Politics of Frenchness in Australia, 1890–1914' (PhD Thesis, The Australian National University, 2016), 11.
11. Stuart Ward, 'Security: Defending Australia's Empire', in *Australia's Empire*, Stuart Ward and Deryck M Schreuder (eds) (Oxford: Oxford University Press, 2008), 234; Henry Parkes, *Fifty Years in the Making of Australian History*, Vol. I, 1972, 139.
12. *The Australian, Windsor, Richmond, and Hawkesbury Advertiser*, 22 April 1882, 2; *Moreton Bay Courier*, 19 November 1853, 2.
13. *Argus*, 28 November 1891, 13; Corille Fraser, *Come to Dazzle: Sarah Bernhardt's Australian Tour* (Sydney: Currency Press, 1998). On Sarah Bernhardt's Australian

tour see also John Ramsland and Marie Ramsland, 'Visitors with "An Unusual Charm": French Celebrities at the Australia Hotel, 1891–1932', *Explorations* 34 (June 2003): 3–12.

14 John Rosemberg, 'A Steady Ethnic Group: The Role of the French in Australia', *Ethnic Studies* 2, no. 3 (1978): 52–57; Anny Stuer, *The French in Australia* (Canberra: Australian National University, 1982); Hsu-Ming Teo, 'Multiculturalism and the Problem of Multicultural Histories: An Overview of Ethnic Historiography', in Richard White and Hsu-Ming Teo (eds), *Cultural History in Australia* (Sydney: University of New South Wales Press, 2003), 142–58.

15 Paul Maistre, *Dans la Brousse Australienne: Scènes de Chasse* (Paris: Montgredien, 1901), 4.

16 Raymond Williams, *Keywords: A Vocabulary of Culture and Society* (New York: Oxford University Press, 1985), 57; Norbert Elias, *The Civilizing Process* (Oxford: Blackwell, 1978).

17 Penny Russell, *Savage or Civilised? Manners in Colonial Australia* (Sydney: University of New South Wales Press, 2010).

18 *Argus*, 1 June 1895, 5; *Table Talk*, 5 June 1891, 13, both quoted in Charles Sowerwine and Gabrielle Wolf, 'Echoes of Paris in the Antipodes: French Theatre and Opera in Melbourne (1850–1914)', *Australian Journal of French Studies* 45, no. 1 (2008): 93.

19 Pierre Bourdieu, *Distinction: A Social Critique of the Judgement of Taste* (London: Routledge & Kegan Paul, 1984). On the impact of Elias on Bourdieu, see Paulle Bowen, Bart von Heerikhuizen and Mustafa Emirbayer, 'Elias and Bourdieu', in *The Legacy of Pierre Bourdieu: Critical Essays*, Simon Susen and Bryan S Turner (eds) (London: Anthem Press, 2011), 145–72. Michel de Certeau proposed 'tactics' as a view from below, instead of Bourdieu's 'strategy', see Roger Chartier's essay on de Certeau and cultural history in *Au Bord de la Falaise: L'histoire entre Certitudes et Inquiétude* (Paris: Albin Michel, 1998); Michel de Certeau, *The Practice of Everyday Life* (Berkeley: University of California Press, 1984).

20 Marilyn Lake, 'White Man's Country: The Trans-national History of a National Project', *Australian Historical Studies* 34, no. 122 (2003): 346–63.

21 Russel Ward, *The Australian Legend* (Melbourne: Oxford University Press, 1966); Marilyn Lake, 'The Politics of Respectability: Identifying the Masculinist Context', *Australian Historical Studies* 22, no. 86 (1986): 116–31; John Docker, *The Nervous Nineties: Australian Cultural Life in the 1890s* (Melbourne: Oxford University Press, 1991); Richard Nile (ed), *The Australian Legend and Its Discontents* (Brisbane: University of Queensland Press, 2000); Graeme Davison, 'Rethinking the Australian Legend', *Australian Historical Studies* 43, no. 3 (2012): 429–51.

22 Colin Nettlebeck, 'The Consul's Treasure', *Explorations* 7 (1988): 18–23; Alexis Bergantz, 'Mapping the Consul's Treasure: A Discussion and Guide to French Consular Archives', *The French Australian Review*, 61 (Australian Summer 2016–2017): 40–46.

1 A glittering, raucous ritual: French cafés and culture

1 *The Lone Hand*, 1 July 1912, 185–93.
2 *The Lone Hand*, 1 May 1909, 16.
3 Patricia Clarke, *Tasma: The Life of Jessie Couvreur* (Sydney: Allen & Unwin, 1994), 70–78; *The Australasian*, 16 April 1881, 488; 29 July 1882, unknown; 11 July 1885, 56, all in Papers of Patricia Clarke, 1887–2010, NLA, MS 8363.

4   Simon James Potter, *News and the British World: The Emergence of an Imperial Press System, 1876–1922* (Oxford: Oxford University Press, 2003).
5   Robert Aldrich, *The French Presence in the South Pacific, 1842–1940* (London: Macmillan, 1990), 122, 199–236.
6   *SMH*, 11 July 1894, 6.
7   George Payne Rainsford James, *The Desultory Man*, vol. 2 (London: Saunders and Otley, 1836), 145–53.
8   Richard Twopeny, *Town Life in Australia* (Melbourne: The Dominion Press, 1976), 73–75.
9   Twopeny, 73–75.
10 Franck L Schoell*, *La Langue Française dans le Monde* (Paris: Bibliothèque du Français Moderne, 1936), 26.
11 *SMH*, 2 May 1906, 5; 26 February 1913, 7.
12 *SMH*, 19 November 1890, 1; 27 December 1890, 1; 2 August 1895, 7; 6 April 1895, 1.
13 Sylvaine Marandon, *L'Image de la France dans l'Angleterre Victorienne, 1848–1900* (Paris: Armand Colin, 1967), 245.
14 Whitney Walton, *France at the Crystal Palace: Bourgeois Taste and Artisan Manufacture in the Nineteenth Century* (Berkeley: University of California Press, 1992), 5–10.
15 Philippe Meyzie, 'La Construction de la Renommée des Produits des Terroirs: Acteurs et Enjeux d'un Marché de la Gourmandise en France (XVIIe–Début XIXe Siècle)', *French Historical Studies* 38, no. 2 (2015): 225–51; Julie McIntyre, *First Vintage: Wine in Colonial New South Wales* (Sydney: NewSouth Publishing, 2012), 2, 23.
16 *SMH*, 19 November 1890, 1; 27 December 1890, 1; 2 August 1895, 7; 6 April 1895, 1.
17 *Argus*, 4 November 1910, 8.
18 Valérie Mars, 'Experiencing French Cookery in Nineteenth-Century London', in *A History of the French in London: Liberty, Equality, Opportunity*, Debra Kelly and Martyn Cornick (eds) (London: Institute of Historical Research, 2013), 219; Denise Gigante, *Taste: A Literary History* (New Haven: Yale University Press, 2005), 14, 167.
19 *Truth*, 13 May 1900, 6; *Punch*, 25 October 1900, 475; *SMH*, 17 August 1896, 8.
20 Paris House Menu, 1904, Private Collection.
21 *CA*, 6 October 1911, 2; 10 December 1904, 1; Ivan Barko, *Vive La Différence! The French in NSW* (Sydney: State Library of New South Wales, 2004), 25. Isadore Brodsky, *Sydney Looks Back* (Sydney: Angus and Robertson, 1957), 128–29.
22 AR Chisholm, *Men Were My Milestones: Australian Portraits and Sketches* (Melbourne: Melbourne University Press, 1958), 90–91; AR Chisholm, *The Familiar Presence and Other Reminiscences* (Melbourne: Melbourne University Press, 1966), 56–61.
23 Richard White, *Inventing Australia: Images and Identity, 1688–1980* (Sydney: Allen & Unwin, 1981), 96.
24 Tony Moore, *Dancing With Empty Pockets: Australia's Bohemians Since 1860* (NSW: Pier 9, 2012), 45.
25 Christopher Campos, *The View of France: From Arnold to Bloomsbury* (London: Oxford University Press, 1965), 6.
26 Henri Murger, *Scènes de La Vie de Bohème* (Paris: Librairie Garnier, 1914); George du Maurier, *Trilby* (New York: Harper, 1894).
27 Sylvia Lawson, *The Archibald Paradox: A Strange Case of Authorship* (Melbourne: The Miegunyah Press, 2006), 28.
28 Moore, 50; *Sunday Herald*, 23 November 1952, 12.

29 Peter Kirkpatrick, *The Sea Coast of Bohemia: Literary Life in Sydney's Roaring Twenties* (Brisbane: University of Queensland Press, 1992), 32–36.
30 Kirkpatrick, 16, 21; Moore, 30–31; on the gendered division of the emerging Australian civic and artistic scenes see especially Lake, 'The Politics of Respectability', 116–31, 119–20.
31 Kirkpatrick, 28–33; White, 96. The development of bohemian subcultures was also a product of the colonial intellectual rivalries between Sydney and Melbourne; see Ken Stewart, 'The Colonial Literati in Sydney and Melbourne', in Susan Dermody, Drusilla Modjeska and John Docker (eds), *Nellie Melba, Ginger Meggs and Friends: Essays in Australian Cultural History* (Malmsbury, Vic: Kibble Books, 1982), 176–91.
32 *The Lone Hand*, 1 May 1909, 12.
33 Joy Hooton, 'Green, Henry Mackenzie (1881–1962)', in *Australian Dictionary of Biography* (Canberra: National Centre of Biography, Australian National University), accessed 3 October 2015, <adb.anu.edu.au/biography/green-henry-mackenzie-10353>.
34 *The Lone Hand*, 1 May 1909, 12.
35 Charles Rearick, *Paris Dreams, Paris Memories: The City and Its Mystique* (Stanford, CA: Stanford University Press, 2011), 22, 38.
36 Dominique Kalifa, *Paris, Une Histoire Érotique, d'Offenbach aux Sixties* (Paris: Payot, 2018), 72–77.
37 Marandon, 336.
38 *SMH*, 28 December 1912, 4.
39 *The Lone Hand*, 1 May 1909, 16.
40 Rearick, 7, 18; Stead, 12.
41 *The Lone Hand*, 1 July 1912 p. 188; Norman Lindsay to JSC Elkington, c. December 1909, in *Letters of Norman Lindsay*, RG Howarth and AW Barker (eds) (London: Angus & Robertson, 1979), 51.
42 Henry James, *The American* (London: Harper Press, 2013), 27; Sian Reynolds, *Paris-Edinburgh: Cultural Connections in the Belle Epoque* (Aldershot, Hants, England: Ashgate, 2007), 9; Colin Jones, *Paris: Biography of a City* (London: Penguin, 2006), 344–96; Stead to Nellie Molyneux, 1 March 1929, 13.
43 Rearick, 12–13.
44 Rearick, 14.
45 Max Kelly, *Faces of the Street: William Street, Sydney 1916* (Sydney: Doak Press, 1982) 3; Max Kelly, (ed), *Nineteenth-Century Sydney: Essays in Urban History* (Sydney: Sydney University Press, 1978); Sowerwine and Wolf, 83.
46 Graeme Davison, *The Rise and Fall of Marvellous Melbourne* (Melbourne: Melbourne University Press, 1988), 230.
47 John William Reps, *Canberra 1912: Plans and Planners of the Australian Capital Competition* (Melbourne: Melbourne University Press, 1997), 110–13.
48 Tombs, 317.
49 Rearick, 19.
50 *SMH*, 25 June 1898, 12; 27 June 1898, 6; Tom Lockley, 'Maurice Guillaux: France's Forgotten Pioneer Airman in Australia', *The French Australian Review*, no. 56 (Winter 2014): 24.
51 *SMH*, 15 January 1908, 5; 7 March 1908, 3; 11 October 1904, 3; *The Lone Hand*, 1 February 1913, 290.
52 *The Lone Hand*, 1 February 1913, 289.

53 Christophe Charle, *Paris Fin de Siècle* (Paris: Éditions du Seuil, 1998), 21–48.
54 *The Lone Hand*, 1 February 1913, 290.
55 *SMH*, 15 January 1908, 5; Charle, 21–48.
56 Margaret Hutchison, *Painting War: A History of Australia's First World War Art Scheme* (Melbourne: Cambridge University Press, 2018), 100–102.
57 *Argus*, 17 June 1911, 7.
58 Jane Hylton, 'Davidson, Bessie Ellen (1879–1965)', in *Australian Dictionary of Biography* (Canberra: National Centre of Biography, Australian National University), <adb.anu.edu.au/biography/davidson-bessie-ellen-9907>.
59 *The Lone Hand*, 1 February 1913, 290.
60 Anne Rees, 'Reading Australian Modernity: Unsettled Settlers and Cultures of Mobility', *History Compass* 15, no. 11 (2017): 124–29; Rearick, 39.
61 Charles, 41; *The Lone Hand*, 1 February 1913, 291.
62 Charles, 41; *The Lone Hand*, 1 February 1913, 291.
63 *SMH*, 15 January 1908, 5; *The Lone Hand*, 1 February 1913, 290.
64 *SMH*, 15 January 1908, 5; *The Lone Hand*, 1 February 1913, 290.
65 *SMH*, 15 January 1908, 5.
66 Anne Gray, 'Art and the Environment: New Visions from Old', in *Australia's Empire*, Deryck M Schreuder and Stuart Ward (eds) (Oxford: Oxford University Press, 2008), 103–39.
67 *Argus*, 28 November 1891, 13.
68 Charle, 11.
69 Dominique Lejeune, *La France de la Belle Époque, 1896–1914* (Paris: Armand Colin, 2011), 11.
70 Jean-Pierre Rioux, *La France de 1900* (Paris: Éditions du Seuil, 2012), 27.
71 Horace Marion, *Il Faut Sauver la France: La Décadence, Ses Causes, Remèdes et Moyens* (Paris: J. Jeannin Trévoux, 1910); *Argus*, 9 August 1892, 6; *SMH*, 26 August 1908, 8.
72 AG Stephens, 'Paul Wenz', in *AG Stephens: His Life and Work*, Vance Palmer (ed.) (Melbourne: Robertson & Mullens Ltd, 1941), 135.
73 *Argus*, 9 August 1892, 6; *SMH*, 18 March 1897, 3.
74 *Argus*, 9 August 1892, 6; *SMH*, 18 March 1897, 3.
75 John Frank Williams, *The Quarantined Culture: Australian Reactions to Modernism 1913–1939*, (Cambridge: Cambridge University Press, 1995); Deana Heath, 'Literary Censorship, Imperialism and the White Australia Policy', in *A History of the Book in Australia 1891–1945: A National Culture in a Colonised Market*, Martyn Lyons and John Arnold (eds) (Brisbane: University of Queensland Press, 2001), 69–74; Frank Bongiorno, *The Sex Lives of Australians: A History* (Melbourne: Black Inc, 2012), 81–87.
76 Chisholm, *Men Were My Milestones*, 106; Stan Scott, 'Chisholm, Alan Rowland (1888–1981)', in *Australian Dictionary of Biography* (Canberra: National Centre of Biography, Australian National University), <adb.anu.edu.au/biography/chisholm-alan-rowland-12315>.
77 *Truth*, 12 November 1895, 8; Bongiorno, *The Sex Lives of Australians*, 70–73.
78 Bongiorno, *The Sex Lives of Australians*, 145; Frank Bongiorno, '"Every Woman a Mother": Radical Intellectuals, Sex Reform and the "Woman Question" in Australia, 1890–1918', *Hecate* 27, no. 1 (2001): 44–64.
79 *The Lone Hand*, 1 May 1909, 12–13.
80 *The Lone Hand*, 1 July 1912, 190.

81 Lindsay, 216.
82 *The Lone Hand*, 1 May 1909, 15–16.
83 Rearick, 34–37; Lindsay.
84 Clair de Pratz, *France from Within* (London: Hodder and Stoughton), 8–9.
85 Colley, 88–90.
86 *The Lone Hand*, 1 May 1909, 13.
87 *The Lone Hand*, 1 July 1912, no page number.
88 *The Lone Hand*, 1 July 1912, 190–91.
89 *Argus*, 6 December 1902, 4.
90 Marilyn Lake, '"Essentially Teutonic": E.A. Freeman, Liberal Race Historian: A Transnational Perspective', in *Race, Nation and Empire: Making Histories, 1750 to the Present*, Catherine Hall and Keith McClelland (eds) (Manchester: Manchester University Press, 2010), 56–73; Marilyn Lake, *Progressive New World: How Settler Colonialism and Transpacific Exchange Shaped American Reform* (Cambridge, Mass: Harvard University Press, 2019); Stuart Ward, *Australia and the British Embrace: The Demise of the Imperial Ideal* (Melbourne: Melbourne University Press, 2001), 2.
91 Georgios Varouxakis, *Victorian Political Thought on France and the French* (New York: Palgrave, 2002); Lucien Febvre, 'Civilisation: Evolution of a Word and a Group of Ideas', in *A New Kind of History: From the Writings of Febvre*, Peter Burke (ed.), trans. K Folca (London: Routledge & Kegan Paul, 1973), 219–57.
92 *SMH*, 15 July 1912, 3.
93 *SMH*, 15 July 1894, 4; *SMH*, 16 July 1900, 5.

2 A battle for control: *Alliance* and misalliance

1 *Age*, 21 April 1908, 5; 22 April 1908, 11.
2 *Age*, 20 April 1908, 6; 23 April 1908, 8.
3 *Age*, 21 April 1908, 4.
4 *Age*, 22 April 1907, 5; *Age*, 23 April 1907, 5, 7; State Library of Victoria (SLV), *Alliance Française de Victoria Minute Books (Minute Books)*, MS Box 3554, 28 April 1908.
5 *Table Talk*, 20 February 1908, 11.
6 Penny Russell, *A Wish of Distinction: Colonial Gentility and Femininity* (Melbourne: Melbourne University Press, 1994).
7 John Drury, 'Berthe Mouchette (1846–1928), Artist and Founder of the First Alliance Française in Australia, and Marie Lion (1855–1922), Artist and Writer', in Barko and Berti (eds), *French Lives in Australia* (Melbourne: Australian Scholarly Publishing), 133.
8 Albert Salon, *L'Action Culturelle de la France dans le Monde* (Paris: Nathan, 1983), 38; Jean Jaurès, 'Discours pour l'Alliance Française à Albi en 1884', in Raoul Girardet, *Le Nationalisme Français 1871–1914* (Paris: Armand Colin, 1966), 94–96.
9 Paul Maistre*, 'Notes sur l'Alliance Française de Victoria: Sa Fondation, ses Statuts, son But et ses Moyens d'Action', 17 July 1907, Ministère des Affaires Etrangères (MAE), 428PO/1/31.
10 Drury, 133.
11 Maistre, 'Notes Sur l'Alliance Française de Victoria'.
12 Maistre, *Dans la Brousse Australienne*, 7; Oscar Comettant, *Au Pays des Kangourous et des Mines d'Or* (Paris: Fischbacher, 1890); CB Thornton-Smith, 'Paul Maistre, Vice-Consul and Later Consul for France in Victoria, 1886–1898, 1901–1908 Part 1', *Explorations* 17 (1994): 3–47.

13 Thornton-Smith, 6.
14 Drury, 131–133; Russell, *A Wish of Distinction*, 7.
15 Linda Colley, 90.
16 Michèle Cohen, 68, 99.
17 Royal Commission on the University of Melbourne: Minutes of evidence on administration, teaching work, and government of the University of Melbourne (Melbourne: Robt. S. Brain, Government Printer, 1903), 326.
18 *Courrier Australien*, 16 December 1905, 3.
19 Sylvia Morrissey, 'Clarke, Sir William John (1831–1897)', in *Australian Dictionary of Biography* (Canberra: National Centre of Biography, Australian National University), <adb.anu.edu.au/biography/clarke-sir-william-john-3229>; Sylvia Morrissey, 'Clarke, Janet Marion (1851–1909)', in Australian Dictionary of Biography (Canberra: National Centre of Biography, Australian National University), <adb.anu.edu.au/biography/clarke-janet-marion-3224>.
21 RG De B Griffith, 'Holroyd, Sir Edward Dundas (1828–1916)', in *Australian Dictionary of Biography* (Canberra: National Centre of Biography, Australian National University), <adb.anu.edu.au/biography/holroyd-sir-edward-dundas-3784>.
21 Russell, *A Wish of Distinction*, 1.
22 Bernice McPherson, 'A Colonial Feminine Ideal: Femininity and Representation', *Journal of Australian Studies* 18, no. 42 (1994): 15; Kylie Mirmohamadi, 'Melbourne's Sites of Reading: Putting the Colonial Woman Reader in Her Place', *History Australia* 6, no. 2 (2010): 15; Woollacott, *To Try Her Fortune in London: Australian Women, Colonialism, and Modernity* (Oxford: Oxford University Press, 2001), 102.
23 Mrs Cave to Maistre, 21 September 1904, MAE, 428PO/1/33; *Table Talk*, 3 October 1901, 27.
24 *Table Talk*, 3 May 1900, 15; see Jacqui Donegan, 'Banned in Boston: A Biography of Annette Kellerman (1886–1975)', Honours Thesis, University of Queensland, 2001, 10–25; Jin Guan Bong, 'Alice Ellen Charbonnet: A French Musician in Nineteenth-Century Australia', Master's Thesis, University of Melbourne, 2006.
25 Thornton-Smith, 4.
26 *Table Talk*, 15 May 1891, 9; 26 December 1890, 5.
27 Maistre to Mrs Cave, 15 August 1905, MAE, 428PO/1/31.
28 Drury, 129–45.
29 Maistre* to Dufourmantelle, Secrétaire Général de l'Alliance Française à Paris, draft letter entitled 'L'Alliance Française du Victoria, ce qu'elle est et ce qu'elle devrait être', December 1907; Paul Maistre, unaddressed note, 20 July 1907, MAE, 428PO/1/31.
30 *Table Talk*, 3 October 1901, 27.
31 Maistre to Dufourmantelle, December 1907, MAE, 428PO/1/31.
32 *Melbourne Punch*, 25 December 1890, 413; *Table Talk*, 19 December 1890, 2.
33 Annual report*, 1893–94, MAE, 428PO/1/31.
34 Ivan Barko, 'La Fondation et les Débuts de l'Alliance Française – Part 1', *Explorations*, no. 26 (2010), 9–17; Barko, 'La Fondation et les Débuts de l'Alliance Française – Part 1', 14–15.
35 Maistre to Mrs James Smith, 15 June 1908, MAE, 428PO/1/33.
36 *Table Talk*, 15 November 1895, 4; *Table Talk**, 24 May 1900, 16.
37 Irma Dreyfus, Candidature to the *Palmes Académiques*, 12 August 1896, 428PO/1/21.
38 Dreyfus* to Maistre, 5 March 1894, 428PO/1/14; Thornton-Smith, 6.
39 Government House invitation, 28 July 1897, MAE, 428PO/1/28.

40 Irma Dreyfus, *Lectures on French Literature* (London Longmans, Green, and Co, 1896); *Age*, 24 June 1898, 4.
41 Irma Dreyfus, Candidature to the *Palmes Académiques*, 12 August 1896, 428PO/1/21.
42 Dreyfus to Maistre, 5 March 1894, 428PO/1/14; Thornton-Smith, 6.
43 Dreyfus* to Maistre, 16 February 1898, MAE, 428PO/1/21.
44 See the booklet of the *Alliance Littéraire, Scientifique et Artistique Franco-Bitannique*, 1907, MAE, 428PO/1/31.
45 *Table Talk**, 24 May 1900, 16.
46 Thornton-Smith, 8.
47 Franck Schoell, 366.
48 *Herald*, 2 October 1906.
49 AR Chisholm, *Men Were My Milestones*, 114; Maurice-Carton to Maistre, 20 November 1905, MAE, 328PO/1/33.
50 Maurice-Carton to Maistre, 20 November 1905, MAE, 428PO/1/33; Program and statutes of the *Club Français*, 1908, MAE, 428PO/1/33.
51 Maurice-Carton to Maistre, 18 May 1905, MAE, 428PO/1/33; Maurice-Carton to Pigeonneau, 20 May 1911; 22 May 1911, MAE, 428PO/1/38; on the creation of the Pierre Corneille Prize see MAE, 428PO/1/40.
52 *Punch*, 17 October 1907, 573.
53 *Punch*, 17 October 1907, 573.
54 *Argus*, 25 October 1919, 22; 17 September 1921, 26; 8 October 1925, 7.
55 Cave to Maistre, 30 July 1901, MAE, 428PO/1/33; Thornton-Smith, 11.
56 Thornton-Smith, 11.
57 Rosa Aarons* to Maistre, undated, MAE, 428PO/1/33.Ê.
58 Thornton-Smith, 7.
59 Maistre to Mrs Cave, 15 August 1905, MAE, 428PO/1/31.
60 Maistre* to Dufourmantelle, draft letter entitled 'L'Alliance Française du Victoria, ce qu'elle Est et ce qu'elle Devrait Être', December 1907, MAE, 428PO/1/31.
61 Maurice-Carton to Maistre, 26 July 1908, MAE, 428PO/1/33.
62 Maurice-Carton* to Maistre, 1 August 1908, MAE, 428PO/1/33.
63 Maurice-Carton to Maistre, 27 June 1905, MAE, 428PO/1/33.
64 Paul Maistre* to Dufourmantelle, draft letter entitled 'L'Alliance Française du Victoria, ce qu'elle Est et ce qu'elle Devrait Être', December 1907, MAE, 428PO/1/31.
65 Alliance Minutes, SLV, 1 October 1907; <www.therealestateconversation.com.au/property/182-fitzroy-street-fitzroy-3065/the-independent-hall-historic-fitzroy-landmark-property>; <www.nelsonalexander.com.au/property/625922/182-fitzroy-street/>.
66 Maistre to Dufourmantelle, draft letter entitled 'L'Alliance Française du Victoria'.
67 *Australasian*, 21 September 1907, 627.
68 Maistre to Dufourmantelle, 30 March 1908, MAE, 428PO/1/31.
69 Alliance Minutes, SLV, 1 October 1907; Maistre to Lady Holroyd, 4 January 1907, MAE, 428PO/1/33.
70 Mrs Cave to M. d'Orgeval, 8 October 1907, MAE, 428PO/1/31; Maistre to Dufourmantelle, 6 May 1908, MAE, 428PO/1/33, *Alliance* Minutes, SLV, 17 March 1908.
71 *Alliance* Minutes, SLV, 13 November 1907.
72 *Table Talk*, 20 February 1908, 11.

73 *Table Talk*, 20 February 1908, 11; *Alliance* Minutes, SLV, 12 December 1907.
74 Thornton-Smith, 20–24; Lady Holroyd to Mrs Aarons, 4 January 1908, MAE, 428PO/1/33.
75 Thornton-Smith, 23; Maistre to Dufourmantelle, 25 March 1908, MAE, 428PO/1/33.
76 Lady Holroyd to Madame Maistre, 18 April 1908, MAE, 428PO/1/33.
77 Copy of a letter from Mrs Aarons, undated, MAE, 428PO/1/31.
78 Pinard to Maistre, 23 April 1908, MAE, 428PO/1/33.
79 MAE* to Maistre, 12 August 1908, MAE, 428PO/1/33.
80 Ivan Barko, 'Maistre, Paul (1851–1932)', French-Australian Dictionary of Biography, *ISFAR*, <www.isfar.org.au/bio/maistre-paul-1851-1932/>.
81 See 'Berthe Mouchette Competition', Alliance Française Melbourne website, <www.afmelbourne.com.au/berthe-mouchette-competition/>.

3   The scum of France: A reckoning with Australia's convict past

1 Biard d'Aunet* to Delcassé, 7 February 1899, Série Océanie, MAE; Ivan Barko, 'Georges Biard d'Aunet: The Life and Career of a Consul General', *Australian Journal of French Studies* 39, no. 2 (August 2002): 271–91.
2 Marilyn Lake, 'The Australian Dream of an Island Empire: Race, Reputation and Resistance', *Australian Historical Studies* 46, no. 3 (2015): 410–24.
3 Stuart Macintyre, *A Concise History of Australia* (Melbourne: Cambridge University Press, 2009), 91–94, 76–77.
4 Peter Cochrane, *Colonial Ambition: Foundations of Australian Democracy* (Melbourne: Melbourne University Press, 2006), 141, 210–11.
5 *SMH*, 24 April 1879, 7.
6 *Courrier Australien*, 21 May 1892, 1.
7 Jean-Paul Faivre, *L'expansion Française dans le Pacifique de 1800 à 1842* (Paris: Nouvelles Éditions latines, 1953), 65–66; Robert Aldrich, 15–19.
8 Aldrich, 17, 34–68.
9 Peter Tremewan, 'La France Australe: From Dream Through Failure to Compromise', *Australian Journal of French Studies* 50, no. 1 (April 2013): 100; Aldrich, 17, 34; Faivre, 443–61.
10 Tremewan; Leslie R Marchant, *France Australe: A Study of French Explorations and Attempts to Found a Penal Colony and Strategic Base in South Western Australia, 1503–1826* (Perth: Artlook, 1982), particularly chapters 8 and 9.
11 Colin Forster, *France and Botany Bay: The Lure of a Penal Colony* (Melbourne: University of Melbourne, 1996), 71, 157.
12 *Moreton Bay Courier*, 19 November 1853, 2, quoted in Rechniewski, 'The Perils of Proximity', *Journal of Multidisciplinary International Studies* 12, no. 1, 69–85.
13 Anthony Burke, *In Fear of Security: Australia's Invasion Anxiety* (Sydney: Pluto Press, 2001), 11.
14 Ward, 'Security: Defending Australia's Empire', 233–34.
15 Henry Parkes, 139.
16 Burke, 12; Neville Meany, *The Search for Security in the Pacific; 1901–14: A History of Australian Defence and Foreign Policy 1901–23, Volume 1* (Sydney: Sydney University Press, 1976), 18.
17 Mark McKenna, *The Captive Republic: A History of Republicanism in Australia 1788–1996* (Cambridge: Cambridge University Press, 1999), 126.

18 *The Queenslander*, 15 August 1874, 8.
19 Charles H Pearson, 'L'Australie dans ses rapports avec la France et l'Allemagne', *Revue Coloniale Internationale* 1, no. 5 (1885): 337–44.
20 Quoted in Nicholas Halter, '"Cannibals and Convicts": Australian Travel Writing About New Caledonia', in *The Palgrave Handbook of Prison Tourism*, eds Jacqueline Z Wilson et al (Basingstoke: Palgrave, 2017), 871.
21 *SMH*, 7 October 1873, 4.
22 *SMH*, 7 October 1873, 4.
23 Isabelle Merle, *Expériences Coloniales: La Nouvelle-Calédonie 1853–1920* (Paris: Belin, 1995), 115.
24 Graeme Davison, John Hirst and Stuart Macintyre (eds), *The Oxford Companion to Australian History* (Oxford: Oxford University Press, 1999), 649; Macintyre, 69–72; Merle, 16–18.
25 Briony Neilson, 'The Paradox of Penal Colonization: Debates on Convict Transportation at the International Prison Congresses 1872–1895', *French History and Civilization: Papers from the George Rudé Seminar* 6 (2015): 208; *The Queenslander*, 8 August 1874.
26 *SMH*, 3 November 1853 quoted in both Forster, 168 and in Pierre-Henri Zaidman, 'Les condamnés de Nouvelle-Calédonie en Australie et en Nouvelle-Zélande', *Criminocorpus, Revue Hypermédia. Histoire de la Justice, des Crimes et des Peines*, 1 January 2010 <criminocorpus.revues.org/176>. See also Rechniewski, 5.
27 Stefan Petrow, '"Convict-Phobia": Combating Vandiemonian Convicts in 1850s and 1860s Victoria', *Journal of Australian Colonial History* 14 (2012): 260.
28 John Rickard, *Australia: A Cultural History* (London; New York: Longman, 1996), 72; Woollacott, 113; *Argus*, reproduced in *SMH*, 28 October 1854, 2.
29 *SMH*, 4 July 1866, 4.
30 Henri Rochefort, *Retour de la Nouvelle-Calédonie* (Paris: Ancienne Librairie Martinon, 1877), 82.
31 *SMH*, 31 March 1874.
32 Colonial Secretary of New Zealand to Colonial Secretary of New South Wales, 21 August 1876; Colonial Secretary of Queensland to Colonial Secretary of New South Wales, 16 August 1876; Legislative Assembly of New South Wales, 1878–79, *Influx of convicts from New Caledonia*, State Records of New South Wales (hereafter SRNSW), NRS 906 4/960.1.
33 Chief Secretary of Victoria to Colonial Secretary of New South Wales, 17 August 1876, SRNSW, NRS 906 4/960.1.
34 Chief Secretary of South Australia to Colonial Secretary of New South Wales, 18 August 1876, SRNSW, NRS 906 4/960.1; *SMH*, 24 April 1879, 7.
35 Colonial Secretary of New South Wales to Colonial Secretary of Queensland, 31 August 1876; Circular from Downing Street, 1 January 1877; Lord Lyons to Duc Decazes, 13 December 1876; Duc Decazes to Lord Lyons, 13 February 1877, SRNSW, NRS 906 4/960.1.
36 Duc Decazes to Lord Lyons, 13 February 1877; Colonial Secretary of New South Wales to Colonial Secretary of Queensland, August 1876; Eugène Simon to Hercules Robinson, 12 September 1876; Earl of Derby to Lord Lyons, 8 December 1876, SRNSW, NRS 906 4/960.1.
37 *Journal Officiel*, 29 August 1876, SRNSW, NRS 906 4/960.1.

38 Alice Bullard, *Exile to Paradise: Savagery and Civilization in Paris and the South Pacific, 1790–1900* (Stanford: Stanford University Press, 2000), 236–38; Ann Stephen (ed.), *Visions of a Republic: The Work of Lucien Henry – Paris – Noumea – Sydney* (Sydney: Powerhouse Publishing, 2001).
39 *SMH*, 18 September 1872.
40 *SMH*, 22 July 1872, 5.
41 *SMH*, 24 April 1879, 7; Castelnau to Robinson, 31 January 1878, SRNSW, NRS 906 4/960.1.
42 *Queenslander*, 12 August 1871, 8.
43 *Morning Bulletin*, 28 June 1882, 1; 6 April 1912, 7; *Brisbane Courier*, 6 March 1879, 3; 8 March 1879, 3.
44 Le bagnard devenu baron, Les Nouvelles Calédoniennes, 16 May 2015, <www.lnc.nc/article/pays/le-bagnard-devenu-baron>.
45 Trottet* to Grattepin, 1885; Paul Trottet, *Extrait de la matricule générale*, MAE, 428PO/1/2.
46 Trottet* to Grattepin, 1885; Paul Trottet, *Extrait de la matricule générale*, MAE, 428PO/1/2.
47 Merle, *Expériences Coloniales*, 126, 194–98.
48 Chevalier, 'L'Émigration Française au XIXe Siècle', 130–71; Annick Foucrier, *Le Rêve Californien*; Laurent Vidal and Tania Regina De Luca (eds), *Les Français au Brésil: XIXe–XXe Siècles*.
49 Trottet* to Grattepin, 1885.
50 Verleye to MAE, 3 July 1889, MAE, 2CPC/101.
51 French Consulate in Melbourne to MAE, 1887, MAE, 378PO/K/680.
52 Zaidman gives the figure of 570 between 1866 and 1913 while Merle estimates that of the total number of convicts sent to New Caledonia during the *bagne*, 2.4 per cent (720 convicts) managed to escape between 1864 and 1912. See Merle, *Expériences Coloniales*, 135–37; Zaidman.
53 Biard d'Aunet to Forrest, 1 September 1898, MAE, 662PO/1/1-3 *Signalement de Vernay Antoine*, 1898, MAE, 662PO/1/1–3.
54 *SMH*, 31 March 1874, 4; *The Brisbane Courier*, 2 May 1879, 2.
55 Etienne de Vazelhes, *Etude sur l'Extradition: Suivie du Texte de Traités Franco-Belge de 1874 et Franco-Anglais de 1843 et 1876* (Paris: P. Pichon, 1876).
56 'Application of the Consul for France for the Extradition of One Colouma Recently Escaped from New Caledonia', Attorney General NSW, 12 March 1879, SRNSW, NRS 906 4/960.1.
57 *Argus*, 14 July 1890, 6. My emphasis.
58 *A Bill to Make Provision Against the Influx of Certain Foreign Criminals into New South Wales*, Legislative Assembly of New South Wales, 1879, SRNSW, NRS 906 4/960.1.
59 Vazelhes, 642; David Roberts, 'Beyond "The Stain": Rethinking the Nature and Impact of the Anti-transportation Movement', *Journal of Australian Colonial History*, vol. 14 (2012), 210.
60 Federal Council of Australasia, Address to Her Majesty's Government, 18 January 1888, SRNSW, NRS 906 4/960.1.
61 Merle, 196–97; Zaidman.
62 Trottet to Grattepin, 1885; Trottet, Paul, *Extrait de la Matricule Générale*, MAE, 428PO/1/2;

63 *SMH*, 2 May 1894, 6; 5 May 1894, 10; 22 February 1897, 3; 8 April 1897, 6.
64 See Stephen, *Visions of a Republic*; Terry H Irving and Rowan J Cahill, *Radical Sydney: Places, Portraits and Unruly Episodes* (Sydney: University of New South Wales Press, 2010), 67–74.
65 *Illustrated Sydney News*, 4 April 1889, 19.
66 Clem Lack, 'The Problem of the French Escapees from New Caledonia', *Journal of the Royal Historical Society of Queensland* 5 (1955), 1049–50; *Australian Town and Country Journal*, 24 May 1879, 13.
67 Merle, 125; *Australian Town and Country Journal*, 4 December 1886, 18.
68 *Queensland Figaro and Punch*, 6 February 1886, 2.
69 *Australian Town and Country Journal*, 27 March 1907, 51.
70 *A Bill to Prevent the Introduction of Foreign Criminals into New South Wales*, March 1887, MAE, 378PO/K/680; Stuer, 131–136.
71 Deputy Administrator Girette to Directeur Général, 27 August 1887, MAE, Ambassade de France à Londres (Fonds K), box 680 (hereafter 378PO/K/680).
72 Directeur Général des Postes et des Télégraphes to MAE, 1 September 1887, MAE, 378PO/K/680.
73 Alison Bashford and Catie Gilchrist, 'The Colonial History of the 1905 Aliens Act', *The Journal of Imperial and Commonwealth History* 40, no. 3 (2012): 423, 433.
74 Geoffrey Serle, 'The Victorian Government's Campaign for Federation, 1883–1889', in Allan William Martin (ed.), *Essays in Australian Federation* (Melbourne: Melbourne University Press, 1969); Geoffrey Serle, 'Service, James (1823–1899)' in *Australian Dictionary of Biography* (Canberra: National Centre of Biography, Australian National University), <adb.anu.edu.au/biography/service-james-4561>.
75 *Queenslander*, 10 May 1884, 746.
76 French consul* to MAE, 31 March 1889, MAE, 378PO/K/680.
77 Speedy, Karen, '"Arab Castaways/French Escapees": Mobilites, Border Protection and White Australia'. *Law, Crime and History*, no. 2 (2016): 21–29.
78 Maistre* to MAE, 29 March 1892, MAE, Correspondance Politique et Commerciale, volume 94.
79 French Consulate in Melbourne to MAE, 1887, MAE, 378/K/680.
80 *Argus*, 24 April 1873, 7; Marcus Clarke, *For the Term of His Natural Life* (Sydney: New Holland, 2008).
81 *Argus*, 24 April 1873, 7; *SMH*, 28 April 1873, 7.
82 Lack, 1049–50.
83 *Australian Town and Country Journal*, 24 May 1879, 13.
84 *The Australian, Windsor, Richmond, and Hawkesbury Advertiser*, 22 April 1882, 2.
85 *Punch*, 29 October 1908, 6; Georges M Crivelli and Pierre Louvet*, *L'Australie et le Pacifique* (Paris: G. Cres et Cie, 1923), 182.

4 French migrants: The 'crème de la crème'

1 Antoine Fauchery, *Letters from a Miner in Australia*, trans. Alan R Chisholm (Melbourne: Georgian House, 1965), 1.
2 Diane Reilly, 'Fauchery, Antoine Julien (1823–1861)', ISFAR, <www.isfar.org.au/bio/fauchery-antoine-julien-1823-1861/>.
3 Only a few of the letters received by the consulates survive. I have excluded from my corpus letters that had no information about their senders or the missing people other than their names. To give an order of scale about the corpus, in the archives of

the consulates of Melbourne and Sydney I have found 69 letters produced during the period between 1860 and 1914. Yet we know that, for just one year in 1909, the consulate in Melbourne received 169 letters from private individuals (135 from French nationals and 34 from 'foreigners'). In 1910 it received 159 (112 from French nationals and 47 from 'foreigners'). So for a period of about fifty-five years, the corpus represents roughly just over a third of the letters that each consulate would have received for any given year. Since the sample is rather small I do not make claims that the corpus is representative of French emigration in general.

4 Gustave Flaubert, *Dictionary of Accepted Ideas*, trans. Jacques Barzun (New Directions Publishing, 1968), 25; Raoul Girardet, *L'Idée Coloniale en France de 1871 à 1962* (Paris: La Table Ronde, 1972), 4.
5 Eugène Poiré, *L'Émigration Française aux Colonies* (Paris: Plon, 1897), 50.
6 Gerrit Verschuur*, *Aux Antipodes: Voyage en Australie, La Nouvelle-Zélande, aux Fidji, à la Nouvelle-Calédonie, aux Nouvelles-Hébrides et dans l'Amérique du Sud, 1888–1889* (Paris: Librairie Hachette et Cie., 1891), 122.
7 Verschuur, 121.
8 Isabelle Merle, *Expériences Coloniales*, 57.
9 Philippe Ariès, *Histoire des Populations Françaises et de Leurs Attitudes Devant la Vie Depuis le XVIIIe Siècle*, (Paris: Éditions du Seuil, 1971).
10 Jens Lyng, *Non-Britishers in Australia: Influence on Population and Progress* (Melbourne: Melbourne University Press, 1935), 116.
11 Louis Chevalier, 127–71; Poiré, 3, 220–34.
12 Charles-Robert Ageron, *France Coloniale ou Parti Colonial?* (Paris: Presses Universitaires de France, 1978); Isabelle Merle, 'Drawing Settlers to New Caledonia: French Colonial Propaganda in the Late Nineteenth Century', in Tony Chafer and Amanda Sackur (eds), *Promoting the Colonial Idea: Propaganda and Visions of Empire in France* (Houndmills, Basingstoke Hampshire; New York: Palgrave, 2002), 40–52.
13 See the introduction in Tony Chafer and Amanda Sackur (eds), *Promoting the Colonial Idea*, particularly 4–5.
14 Clément Trouillas* to Consul Melbourne, 17 July 1913, MAE, 428PO/1/42.
15 Marie le Callee to Consul Melbourne, 9 May 1905, MAE, 428PO/1/30.
16 Fauchery, 7.
17 Fauchery, 9.
18 Fauchery, 9–10, 18.
19 KM O'Neill, 'Fauchery, Antoine Julien (1827–1861)', in *Australian Dictionary of Biography* (Canberra: National Centre of Biography, Australian National University), <adb.anu.edu.au/biography/fauchery-antoine-julien-3504>; Anny Stuer, 67–68.
20 Stuer, 73.
21 Stuer, 86–108.
22 Tasma, 'L'Australie et les Avantages Qu'elle Offre à L'Émigration Française', *Bulletin de Géographie Commerciale de Paris* (1880), 13.
23 Alexis Bergantz, 'French Connection: The Culture and Politics of Frenchness in Australia, 1890–1914' (PhD Thesis, Australian National University, 2016), 103–4; Stuer, 87.
24 Fauchery, 37–44.
25 See the introduction by Patricia Clancy and Jeanne Allen in Céleste de Chabrillan, *The French Consul's Wife: Mémoirs of Céleste de Chabrillan in Gold-Rush Australia*, trans. Patricia Clancy and Jeanne Allen (Melbourne: The Miegunyah Press, 1998), 6–7.

26 Bernard Smith, *European Vision and the South Pacific* (Melbourne: Oxford University Press, 1989); Paul Arthur, 'Antipodean Myths Transformed: The Evolution of Australian Identity', *History Compass* 5, no. 6 (2007): 1862–78.
27 Jennifer Génion, 'The Adventure Playground: Australia in the Popular Literature of Nineteenth-Century France' (PhD Thesis, University of Sydney, 2007), 2; See also Jennifer Génion, 'The Classroom on the Other Side of the World: The Redemption Narrative in Nineteenth-Century French Popular Literature Set in Australia', *Explorations* 38 (June 2005): 29–60.
28 Colin Forster, 8.
29 Citizen Gamas, *The First 'Australian' Play: Les Émigrés aux Terres Australes (1792)*, ed. and trans. Patricia Clancy (Melbourne, Monash University, 1984).
30 Génion, 'The Adventure Playground', 11, 247, 253–63.
31 Génion, 'The Adventure Playground'.
32 Jules Verne, *A Voyage Round the World: In Search of the Castaways* (Philadelphia: Lippincott, 1873); Alexandre Dumas, *The Journal of Madame Giovanni* (London: Liveright Publishing Corporation, 1944).
33 Céleste de Chabrillan, Edouart Marcet, Paul Maistre and Alfred de la Chapelle, in Génion, 'The Adventure Playground', 269.
34 Girardet, 16–17; see also Dominique Lejeune, *Les Sociétés de Géographie en France et l'Expansion Coloniale au XIX Siècle* (Paris: Albin Michel, 1993); Fauchery, 2.
35 Génion, 'The Adventure Playground', 265.
36 Viviane Fayaud, 'Le Temps du Rêve Français: L'Australie dans l'Iconographie au XIXe Siècle', *Le Journal de la Société des Océanistes*, no. 129 (2009): 223.
37 Unknown* to consul Melbourne, 25 February 1910, MAE, 428PO/1/36.
38 Henriette Repiquet* to consul Melbourne, 29 April 1899, MAE, 428PO/1/12.
39 Dr Essely to consul Melbourne, 1892, MAE, 428PO/1/11.
40 Tasma*, 12–13.
41 Oscar Comettant*, 210–11.
42 Tasma, 14.
43 Madame Laborie to consul Melbourne, 28 May 1891, MAE, 428PO/1/10; Pierre Gavi to consul Melbourne, 19 November 1918, MAE, 428PO/1/42; Clément Adrien to consul Melbourne, 12 August 1893, MAE, 428PO/1/12; Victor Crémieux to consul Melbourne, 1 November 1891, MAE, 428PO/1/10; Henry Lecomte to consul Melbourne, 12 October 1905, MAE, 428PO/1/30; Marie Reynand to consul Melbourne, 6 October 1900, MAE, 428PO/1/23.
44 *SMH*, 2 September 1893, 5.
45 Stuer, 116–25.
46 Stuer, 61–65. Geoffrey de Lassus, *The History of BNP Paribas in Australia and New Zealand 1881–2011* (BNP Paribas Australia & New Zealand in collaboration with Group Heritage and Historical Archives of BNP Paribas and BNP Paribas Historical Association, 2011), 41.
47 Jacqueline Dwyer, *Flanders in Australia: A Personal History of Wool and War* (Sydney: Kangaroo Press, 1998), 32, 207–8.
48 Stuer, 110, 139; Michel Rapoport, 'The London French from the Belle Epoque to the End of the Inter-War Period (1880–1939)', in *A History of the French in London: Liberty, Equality, Opportunity*, Debra Kelly and Martyn Cornick (eds) (London: Institute of Historical Research, 2013), 244.

49 Nancy Green, *Repenser Les Migrations* (Paris: PUF, 2002), 82–84.
50 John Torpey, *The Invention of the Passport: Surveillance, Citizenship and the State* (Cambridge: Cambridge University Press, 2000), 1, 93.
51 David Dutton, *One of Us?: A Century of Australian Citizenship* (Sydney: University of New South Wales Press, 2002), 25.
52 Dutton, 42.
53 Dutton, 13.
54 Green, 112.
55 *SMH*, 2 September 1893, 5.
56 Wolfgang Helbich and Walter D Kamphoefner, 'How Representative Are Emigrant Letters? An Exploration of the German Case', in Bruce S Elliott, David A Gerber and Suzanne M Sinke (eds), *Letters Across Borders: The Epistolary Practices of International Migrants* (Basingstoke: Palgrave Macmillan, 2006), 29–30.
57 Silvain d'Héron to consul Melbourne, 24 May 1886, MAE, 428PO/1/1.
58 A Dennemont* to consul Melbourne, 7 July 1886, MAE, 428PO/1/1.
59 M Paysan to consul Melbourne, 26 November 1888, MAE, 428PO/1/3.
60 Pierre Guillerie to consul Sydney, 8 May 1888, MAE, 662/PO/1/3.
61 David Fitzpatrick, *Oceans of Consolation: Personal Accounts of Irish Migration to Australia* (Melbourne: Melbourne University Press, 1995), 3.
62 Chevalier, 127–71; Green.
63 Marie Coing* to consul Melbourne, 14 July 1913; internal note, 21 July 1913, MAE, 428PO/1/42.
64 George Henri d'Alphonse* to consul Melbourne, 2 November 1886, MAE 428PO/1/1.
65 Stuart Macintyre, 122–30.
66 Ivan Barko, 'Felicite Cochard and the Foundation of the Sydney French Benevolent Society', *Explorations* 44 (June 2008).
67 Consul Melbourne* to Marie le Callee, 15 June 1905, MAE, 428PO/1/30.
68 Unknown* to consul Melbourne, 25 February 1910, MAE, 428PO/1/36.
69 Macintyre, 130.
70 *SMH*, 2 September 1893, 5; consul Melbourne* to Henry Lecomte, 15 December 1905, MAE, 428PO/1/30.
71 *SMH*, 2 September 1893, 5.
72 Consul Melbourne* to MAE, 11 December 1906, MAE, 139CPCOM/13; Chris Cunneen, 'Jersey, Seventh Earl of (1845–1915)', in *Australian Dictionary of Biography* (Canberra: National Centre of Biography, Australian National University), <adb.anu.edu.au/biography/jersey-seventh-earl-of-6844>.
73 Consul Melbourne* to MAE, 11 December 1906, MAE, 139CPCOM/13.
74 Fernand Gracin* to consul Melbourne, 14 July 1914, MAE, 428PO/1/44.
75 Dannie Favre* to consul Melbourne, 2 February 1888, MAE, 428PO/1/3.
76 Madame Lusanne Chalauser to consul Melbourne, 1891, MAE, 428PO/1/11.
77 Suzanne Thibault to consul Melbourne, c. 1910–20, MAE, 428PO/1/38.
78 Monsieur Borelle to consul Melbourne, 12 January 1886; Monsieur Guiniac to consul Melbourne, 15 May 1886; Madame Borelle* to Consul Melbourne, 22 February 1886; Monsieur Borelle to consul Melbourne, 20 December 1887; Monsieur Borelle* to Mademoiselle Isoline Pédron, 20 December 1887, MAE, 428PO/1/3.
79 *Age*, 26 July 1886, 7.

80 Dossier Bocquet (Henri)*, July 1886 ; Madame Bocquet to consul Melbourne, 30 January 1887, MAE, 428PO/1/1; *Age*, 26 July 1886, 7; *Argus*, 26 July 1886, 6; 7 August 1886, 5.
81 Georges M Crivelli and Pierre Louvet*, 182.

5 A matter of honour: Frenchness on trial

1 'Hunters Hill Property Market, House Prices, Suburb Profile & Investment Data', <www.realestate.com.au/neighbourhoods/hunters-hill-2110-nsw>.
2 *SMH*, 2 September 1893, 5.
3 Linda Emery, *Hunters Hill: Pictorial History*, Alexandria, NSW: Kingsclear Books, 2011, 70; The Hunter's Hill Trust, *Heritage of Hunter's Hill* (Sydney: The Hunter's Hill Trust, 2002), 5.
4 'Hunters Hill', The Dictionary of Sydney, <dictionaryofsydney.org/entry/hunters_hill>; Emery 13–14; The Hunter's Hill Trust, 3.
5 Beverley Sherry, *Hunter's Hill, Australia's Oldest Garden Suburb* (Sydney: David Ell Press, 1989), 52.
6 *SMH*, 2 January 1858, 4.
7 'Hunters Hill', The Dictionary of Sydney.
8 *SMH*, 2 September 1893, 5.
9 Patricia Thompson, *Hunter's Hill Sketchbook* (Adelaide: Rigby, 1973), 6.
10 *SMH*, 2 September 1893, 5.
11 *SMH*, 2 September 1893, 5.
12 Robert Aldrich, 205.
13 *The Lone Hand*, 1 July 1912, 188.
14 Jacqueline Dwyer, 24.
15 Alexis Bergantz, 'Remembering *Australasie*: Trans-Imperial Thinking and Migrant-Settler Legitimacy in *Le Courrier Australien* (1892–1896)', in *Voices of Challenge in Australia's Migrant and Minority Press*, Catherine Dewhirst and Richard Scully (eds) (Palgrave, forthcoming); Alexis Bergantz, 117–18.
16 Dwyer, 34–35, 39; Personal correspondence with Jacqueline Dwyer, 6 May 2016.
17 Bergantz, 'Remembering *Australasie*'.
18 Edmond Marin la Mesleé, *The New Australia*, trans. Russel Ward (London: Heinemann Educational, 1979).
19 Georges M Crivelli and Pierre Louvet, 182.
20 Jill Donohoo, 'NSW Premier William Holman and the "Inexhaustible Interest of French Literature and Affairs"', *The French Australian Review*, 61 (Australian Summer, 2016–2017), 3–18.
21 Nancy L Green, 'Classe et Ethnicité, Des Catégories Caduques de l'Histoire Sociale?', in *Les Formes de l'Expérience: Une Autre Histoire Sociale*, Bernard Lepetit (ed) (Paris: Albin Michel, 1995), 180–81.
22 *Argus*, 26 November 1898, 13.
23 Vincent Duclert, *L'Affaire Dreyfus* (Paris: La Découverte, 2012), 141; Pascal Ory and Jean-François Sirinelli, *Les Intellectuels en France: De l'Affaire Dreyfus à Nos Jours* (Paris: Albert Colin, 2002), 5–27; Michel Winock, *Le Siècle des Intellectuels* (Paris: Seuil, 1997), 11–55; Christopher E Forth, *The Dreyfus Affair and the Crisis of French Manhood* (Baltimore: Johns Hopkins University Press, 2004); Signed protest letter from the French notables of Sydney to the consul general in reaction to the Cobar incident, undated, MAE, 139CPCOM/9.

24 *The Evening News*, 5 October 1899, 4.
25 Duclert, 60; Martyn Cornick, 'La Réception de l'Affaire en Grande-Bretagne', in Michel Drouin (ed.), *L'Affaire Dreyfus de A à Z: Histoire et Dictionnaire* (Paris: Flammarion, 1994), 441–47; *Courrier Australien*, 23 April 1904, 2.
26 CA*, 3 September 1898, 2.
27 *Evening News*, 5 October 1899, 4.
28 CA, 20 May 1899, 2; 4 November 1899, 3.
29 CA, 4 November 1899, 3; 12 March 1898, 1.
30 CA, 23 September 1899, 3.
31 *The Cobar Herald*, 30 September 1899, 2.
32 *The Cobar Herald*, 30 September 1899, 2.
33 *The Cobar Herald*, 7 October 1899, 2; *SMH*, 28 September 1899, 7.
34 *The Bulletin*, 14 October 1899, 9; *Evening News*, 5 October 1899, 4.
35 *The Daily Telegraph*, 28 September 1899, 5.
36 *The Cobar Herald*, 30 September 1899, 2.
37 Cameron Hazlehurst, 'Beauchamp, Seventh Earl (1872–1938)', in *Australian Dictionary of Biography* (Canberra: National Centre of Biography, Australian National University), <adb.anu.edu.au/biography/beauchamp-seventh-earl-5174>; William Lygon, 7th Earl of Beauchamp, Diary Written While Governor of New South Wales, 1899 – ca. 1900, Mitchell Library, SLNSW.
38 Ivan Barko, 'The Cobar Incident, Its Antecedents and Sequels 1899–1900', *JRAHS* 86, no. 2 (2000), 139.
39 Barko, Cobar Incident, 143–45
40 CA, 14 October 1899, 3.
41 Barko, Cobar Incident, 148.
42 The *Bulletin*, 14 October 1899, 9.
43 *Truth*, 15 October 1899, 8.
44 Robert Nye, *Masculinity and Male Codes of Honor in Modern France*, Studies in the History of Sexuality (New York: Oxford University Press, 1993), 8.
45 Penny Russell, see in particular 165–92.
46 *SMH*, 4 October 1899, 6.
47 *Signed protest letter from the French notables of Sydney to the consul general in reaction to the Cobar incident, no date, MAE, 139CPCOM/9.
48 *Signed protest letter from the French notables of Sydney to the consul general in reaction to the Cobar incident, no date, MAE, 139CPCOM/9.
49 Duclert, 57–64.
50 Maurice Agulhon, *The French Republic, 1879–1992*, English edition, *History of France* (Oxford: B. Blackwell, 1993).
51 CA, 14 October 1899, 3.
52 *Truth*, 15 October 1899, 1; *SMH*, 5 October 1899, 5; *Argus*, 5 October 1899, 4.
53 *The Bulletin*, 14 October 1899, 1.
54 Beauchamp to Chamberlain, 9 December 1899, quoted in Barko, Cobar Incident, 150.
55 *Punch*, 29 October 1908, 6.
56 *Argus*, 9 February 1899, 7; *Champion*, 4 July 1896, 4; *Age*, 26 June 1896, 6.
57 *Western Australian Goldfields Courier*, 25 July 1896, 10.
58 Alan Atkinson, *The Europeans in Australia: A History*, Vol. 3 (Sydney: NewSouth Publishing, 2014), 163.
59 *Age*, 7 December 1895, 4.

60 *Punch*, 29 October 1908, 6.
61 *Age*, 1 September 1898, 5.
62 *Age*, 1 September 1898, 5; Paul Maistre, Note pour Monsieur Joseph Woolf, Avocat du Consulat Général de France. Affaire Cayron c/ Crivelli, 7 August 1896, MAE, 428PO/1/21.
63 *Evening News*, 15 August 1898, 5; *Age*, 1 September 1898, 5; *Punch*, 29 October 1908, 6.
64 Paul Maistre, Note pour Monsieur Joseph Woolf, Avocat du Consulat Général de France. Affaire Cayron c/ Crivelli, 7 August 1896, MAE, 428PO/1/21.
65 Cayron to MAE, 30 January 1897, MAE, 428PO/1/21.
66 Cayron* to MAE, 30 January 1897, MAE, 428PO/1/21.
67 Woolf to Déjardin, 27 May 1898; 1 June 1898; 6 June 1898; MAE to Déjardin, 27 March 1897, MAE, 428PO/1/21.
68 *Punch*, 29 October 1908, 6.
69 Woolf to Déjardin, 27 May 1898; 1 June 1898; 6 June 1898; MAE to Déjardin, 27 March 1897, MAE, 428PO/1/21.
70 *Age*, 17 August 1898, 6; *Age*, 1 September 1898, 5.
71 Woolf to Déjardin, 27 May 1898; 1 June 1898; 6 June 1898; MAE to Déjardin, 27 March 1897, MAE, 428PO/1/21. On the consul's duties and whether he should have forwarded a copy of the interview to Cayron see Notes sur le Dossier Cayron vs. Crivelli, 24 December 1896, MAE, 428PO/1/30.
72 *Argus*, 9 February 1899, 7.
73 *Evening News*, 19 August 1898, 3.
74 *Argus*, 16 August 1898, 7; 17 August 1898, 5; 20 August 1898, 14; *Age*, 19 August 1898, 5; 20 August 1898, 9.
75 George Robb, *White-Collar Crime in Modern England: Financial Fraud and Business Morality, 1845–1929* (Cambridge: Cambridge University Press, 2002), 94–124; David Kynaston, *City of London: The History* (London: Random House, 2012), 179–80; *Age*, 16 August 1898, 4.
76 *Argus*, 13 August 1898, 11; *Age*, 13 August 1898, 9.
77 *Argus*, 13 August 1898, 11; 16 August 1898, 11; *Age*, 16 August 1898, 6.
78 *Argus*, 13 August 1898, 11.
79 *Argus*, 23 August 1898, 6.
80 *Argus*, 3 December 1898, 6; 1 September 1898, 9.

6 Fading family ties to France: Two diarists' views

1 Lydia Delarue, 'Diary 2/2', 12. Lydia's diary is composed of two small volumes that I have simply numbered 1 and 2. They are located within the Delarue Family Papers in the Mitchell Library in Sydney, ML MSS 5106, Box 01. Leopold's single-volume diary is in a private collection.
2 Ros Pesman, *Duty Free: Australian Women Abroad* (Oxford: Oxford University Press, 1996).
3 Ivan Barko, *Vive la Différence! The French in NSW* [Catalogue of the Exhibition] (Sydney, 2004).
4 Eugénie Crawford, *A Bunyip Close Behind Me* (Melbourne: Hawthorn Press, 1972); Barko, *Vive la Différence*, 18.
5 John Bernard Hawkins, *19th Century Australian Silver* (Woodbridge, Suffolk, England: Antique Collectors Club, 1990), 4, 179, 291–92, 303–4.

6 *Catalogue of the Natural and Industrial Products of New South Wales Forwarded to the Paris Universal Exhibition of 1867 by the New South Wales Exhibition Commissioners* (Sydney, 1867), 28.
7 Hawkins, 4, 179, 291–92, 303–4.
8 Crawford, *A Bunyip Close Behind Me*, 5.
9 Jules Joubert to Hippolyte Felix Delarue, 7 June 1878, Delarue Family Papers, SLNSW, ML MSS 5106; Martha Rutledge, 'Joubert, Jules François de Sales (1824–1907)', in *Australian Dictionary of Biography* (Canberra: National Centre of Biography, Australian National University), <adb.anu.edu.au/biography/joubert-jules-francois-de-sales-3874>.
10 Leopold Delarue, 'Diary', Friday 31/5/1878.
11 Leopold Delarue, Tuesday 23/4/1878, Wednesday 24/4/1878, Thursday 25/4/1878; *Official Catalogue of the Natural and Industrial Products of New South Wales Forwarded to the Universal Exhibition of 1878 at Paris*, 1878, 8.
12 Leopold Delarue, 'Diary', Friday 26/4/1878, Monday 6/5/1878, Tuesday 7/5/1878, Wednesday 8/5/1878, Thursday 9/5/1878, Friday 10/5/1878, Saturday 11/5/1878.
13 Leopold Delarue, Sunday 18/8/1878.
14 Eugénie Crawford, *Ladies Didn't: Recollections of an Edwardian Girlhood* (Melbourne: Penguin Books, 1984), 3.
15 John Firth, 'History of Tuberculosis: Part 1 – Phthisis, Consumption and the White Plague', *Journal of Military and Veterans' Health* 22, no. 2, June 2020 <jmvh.org/article/history-of-tuberculosis-part-1-phthisis-consumption-and-the-white-plague/>.
16 *SMH*, 21 September 1891, 4; Barko, *Vive la Différence!*, 18.
17 Crawford, *Ladies Didn't*, 3.
18 Crawford, *A Bunyip Close Behind Me*, 101, 106, 53.
19 Crawford, *A Bunyip Close Behind Me*, 5
20 Richard Twopeny, 40.
21 Angela Woollacott, 6.
22 Richard White, *On Holidays: A History of Getting Away in Australia* (Melbourne: Pluto Press Australia, 2005), 26–29; Kenneth S Inglis, 'Going Home', in *Home or Away?: Immigrants in Colonial Australia*, David Fitzpatrick (ed) (Canberra: Australian National University, 1992), 105–30; Andrew Hassam, *Through Australian Eyes: Colonial Perceptions of Imperial Britain* (Melbourne: Melbourne University Press, 2000), 9–29.
23 The original manuscript of Daisy's diary is at the National Library of Australia, MS 9247. For convenience I am referencing the published edition, Daisy White, *Daisy in Exile: The Diary of an Australian Schoolgirl in France (1887–1889), Introduced and Annotated by Marc Serge Rivière* (Canberra: National Library of Australia, 2003).
24 Patrick White, *Flaws in the Glass: A Self-Portrait* (London: Penguin Books, 1983), 4.
25 Patrick White, 18.
26 Ros Pesman, David Walker and Richard White (eds), *The Oxford Book of Australian Travel Writing*, Melbourne: Oxford University Press, xxi; see also Woollacott, *To Try Her Fortune in London: Australian Women, Colonialism, and Modernity*, 4; Penny Russell, 'Cultures of Distinction', in Richard White and Hsu-Ming Teo (eds), *Cultural History in Australia* (Sydney: University of New South Wales Press, 2003), 158–71.
27 Crawford, *A Bunyip Close Behind Me*, 96, 128–9; see also Papers of the Delarue and de Lostalot families, 1877–1911, Mitchell Library, MLMSS 4972.
28 Delarue, 'Diary 1/2', 67.i.
29 Crawford, *Ladies Didn't*, 4.

30   Crawford, *Ladies Didn't*, 4, 10.
31   Crawford, *A Bunyip Close Behind Me*, 129.
32   Julie Rak, 'Dialogue with the Future: Philippe Lejeune's Method and Theory of Diary', in Jeremy D Popkin and Julie Rak (eds), *On Diary* (Honolulu: University of Hawai'i Press, 2009), 19; see in particular David Rasmussen, 'Rethinking Subjectivity: Narrative Identity and the Self', *Philosophy and Social Criticism* 21, no. 5 (1995): 159–72.
33   Lynn Z Bloom, '"I Write for Myself and Strangers": Private Diaries as Public Documents', in Suzanne L Bunkers and Cynthia A Huff (eds), *Inscribing the Daily: Critical Essays on Women's Diaries* (Massachusetts: University of Massachusetts Press, 1996), 23–37.
34   Daisy White, *Daisy in Exile*, 54.
35   Delarue, 'Diary 1/2', 14; Atkinson, 88. Philippe Lejeune, 'The "Journal de Jeune Fille" in Nineteenth-Century France', in Jeremy Popkin and Julie Rak (eds), *On Diary* (Honolulu: University of Hawai'i Press, 2009), 136–7.
36   Inglis, 129.
37   Leopold Delarue, 'Diary', Tuesday 30/7/1878; Thursday 10/10/1878.
38   Leopold Delarue, 'Diary', 9/4/1878; Saturday 20/4/1878.
39   Richard White, 'Bluebells and Fogtown: Australians' First Impressions of England 1860–1940', *Australian Cultural History*, 1986, 44.
40   White, Bluebells and Fogtown, 47.
41   Leopold Delarue, 'Diary', no date.
42   White, Bluebells and Fogtown, 48.
43   Lydia Delarue, 'Diary 1/2', 32–43.
44   Lydia Delarue, 'Diary 1/2', 60, 97; Karl Baedeker, *Paris and Its Environs with Routes from London to Paris, and from Paris to the Rhine and Switzerland: Handbook for Travellers* (Leipsig: K. Baedeker, 1878), 4.
45   Lydia Delarue, 'Diary 1/2', 61, 85–86.
46   *Argus*, 20 May 1899, 13.
47   Sylvaine Marandon, 283.
48   Marandon, 283.
49   Delarue, 'Diary 2/2', 12.
50   Delarue, 'Diary 1/2', 35; Crawford, *Ladies Didn't*, 18.
51   Delarue, 'Diary 2/2', 9.
52   Delarue, 'Diary 2/2', 12.
53   Pierre Tucoo-Chala, *Pau, Ville Anglaise* (Orthez: Editions Gascogne, 2013), 56–58.
54   Tucoo-Chala, 10, 14.
55   Tucoo-Chala, 49.
56   Robert Tombs, 22–28.
57   Lydia Delarue, 'Diary 1/2', 97.
58   Lydia Delarue, 'Diary 1/2', 97.
59   Marandon, 309–12; Rioux, 10; Walton, 5.
60   Tombs, 22–28.
61   Henry James, *A Little Tour in France* (Penguin Books, 1984), 1.
62   James, xvi–xviii.
63   Lydia Delarue, 'Diary 1/2', 97.
64   Anne-Marie Thiesse, *La Création des Identités Nationales, Europe XVIII–XIX Siècles* (Paris: Seuil, 2001), 201–2; Theodore Zeldin, *Histoire des Passions Françaises 1848–1945*, trans. Denise Demoy, Vol. 1 (Oxford: Oxford University Press, 1978), 161–66.

65 Consul general for Denmark to vice-consul for France, 15 August 1903, MAE, 428PO/1/28.
66 Lydia Delarue, 'Diary 1/2', 97.
67 Leopold Delarue, 'Diary', Saturday 20/4/1878.
68 Leopold Delarue, 'Diary', 26/7/1878.
69 Lydia Delarue, 'Diary 2/2', 54.
70 John Gascoigne, *The Enlightenment and the Origins of European Australia* (Cambridge: Cambridge University Press, 2005), 69, 71, 99.
71 Bill Gammage, *The Biggest Estate on Earth: How Aborigines Made Australia* (Sydney: Allen & Unwin, 2012), 298–303; Woollacott, 12.
72 *SMH*, 6 July 1871, 2; 12 September 1913, 8; *Brisbane Courier*, 8 May 1909, 13.
73 Charles EW Bean, *Letters from France* (London, New York: Cassell and Company, Ltd, 1917), 27.
74 Bean, 8.
75 *SMH*, 28 June 1924, 14; Delarue, 'Diary 2/2', 47; Crawford, *Ladies Didn't*, ii.

Epilogue: France and ideas of the 'feminine' in 20th-century Australia

1 'France country brief', Australian Government, Department of Foreign Affairs and Trade website, <www.dfat.gov.au/geo/france/Pages/france-country-brief>.
2 Sarah Turnbull, *Almost French* (Melbourne: Penguin, 2002).
3 Juliana de Nooy, *What's France Got to Do with It?* (Canberra: ANU Press, 2020), 1–4.
4 De Nooy, 4.
5 De Nooy; see chapter 10.
6 Homéry*, vice-consul for France to MAE, 16 July 1915, MAE, 139CPCOM/20; *Argus*, 15 July 1915, 8.
7 Ivan Barko, *Vive la Différence!* 29.
8 Anny Stuer, 167.
9 Romain Fathi, *Our Corner of the Somme: Australia at Villers-Bretonneux* (Cambridge: Cambridge University Press, 2019).
10 Briony Neilson, 'Settling Scores in New Caledonia and Australia: French Convictism and Settler Legitimacy', *Australian Journal of Politics & History* 64, no. 3 (2018): 391–406.
11 Nicholas Halter, 867–84.
12 Wilfred Burchett, *Pacific Treasure Island: New Caledonia: Voyage Through Its Land and Wealth, the Story of Its People and Past* (Melbourne: Cheshire, 1941), 11, 13.
13 Véronique Duché and Diane de Saint Léger, 'Aussie, Code-Switching in an Australian Soldier's Magazine – an Overview', in *Languages and the First World War: Representation and Memory*, Julian Walker and Christophe Declercq (eds) (London: Palgrave, 2016), 80.
14 James Curran, '"Bonjoor Paree!" The First AIF in Paris, 1916–1918', *Journal of Australian Studies* 23, no. 60 (1999), 18.
15 Curran, 26.
16 Quoted in Curran, 21.
17 Halter, 'Cannibals and Convicts'.
18 Michael Symons, *One Continuous Picnic: A History of Eating in Australia* (Adelaide: Duck Press, 1982), 223.
19 Symons, 223; Donna Lee Brien and Alison Vincent, 'Oh, for a French Wife?: Australian Women and Culinary Francophilia in Post-War Australia', *Lilith: A Feminist History Journal*, no. 22 (2016), 82.

20 Nic Maclellan and Jean Chesneaux, *After Moruroa: France in the South Pacific* (Melbourne: Ocean Press, 1998), 84–85.
21 *Le Monde*, 28 June 1995, trans. Australian Government, Department of the Prime Minister and Cabinet, <pmtranscripts.pmc.gov.au/release/transcript-9649>.
22 Maclellan and Chesneaux, 104.
23 Symons, 224–26.
24 Donna Lee Brien and Alison Vincent, 79.
25 Johnnie Walker, 'What Goes on in Cook's School', *Sun Herald*, 24 September 1967, quoted in Brien and Vincent, 86.
26 Brien and Vincent, 89.
27 Barko, *Vive la Différence*, 7; Brien and Vincent, 82.
28 Margot Riley, 'Fashioned from Fleece: Australian Wool and French Haute Couture', *Explorations* 46 (June 2010): 21–42.
29 Margaret Maynard, 'Fashion Modelling in Australia', in *Fashioning Models: Image, Text and Industry* (New York: Berg Publishers, 2012), 83.
30 Riley, 36; Maynard, 90.
31 Riley, 36.
32 Riley, 39.

Acknowledgments

I started writing this book a few years after completing the PhD Thesis on which it is based. I owe a debt of gratitude to many people whose paths I have crossed along the way since the inception of the project in 2011.

The support of family and friends cannot be overstated. My parents, Hubert and Sonia Bergantz, have been there all along, and have trusted me with blind faith. This included financial help without which I would never have had the privilege to uproot myself to the other side of the world to study and start a different and fulfilling life in a foreign country. Dedicating this book to them seems an inadequate repayment for the sacrifices they have made for me to live this life. *Papa, Maman, ce livre est pour vous.* Elizabeth Kinne, Paul Smith and Ibrahim have been anchors along the choppy waters of postgraduate studies, work and life.

At the University of Sydney, Iain McCalman ran an inspiring postgraduate seminar that made me want to keep researching and writing, and made me feel that I could make a contribution, too. Robert Aldrich supported my first foray into researching the French-speaking Pacific and has provided generous and ongoing mentorship since. The Australian National University gave me the opportunity to pursue further research through an International Postgraduate Research Scholarship and an ANU College of Arts and Social Science PhD Scholarship. Peter Brown provided early support and encouragement, and the School of History offered an exceptional intellectual environment in which to explore ideas and learn the craft of history. I particularly benefited from the mentoring and guidance of Frank Bongiorno, Alexander Cook, Tom Griffiths, Carolyn Strange and Angela Woollacott.

Research is a collective enterprise underpinned by research institutions and their staff. I warmly thank the dedicated curators and librarians at the Mitchell Library in Sydney, especially Margot Riley, at the State Records of New South Wales, the National Library of Australia, the National Archives of Australia and the State Library of Victoria. In France, I thank the staff of the Archives of the Ministry of Foreign Affairs and the Bibliothèque Nationale.

Julie Robert at UTS has been the best mentor and friend anyone could ask for. Her invaluable guidance and encouragements helped me navigate the uncertainties of the post-PhD period. I also thank Andrew Walker for vital ongoing research assistant work on a different project during and after the PhD. My colleagues in Global and Language Studies at RMIT have unreservedly welcomed me and offered their friendship since my move to Melbourne, and I also thank the university for affording me a semester without teaching or administrative duties to finish this book. Everyone at the Institute for the Study of French–Australian Relations (ISFAR) has helped keep the passion alive. Ivan Barko and Colin Nettlebeck deserve particular mention for their relentless commitment to the field and to others for well over the thirty-five years of the existence of ISFAR.

Since I arrived in Melbourne the members of my early-career research writing group have been brilliant companions and have provided a motivating and intellectually rewarding platform to help think through and refine both ideas and writing: Alessandro Antonello, Ruth Gamble, Kyle Harvey, Sianan Healy, Ben Huf, Yves Rees and Alexandra Roginski.

I am lucky enough that my professional life straddles two academic communities. It can take more than one village! I thank everyone in the history community here and abroad and in French studies in Australia who have played a role in helping me put this book together. For reading drafts, providing comments, giving me advice, being sounding boards, for lending a listening ear, and for offering their friendship I thank Brett Bennett, Kim Doyle, Hannah Forsyth, Niki Francis, Valentina Gosetti, Meggie Hutchison, Gemma King, Elaine Lewis, Tristan Moss, Briony Neilson, Shannyn Palmer, Jayne Persian, Elizabeth Rechniewski, Noah Riseman, Blake Singley, Clara Sitbon and Karen Smith.

At NewSouth, Phillipa McGuinness was the first to believe in the book and I thank Elspeth Menzies, Paul O'Beirne and Jocelyn Hungerford for shepherding it through with kindness and patience.

Ideas developed in chapter 6 were first aired in the *New Zealand Journal of French Studies and French History and Civilization: Papers of the George Rudé Seminar*. Parts of chapter 3 appeared in '"The scum of France": Australian Anxieties Towards French Convicts in the Nineteenth Century', *Australian Historical Studies* 49, 2 (2018): 150–66. I am grateful to the editors and reviewers for their comments, and to the publishers for permission to reproduce these works here.

Finally, to the descendants of French migrants who showed such enthusiasm and contributed all they could to the project, a heartfelt thank you, particularly to the late Jacqueline Dwyer, the *doyenne* of the old French community and the French and Belgian wool-buying world, and to Michel Reymond, Gaston Liévain and Liz de Chastel. Writing about the past is an endless present endeavour; if other descendants are out there and pick up this book, I invite them to come find me!

Index

Illustrations from the photo section are indicated by *ill.*

Aarons, Rosa 45, 52
Académie Colarossi 25
Académie Delécluze 25
Académie Julian 25
'Adolphe's Diner Parisien', Melbourne 17
Agache, Hubert 22–23, *ill.* 4–7
AIF 136, 137, 138–39
Allen, Charlotte *see* Maistre, Charlotte
Alliance Contracting Company 112, 113
Alliance Française 8, 102
    Melbourne 6, 8–9, 35–58, 89, 118
    Paris 37–38, 39, 42, 50, 51, 56, 57
    Sydney 40, 44, 50
Alliance littéraire, scientifique et artistique Franco-Britannique 46
anti-Semitism 104–5
anti-transportation campaign 65, 75, 76
Archibald Fountain, Sydney 19, 22
Archibald, JF 19
Arnold, Matthew 32, 33
Astruc, Maurice 38
Athenaeum Club 41, 44
Austral Salon 41, 43, 51
Australian Imperial Force 133 *see also* AIF

Bankstown, Sydney 122, 125, 132
Banville, Théodore de 81
Baptiste, J. 90, *ill.* 9–10
Barney, Nathalie 124
Bashkirtseff, Marie 126
Bastille Day 71–72, 96, 103, 136, 144
Baudelaire, Charles 81
Bean, Charles 133
Beauchamp, Earl of *see* Beauchamp, Lord
Beauchamp, Lord 105–9, 110–11, 115 *see also* Lygon, William

Beer, Leslie 24
Benjamin, Walter 21
Bent, Sir Thomas 1–2
Bernhardt, Sarah 5, 7–8, 42
'The Bistro', Sydney 142
Bocquet, Henri 97–98
Boer War, The 5, 27, 117
Bohemianism 18–19
border protection, Australia 58–73
Bordier, Leonard 100
Botany Bay 60, 61
Bougainville, Louis-Antoine de 87
Brennan, Christopher 18, 20
Brereton, John Le Gay 20
Buckie, Harry 139
Bulletin, The 18, 19, 106, 110,
Bunny, Rubert 25
Burchett, Wilfred 138
Burley Griffin, Walter 23
Bussy, Dorothy 124

'Café Estaminet Français', Melbourne 86
'Café Français', Sydney 18, *ill.* 3
'Café Tourtel', Paris 12
café culture, Parisian 12–13, 20–22, 29–30, *ill.* 8
Canberra 22–23, *ill.* 4–7
Cave, Sybil Maude 49, 50, 53, 54–56
Cayron, Léonce 111, 112–14, 115–18
Cercle littéraire français 74
Chabrillan, Céleste de 86
Chabrillan, Lionel de 86, 97
Chalauser, Lusanne 96
Charbonnet, Alice 42 *see also* Charbonnet-Kellerman, Madame
Charbonnet-Kellerman, Madame 103

Index

Charmier, Claude-Emile 68–69 *see also* Chastel, Baron Emile de
Chastel, Baron Emile de 68–69, 70
Chisholm, Alan Rowland 28–29
Chrétien, Louis 70
Clarke, Lady Janet 40–42, 53
Clarke, Marcus 78
Clarke, Sir William 40–41
'Cliveden' 41, 43
Cobar, New South Wales 105, 106, 108
Cochelet, G 109
Coing, Marie 94
Coleman, Louise 140
Coleman, Loyd 140
Communards 64, 66–68, 73–74, 78–79, 120–21
Comptoir National d'Escompte de Paris 44, 54–56, 101, 109 *see also* French Bank of Melbourne
convicts, French 60–75, 92, 98, 137–38 *see also récidivistes*
Cook, James 87
Coolgardie, Western Australia 111–12
Cormon, Fernand 25
Courrier Australien 102, 105, 107, 108
Couvreur, Jessie 14 *see also* Tasma
Crawford, Eugénie 134
Crimean War 5, 62
Crivelli, Charlotte 49–50, 56, 57, 79
Crivelli, Georges 79–80, 98–99
Crivelli, Marcel 49–50, 103, 114
cuisine, French 17, 135, 140

D'Alphonse, George Henri 94
D'Aunet, Georges Biard 44, 59, 79, 107, 108, 109
D'Aunet, Léonie 59
D'Héron, Sylvain 93
D'Orgeval, Pierre Le Barrois 54, 55–56, 109
D'Urville, Durmont 87
Dante Society 41
David Jones department store 16, 143–44
Davidson, Bessie 25
Deakin, Alfred 28
Decaze, Duc 67
Déjardin, Léon 38, 114–15
Delarue, Eugénie 120, 123, 125, 127, 130, 134

Delarue, Hippolyte Felix 120–21, 125, 132
Delarue, Leopold Hippolyte 119–20, 121–22, 123, 125, 126, 127, 128, 132–33
Delarue, Lydia 9–10, 52, 119–20, 121, 122, 123, 125, 126–34
Delarue, Lydia, snr. *see* Knight, Lydia
Delarue, Kate 121, 125, 127
Delarue shop, Sydney 120–21, 122–23, *ill.* 11
Dennemont, Emile 93
Deutsche Schulverein von Victoria 47
Dior, Christian 143–44
Doyle, Arthur Conan 14–15
Dreyfus Affair 2, 5, 27, 45–46, 103, 104–5, 106, 108, 109–10
Dreyfus, Alfred 45–46, 104, 105, 108, 109–10
Dreyfus, Irma 45–46, 48–49, 52, 118
Du Maurier, George 19
Dumas, Alexandre 6, 86, 87
Dunstan, Don 140
Duret, Charles 49, 103

Eaux Bonnes 122
Eaux Chaudes 122
École des Beaux Arts, Paris 25
École Nationale d'Agriculture 90
'Eildon Mansion' 38
Les émigrés aux terres australes 87
Entente Cordiale 5
Exposition Universelle 119, 121, 122
extradition, French convicts 65, 71, 77

Farmers department store 143
fashion, French 16, 143–44
Fashoda Incident 5, 27,
Fauchery, Antoine 81, 84–86, 88
Favre, Dannie 96
Federal Council of Australasia 62, 72
Federation 13, 26, 36, 59, 60, 77, 92, 105, 107, 110, 127, 137
Feildel, Manu 142
Fiji 62
First World War 19, 133, 136, 137, 138–39
Flaubert, Gustave 6, 18, 82
Fort Denison 5, 62
Fox, Emanuel Phillips 25
Foy, Alice 24, 25–26

Francophilia 7, 19, 28, 31, 38, 58, 59, 89, 102, 103
Francophobia *see* convicts, French
Franklin, Miles 20
French Bank of Melbourne 90 *see also* Comptoir National d'Escompte de Paris
French Benevolent Society, Sydney 94–95
French Chamber of Commerce 101, 102, 107, 109
'The French Kitchen', Melbourne 142
French Prospecting Syndicate 111, 112–16
Fromelles 137

Geelong, Victoria 90
gender 3, 19, 29, 30–32, 36, 37, 38–42, 49, 52, 53, 88, 92, 103, 108, 112, 115, 123–24, 129, 135–36, 139, 142–44
Geographical Society of Australia 103
Gilmore, Mary 20
Gippsland, Victoria 6–7, 138
gold rush, Victoria 81, 85–86, 90
Gracin, Fernand 96
Green, Henry Mackenzie 13, 20, 21–22, 29–30, 31, 32, 120, 135–36, 139, 140–41
Greenpeace 141
Guillaux, Maurice 23
Guillerie, Pierre Marie 93
Guizot, Guillaume de 33

Haussmann, Georges-Eugène 22, 23
Henry, Juliette 73–74
Henry, Lucien 73–74, 120–21
Heidelberg, Victoria 85
Heidelberg School 24–25, 26
Hickson, Dolly 97
Hill End, New South Wales *ill.* 9–10
Hobart 87
Holman, William 103
Holroyd, Lady 41, 46, 53, 56
Holuigue, Diane 142
Homéry, Jules 137
honour, masculine 2–3, 15, 99, 103, 108–9, 112, 114, 117
Hordern, Mary 143
Hôtel de Savoie, Paris 89
House of Dior 143
Hugo, Victor 27, 59

Hunters Hill, Sydney 100, 101, 102, 119, 121, 122, 125

immigration restriction 73, 76 *see also* border protection, Australia
Immigration Restriction Act 76
Imperial Federation League 41
'Independent Hall', Fitzroy 53, 55
Intercolonial Convention 62
Intercolonial Trade Union Conference 77

James, George PR 15, 30
James, Henry 22, 131–32
Jaurès, Jean 37–38
Jeanneret, Edward 100
Jersey, Lord 95–96
Jones, Charles Lloyd 143
Joubert, Didier Numa 100–1
Joubert, Jules 100–1, 119, 122
Journal of Madame Giovanni 87

Kalgoorlie, Western Australia 111
Kambala Girls' School 40
Keating, Paul 141
Kellerman, Annette 42
Kingsford Smith, Charles 23
Knight, Lydia 121
Kowalski, Henry 103

La Pérouse expedition 61
Lamotte, Henriette 140, 143
Languer, Eugène 108
Laure, Dr 94–95, 109
Laurent, Ernest 70
Lawrence, Cyril 139
Lawson, Henry 18
Le Callee, Marie 83
'Le Louvre', Melbourne 143
Liberty Consolidated Gold Mines 112
Liévain, Gaston 17
Lindsay, Norman 8, 12, 13, 21–22, 29, 30, 31–32, 101–2, 120, 135–36, 140–41, *ill.* 8
Lion, Marie 37, 42, 89
Liversidge, Archibald 122
Longstaff, John 25
'Luca's Town Hall Café', Melbourne 17
Lucas, Dione 142

Index

Lucciardi, Eugène 1, 2, 49, 136
Lygon, William 2–3 *see also* Beauchamp, Lord
Lyng, Jens 83

'Maison Dorée', Melbourne 18
Maistre, Charlotte 39
Maistre, Paul 6–7, 8–9, 36, 39–40, 42, 43, 45, 46, 49–52, 54–57, 95, 96, 118
Manning, Edye 100
Marin La Meslée, Edmond 103
Marist Orders 61, 101
Marquesas Islands 61
Maupassant, Guy de 28
Maurice-Carton, Fernand Isidore 40, 46–47, 48–49, 52
McNeil, Eugénie *see* Crawford, Eugénie
Melba, Nellie 42
Melbourne 1, 2, 6, 8–9, 10, 14, 15, 17, 18, 22, 28–29, 32, 35–36, 38–58, 70, 71–72, 77, 78, 81, 86, 88, 89, 90, 91, 93, 94, 95–96, 97, 98, 99, 101, 102–3, 107, 111, 113–15, 118, 132, 136, 137, 140, 142, 143, 144
Messageries Maritimes 14, 76, 84, 89, 93, 102–3, 109, 111
Metropolitan Intercolonial Exhibition 121
Migration, French 81–99
Milhau, Baron de 100
Mill, John Stuart 33
Minto, New South Wales 95
Molnar, George 140
Moloney, Ted 140
Moore, George 18
Mororoa 141
Mosman, Sydney 102
Mouchette, Berthe 37, 38–39, 40, 42, 57, 89
Murger, Henri 18–19, 81
Myer, Norman 143

nationalism, Australian 10, 13, 18, 26, 32–33, 60, 73, 107
Naturalization Act of 1903 92
Nerval, Gérard de 81
New Caledonia 5, 9, 14, 58, 60–73, 78, 79, 89–90, 92, 102–3, 120–21, 125, 133, 138
Newcastle, New South Wales 66
New Guinea 59–60, 62

New Hebrides 60, 61, 62, 76

'Oberwyl' 37, 38
Oh, for a French Wife! 140, 143
'Olympia Café', Paris 30, *ill.* 8

Papua New Guinea 70
Pacific, French presence 59–80, 86–88, 137–38, 141
Paris 1, 12–14, 18–19, 20–31, 37, 38–39, 42, 46, 50, 51, 52, 56, 57, 59, 64–65, 73, 81, 86, 87, 89, 90, 101, 114–15, 120, 121, 122, 124, 126, 127, 128, 129–30, 131–32, 133, 134, 135, 138–39, 143–44
Paris Commune *see* Communards
'Paris House', Sydney 17–18, *ill.* 1–2
Parkes, Henry 62, 72, 76
'Passy House', Hunters Hill 101
Pasteur Institute 103, 109
Paterson, AB 18
Pau 9, 119, 125, 127, 128, 130
Paysan, Victor 93
Pearson, Charles 63
Pellier, Paulette 140, 143
Playoust, George 101–2, 109, 111, 114, 117, 118, 143
Port Arthur 87
Poussard, Henri 103
Pozières 137
Pratz, Claire de 21, 31
Presbyterian Ladies' College, Croydon 40

Rainbow Warrior 141
Randwick, Sydney 102
récidivistes 64, 74–76, 77 *see also* Communards; convicts, French
Red Cross 136
Reid, George 103
Repiquete, Henriette 88
Reynand, Marie 90
Robinson, Sir Hercules 67
Roca, François 70
Rochefort, Henri 66
Rockhampton, Queensland 68, 78
Roosevelt, Eleanor 124
Rose, George 139
Rougier, Dr 109
Les Ruches 124

Russell, Adolphe de la Cour 111, 112, 113, 114, 115–17, 118
Russian invasion, fear of 5, 60, 62

Salon de la Société des Artistes Français 25
Savage Club 41
See, John 103
Seguin, Lisbeth 129
Seringue, Michel 78
Serlopette, Madame 23
Service, James 62, 77, 79
Simon, Eugène 67
sociability, feminine 8, 36, 38–43, 46, 49, 53, 58, 123–24
Société de Géographie Commerciale de Paris 89
Société Nationale des Beaux-Arts 25
South African War *see* Boer War
St Catherine's Clergy Daughters 40
St Catherine's School, Waverley 40
St Joseph's College, Hunters Hill 101
St Mary's Cathedral, Sydney 121
Stead, Christina 1, 2, 21, 22
Stephens, AG 18, 27
Stoop, Wivine de 142
Strauss, Jean 140
Sydney 2, 5, 9, 10, 14, 16, 17–18, 19, 20, 22, 23, 24, 26, 39, 40, 44, 49, 50, 57, 59, 61, 62, 65, 66, 67, 68, 71, 73–74, 78–79, 81, 91, 93, 94, 95, 99, 100–1, 102–3, 105, 107, 109, 111, 114, 118, 120–21, 122, 134, 140, 142, 143,
Sydney International Exhibition 121, 122
Sydney Technical College 74, 120–21

Sydney Town Hall 74

Tasma 14, 89, 95
Thibault, Suzanne 97
Thomas, Julian 63
Tischbauer, Alfred 120–21, *ill.* 11
Trottet, Paul 69–70, 73
Turnbull, Sarah 135
Twopeny, Richard 15

University of Melbourne 28, 40, 46–47, 52
University of Sydney 20, 122

Vanuatu *see* New Hebrides
Vernay, Antoine 70–71
Verne, Jules 87
Verschuur, Gerrit 82–83
Victoria League of Help 49
Villa Maria, Hunters Hill 101
Villers-Bretonneux 137
Vizetelly, Henry 28
Les voleurs d'Or 86

Wenz, Paul 27
White, Dorothy 124
White, Margaret Isabella 'Daisy' 124, 126
White, Patrick 124
White Australia Policy 92
wool trade 2, 9, 14, 89, 90–91, 101, 102, 111, 142, 143
Woolf, Joseph 38–39, 56

Zola, Emile 27, 28, 29, 129

www.ingramcontent.com/pod-product-compliance
Lightning Source LLC
Chambersburg PA
CBHW071957240426
43669CB00049B/2681